JavaScript
Manual of Style

JAVASCRIPT
MANUAL
OF STYLE

Marc Johnson

Ziff-Davis Press
An imprint of Macmillan Computer Publishing USA
Emeryville, California

Acquisitions Editor	Suzanne Anthony
Coordinating Editor	Kelly Green
Editor	Deborah Craig
Technical Reviewer	Luke Cassady-Dorion
Project Coordinator	Barbara Dahl
Cover Illustration	Regan Honda
Cover Design	Regan Honda and Megan Gandt
Book Design	Gary Suen
Word Processing	Howard Blechman
Page Layout	Janet Piercy
Indexer	Valerie Robbins

Ziff-Davis Press, ZD Press, and the Ziff-Davis Press logo are trademarks or registered trademarks of, and are licensed to Macmillan Computer Publishing USA by Ziff-Davis Publishing Company, New York, New York.

Ziff-Davis Press imprint books are produced on a Macintosh computer system with the following applications: FrameMaker®, Microsoft® Word, QuarkXPress®, Adobe Illustrator®, Adobe Photoshop®, Adobe Streamline™, MacLink® Plus, Aldus® FreeHand™, Collage Plus™.

Ziff-Davis Press, an imprint of
Macmillan Computer Publishing USA
5903 Christie Avenue
Emeryville, CA 94608

ISBN 1-56276-423-3

Manufactured in the United States of America
10 9 8 7 6 5 4 3 2 1

CONTENTS AT A GLANCE

Introduction   xiii

Part 1   Welcome to JavaScript

1   What Is JavaScript?   2
2   What Can You Do
    with JavaScript?   10
3   Style   26

Part 2   The Examples

4   URL Patch   42
5   An Outlined Document   50
6   Color Chooser   78
7   Form Validation   102
8   Form Modification   128
9   Games   152

Part 3   Quick Reference

A   ISO Latin-1 Character Set   185
B   JavaScript Reserved Words   192
C   A Review of HTML   193
D   JavaScript Operators   225
E   Built-in Objects and Functions   237
F   Online Resources   265
    Index   269

TABLE OF CONTENTS

Introduction   **xiii**

Part 1   Welcome to JavaScript

Chapter 1   What Is JavaScript?   **2**

The History of JavaScript   3

    HTML 1.0 and 2.0   4

    HTML 3.0 and NHTML   4

    LiveScript   6

What JavaScript Isn't   6

    CGI   6

    Java   8

Platforms and Browsers   8

**Chapter 2   What Can You Do
               with JavaScript?**   **10**

Multipart Documents with Frames   11

    Reloading Part of the Window   14

    Creating Interactive Documents   14

More Control over User Interaction   16

Documents with Memory   20

Live Documents   21

    Scrolling Messages   21

    Clocks   23

    Countdown Timers   24

    Self-updating Documents   25

Chapter 3   Style   **26**

Image is Everything   27

    Content   27

    Presentation   31

Protecting Your Document from Rogue Users   35

     Make Sure Your Functions Are Loaded   35

     Validate Input   35

     But Surely No One Would Do That!   36

     Not All Platforms Are Created Equal, Part 2   36

Document Maintenance   37

     Comment, Comment, Comment   37

     Consistent Internal Style   38

The Last Rule   38

Part 2   The Examples

Chapter 4   URL Patch   42

The Scenario   43

The Requirements   43

The Solution (without JavaScript)   43

The Solution (with JavaScript)   44

Modifying the Example for Your Own Use   48

Chapter 5   An Outlined Document   50

The Scenario   51

The Requirements   51

The Solution (without JavaScript)   52

The Solution (with JavaScript)   55

     Frame in the Outline   55

     Make the Document Outline Smarter   55

Improving the Solution   76

Modifying the Example for Your Own Use   77

Chapter 6   Color Chooser   78

The Scenario   80

The Requirements   80

The Solution (without JavaScript)   81

The Solution (with JavaScript)   83
    The Form   83
Improving the Solution   100
Modifying the Example for Your Own Use   101

Chapter 7   Form Validation   102

The Scenario   103
The Requirements   103
The Solution (without JavaScript)   104
The Solution (with JavaScript)   107
Improving the Solution   126
Modifying the Example for Your Own Use   126

Chapter 8   Form Modification   128

The Scenario   129
The Requirements   130
The Solution (without JavaScript)   130
The Solution (with JavaScript)   131
    Laying Out the Controls   134
    Laying Out the Window   138
    Adding Functionality to the Controls   139
    Putting Everything Together   144
Improving the Solution   150
Modifying the Example for Your Own Use   151

Chapter 9   Games   152

The Scenario   153
The Requirements   153
The Solution (without JavaScript)   155
The Solution (with JavaScript)   156
Improving the Solution   181
Modifying the Example for Your Own Use   181

Part 3   Quick Reference

Appendix A   **ISO Latin-1 Character Set**   **185**

Appendix B   **JavaScript Reserved Words**   **192**

Appendix C   **A Review of HTML**   **193**

Appendix D   **JavaScript Operators**   **225**

Appendix E   **Built-in Objects and Functions**   **237**

Appendix F   **Online Resources**   **265**

Index   **269**

ACKNOWLEDGMENTS

I thank the superb people I worked with at Ziff-Davis—Stacy Hiquet, Suzanne Anthony, Kelly Green, and Barbara Dahl. I thank my incredible editors, Deborah Craig and Luke Cassady-Dorion, without whom this book never would have made it into your hands. I thank my colleagues at Fujitsu Network Switching, who put up with my demented ramblings about the wonders of JavaScript. I thank Chelsea and Trevor for once more putting up with a daddy who never seems to get enough sleep and who is constantly working on the book—again. I thank Joan for putting up with my schedule, and for getting the ball rolling on yet another book, even though she knew what that entailed and the sacrifices she'd have to make—been there, done that, and did it again anyway. Finally, I thank the Lord for this experience, and I thank the woman who taught me to thank Him, even when I don't understand why—Martha Ilene Larson Whitaker. I dedicate this book to her memory.

INTRODUCTION

This is a book about writing exciting Web pages with JavaScript. Before JavaScript or its ancestor, LiveScript, Web pages were written in HTML. The pages could be very sophisticated in their layout, but they just sat there. JavaScript can make your Web pages come alive. Your Web pages can now be dynamic, changing before the user's eyes. JavaScript can make your Web pages both more interesting and more fun.

JavaScript isn't very difficult to learn. I myself picked up the basics in a matter of hours. You can, too.

You don't need to read this book cover to cover, and you don't have to read the chapters in any particular order. Skip around, read what seems interesting, and write some code. It's the best way to learn. You will need a copy of Netscape Navigator, preferably version 2.01 or later, but that's all. I use Web-Mania! to write some of my code, because it takes care of a lot of the details that I might forget, but all you really need is a simple ASCII text editor—vi, emacs, Notepad, whatever.

This book is divided into three parts. The first part includes three chapters. Chapter 1 is a quick introduction to JavaScript that describes what it is and where it came from. Chapter 2 explains what JavaScript is good for, outlining what you can do with it. Chapter 3 lets me get up on my soapbox and do a little preaching about what makes a good Web page, what makes a bad Web page, and what you can do to keep your pages on the good list.

The second section consists of six chapters, all of which contain a complete JavaScript Web page. Each chapter introduces a problem, demonstrates how you might solve it without JavaScript, and then shows how you can craft a much better solution with JavaScript. These chapters all conclude with some thoughts on how you can enhance the solution and how you can adapt the techniques to creating your own Web pages with JavaScript. In every chapter, the JavaScript code is discussed in depth, function by function. No mysteries; there's no one behind the curtain. If you don't understand something about the code, write me at marcj@nando.net. I'll be glad to answer your questions!

Finally, the third section contains six appendices, chock full of useful reference material: the character set, reserved words, a review of HTML, the JavaScript operators, JavaScript's built-in objects and functions, and online resources. Again, if there's something I missed, write me. I want to help.

This book was written on a nameless 486-based desktop system lovingly assembled by Computer Options of Raleigh, North Carolina, and on a

Pentium-based Samsung notebook, using Microsoft Word for Windows 6.0 under Windows 3.1 (the desktop) and Windows 95 (the notebook). The Web pages created were tested on both platforms, as well as on a Sun Microsystems Sparc-10 running Solaris 2.4 and on the desktop system under Linux 1.2.1. Luke Cassady-Dorion, my excellent technical editor, also ran them on his Macintosh. The Web pages were written with WebMania! 1.5. Screen shots were taken with Collage Complete 1.0, and enhanced with Paint Shop Pro 3.12. My Web space provider is Hurricane Electric (he.net; my home page is http://www.he.net/~marcj/index.html), and the Web pages were loaded onto their server for live testing. All of this was accomplished through my Internet service provider, nando.net.

I had a lot of fun writing this book, and I hope it proves to be a useful addition to your library.

Part 1

Welcome to JavaScript

WHAT IS JAVASCRIPT?

WHAT CAN YOU DO WITH JAVASCRIPT?

STYLE

What Is JavaScript?

THE HISTORY OF JAVASCRIPT

WHAT JAVASCRIPT ISN'T

PLATFORMS AND BROWSERS

JavaScript is a lightweight object-based scripting language created by
Netscape Communications Corporation for developing Internet applications. JavaScript is lightweight in that there isn't a great deal to
learn and you can be productive with it very quickly, in contrast to much more
complex languages such as Java. As a scripting language, JavaScript is meant to
tell an application what to do. Unlike languages used to create applications, it
cannot do anything without the application.

You can develop server applications or client applications with JavaScript. In
this book, the term "server" refers to the computer where your Web pages reside.
The term "client" refers to the browser application that loads and displays your
Web pages. This book focuses on teaching you to create client applications with
JavaScript—specifically, documents (Web pages) on the World Wide Web.

You can embed JavaScript statements in Web pages, which are written in
HTML (Hypertext Markup Language). JavaScript is an extension to HTML
that lets you create more sophisticated Web pages than you ever could with
HTML alone. To appreciate this, it helps to know a little history.

THE HISTORY OF JAVASCRIPT

Strictly speaking, HTML is a Standard Generalized Markup Language (SGML),
Document Type Definition (DTD). An SGML document has three parts. The
first part defines the character set to be used and tells which characters in that
set distinguish text from markup tags. Markup tags specify how the viewer
application, or browser, should present the text to the user. The second part of

an SGML document specifies the document type and states which markup tags are legal. The third part of an SGML document, called the document instance, contains the actual text and markup tags. Because there is no requirement that the three parts of an SGML document reside in the same physical file, we can concentrate on the document instance. The Web pages you create are document instances.

Most HTML browsers assume a common definition about the character set used, and about which characters distinguish text from markup tags. They also generally agree about a core set of legal markup tags. They then diverge on which additional new markup tags to permit.

HTML 1.0 AND 2.0

HTML 1.0 refers to the original set of markup tags. HTML 1.0 is so limited that a browser that restricted HTML documents to HTML 1.0 would be a museum piece.

HTML 2.0 includes a more generous set of markup tags than HTML 1.0; in particular, it allows markup tags that define user input fields. As of this writing, HTML 2.0 defines the de facto common core of markup tags. You can create a relatively sophisticated Web page with HTML 2.0 markup tags.

HTML 3.0 AND NHTML

HTML 3.0, still in the process of standardization, adds additional markup tags to those defined in HTML 2.0, such as tags to define tables, figures, and mathematical equations. HTML 3.0 expands some tags to include more functionality, such as centering text or images in the browser, and adding background colors and images.

NHTML, a nickname for Netscape's extension of HTML 2.0, is another set of markup tags that goes beyond those defined in HTML 2.0. Netscape, like other developers of cutting edge Web browsers, is trying to influence the development of the HTML 3.0 standard, and has developed extensions of its own. At the same time, Netscape is making an effort to conform to the evolving HTML 3.0 specification. Furthermore, Netscape continues to support markup tags that the draft HTML 3.0 specification has declared obsolete.

Netscape's browser, Netscape Navigator, is not precisely HTML 3.0–compliant. The best way to find out whether Netscape Navigator supports a particular markup tag is to get the latest version and try a document containing the tag.

Why NHTML isn't proper SGML   Formally, a Web page is the third part of an SGML DTD, and as such, should conform to the SGML DTD specification.

A few features of NHTML do not conform to the rules of the SGML DTD specification. If browsers actually treated a Web page as the third part of an SGML DTD, this would be a problem. However, browsers typically accept a certain hard-coded level of HTML—typically HTML 2.0 with some HTML 3.0 extensions and some NHTML extensions—and ignore markup tags that they do not recognize.

Where this nonconformity does present a problem is in writing tools that validate Web pages. These tools typically use an SGML parser, and they require a page to be part of a properly conforming SGML DTD for the level of HTML they check.

Should you validate your Web pages? I think so, although as of this writing, it's not a viable option for JavaScript pages. So far, no one has come up with a validation tool that recognizes and validates the syntax of JavaScript. But count on it; someone will. And when they do, try it on your pages. Validation tools have saved me countless hours of headaches trying to figure out why my HTML code wasn't working correctly.

Just for the record, here are the nonconforming parts of NHTML:

▶ NHTML makes liberal use of the % character. It's used to specify that certain entities occupy a fixed percentage of the window's real estate, or to specify scaling on images. The problem with this is that the % character is a reserved character in the SGML specification for declaring parameter entities in a DTD. It does not belong in a Web page. There is no workaround to achieve the same effect. An SGML parser-based validation tool will not accept pages with % characters in the attributes.

▶ NHTML allows the BORDER attribute to be specified in two ways:

```
<TABLE BORDER>
```

and

```
<TABLE BORDER="1">
```

The SGML DTD specification does not allow an attribute to be specified in two entirely different fashions like this. While a grammatically correct SGML DTD cannot handle both forms simultaneously, a grammatically correct SGML DTD can handle either form. Since BORDER alone means the same thing as BORDER="1", BORDER alone is redundant, and you can write a DTD that says the BORDER attribute always takes a numeric argument. From the standpoint of making your pages clear and easy to maintain, it's always a good idea to state the border size explicitly.

▶ SGML parsers will not accept tags like <FONT SIZE=+3> and <FONT SIZE=-2>. Fortunately, this one is easy to work around: Place the value in double quotes, like this:

```
<FONT SIZE="+3">
```

and

```
<FONT SIZE="-2">
```

▶ Color attributes specified as six-digit hexadecimal values will not pass an SGML parser if written like this:

```
<BODY BGCOLOR=#123456>
```

As with the incremented or decremented font sizes, you can fix this problem by placing the offending value inside double quotes.

```
<BODY BGCOLOR="#123456">
```

LIVESCRIPT

Netscape began working on a scripting language called LiveScript, which quickly evolved into what is now JavaScript. Although JavaScript and Java are not the same thing, Netscape intends JavaScript to tie into Java; hence the name change. Netscape and Sun Microsystems (the developers of Java) are working closely on the development of the two languages. There are few other major differences between LiveScript and JavaScript, the biggest being that LiveScript was case-insensitive and JavaScript is case-sensitive.

WHAT JAVASCRIPT ISN'T

JavaScript can provide a high degree of user interaction like some other systems, including CGI and Java.

CGI

The Common Gateway Interface (CGI) provides a mechanism for a program on the server to interact with the client's browser. You can use any language to write CGI programs, and CGI programs may be interpreted (PERL scripts, for instance) or compiled (C or C++). One popular use of CGI is in hit counters—programs that modify the page to show how many times that page has been visited. Another popular use of CGI is in form handling, where a program on the server reads the data from the user input fields and does some work based on that data.

JavaScript, which does its work in the client's browser, cannot entirely replace CGI. For instance, a hit counter has to update a file on the server so it can remember how many times the page has been visited by all visitors. That's a little difficult for JavaScript, but a JavaScript Web page *can* keep track of how many times a given visitor has visited the page. So can CGI, but only if given an endless supply of disk space on the server.

JavaScript can do a lot of the same things CGI can do, and it can often do them much more efficiently. For example, JavaScript can do form validation more efficiently than CGI. When a non-JavaScript page has user input fields, it sends all the field values to a CGI server application. The CGI application then has to figure out whether the data in each field makes sense before doing something with the data. A JavaScript page, however, can validate the data entered before it is sent to the server. If the data is invalid, JavaScript can block transmission to the server. Because all of this work is performed on the client side, JavaScript does not waste bandwidth transmitting bad data and then receiving an error page from the server.

JavaScript can also replace some of the animation and page-reloading functionality of CGI. To perform animation and page-reloading, CGI provides mechanisms called "server push" and "client pull." With server push, the Web page server maintains a connection between the client (the browser) and server. Server push restricts the number of simultaneous connections the Web page server can maintain—a popular page using server push will frequently reward potential visits with a "sorry, not now, try later" message. Client pull, on the other hand, involves the client frequently re-establishing its connection to the server, artificially adding to the traffic at the server. You can use JavaScript to create dynamic documents that would have required either server push or client pull in CGI, but that involve no additional traffic or long, drawn-out connections between the client and the server.

JavaScript is independent of the server platform, the hardware and software that your server uses. CGI has to be written in a language that your server platform supports. No single language is supported by all server platforms. If your Web pages rely on CGI, what happens if the company that provides your server changes platforms? What happens if they go bankrupt and you have to take your pages and their CGI applications to another server?

Finally, not all Web space providers allow Web pages to use CGI. CGI requires that the program be executed on the server, but some Web space providers are nervous about the possible side effects of badly written or maliciously written CGI programs being executed on their machines. Some providers only allow the use of a limited set of applications. Many providers do not support server push CGI. JavaScript running on the client browser is perfectly safe to the server, and affords you, the creator of the JavaScript document, much greater flexibility in how your document interacts with the reader.

JAVA

Many people confuse JavaScript with Java, which is a programming language developed by Sun Microsystems, Inc. Each has its own Usenet newsgroup, yet people frequently post questions about Java to the JavaScript newsgroup, and vice versa.

Java is a programming language and JavaScript is a scripting language. Java programs are compiled on the server. You can write stand-alone programs in Java. Scripts written in JavaScript are interpreted by the browser. You cannot write stand-alone programs in JavaScript—you need a browser to interpret JavaScript.

Java is object-oriented. It employs classes and inheritance. It provides encapsulation of data. JavaScript is object-based. There are no classes. There is no inheritance. Data within objects is readily accessible.

Java is compiled into "applets" that are accessed from HTML pages. JavaScript is embedded in HTML.

Java requires that data types be strongly typed (if a function expects one of its arguments to be a number, the function will not accept a character string). JavaScript is loosely typed. JavaScript has numbers, character strings, and Booleans (logical yes/no, true/false, on/off data) and freely interchanges them.

Java can be used to create very powerful applications. JavaScript scripts cannot really do all the neat things that Java applets can. On the other hand, it is much more difficult to write programs in Java than it is to write scripts in JavaScript.

PLATFORMS AND BROWSERS

JavaScript, as described in this book, is supported by Netscape Navigator 2.01 and later releases. It is supported on several architectures, as you can see in Table 1.1.

Table 1.1: Netscape Platforms

Architecture	Operating System
Windows	Windows 3.1
	Windows 3.11
	Windows NT 3.5 and later
	Windows 95
Macintosh	MacOS

Table 1.1: Netscape Platforms (Continued)

Architecture	Operating System
UNIX	DEC Alpha OSF/1 2.0 and later
	HP-UX 9.03
	IBM RS/6000 AIX 3.2
	Irix
	Sun Sparc Solaris 2.3
	Sun Sparc Solaris 2.4
	Sun Sparc SunOS 4.1.3
	BSDI
	Linux 1.1.59 and later

What Can You Do with JavaScript?

MULTIPART DOCUMENTS WITH FRAMES

MORE CONTROL OVER USER INTERACTION

DOCUMENTS WITH MEMORY

LIVE DOCUMENTS

Chapter 2

JavaScript offers you much more expressive power than HTML alone. This chapter touches on a few of the things you can do with JavaScript, such as create multipart documents, build dynamic documents that take you through a Web site from one document to another, and generate documents that interact with the user. It is by no means exhaustive, as you can see by checking out some of the URLs listed in the Quick Reference at the end of this book.

MULTIPART DOCUMENTS WITH FRAMES

You can create documents that split the browser window into pieces—you have probably seen such documents while surfing the Web. The pieces are called *frames,* and much of JavaScript's power derives from what it can do with frames.

Frames give you more control over the layout of your document than conventional HTML allows, and frames let you keep parts of your documents on the screen while other parts change. For example, in one frame you can place a corporate logo, copyright information, and so forth; in another frame, you can place a document describing some particularly interesting information about your company. As the user pages through your Web site, the frame that holds your logo and copyright can remain visible while the information in the other frame changes.

Frames also give you the power to create and present HTML on the fly. Java-Script code in the document of one frame can clear another frame and write new HTML or even more JavaScript code into another frame. Before JavaScript, it was enormously complicated to create, on the fly, a new page tailored to the user's wishes. Now you can do it yourself.

You define frames within a *frame document,* or layout document. A typical Web page is made up of an HTML element that contains a HEAD element and a BODY element. A frame document is usually made up of an HTML element that contains a HEAD element and a FRAMESET element.

FRAME elements are contained within FRAMESET elements, and FRAMESET elements can also contain other FRAMESET elements, allowing you to divide and subdivide the browser window. Be careful with this capability, however: You can easily subdivide the browser window to the point that nothing of value is visible.

Each FRAME element is loaded with its own Web page document. A frame document requires several separate documents; the one in Figure 2.1 requires four documents: one for the frame document itself, and one for each of the three frames.

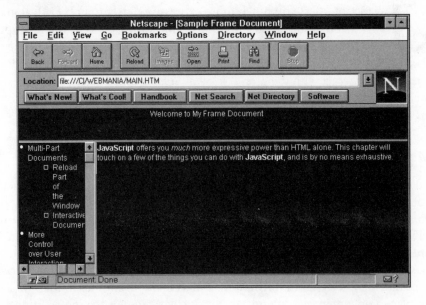

Figure 2.1: A typical frame document

Here are the HTML file listings for the frame document in Figure 2.1. What follows is the file main.htm.

```
<HTML>
    <HEAD>
        <TITLE>Sample Frame Document</TITLE>
```

```
    </HEAD>
    <FRAMESET ROWS="20%,*">
        <FRAME SRC="welcome.htm" NAME="Welcome" SCROLLING="auto"
            MARGINWIDTH=1 MARGINHEIGHT=1 NORESIZE>
        <FRAMESET COLS="20%,80%">
            <FRAME SRC="dir.htm" NAME="Directory" SCROLLING="auto"
                MARGINWIDTH=1 MARGINHEIGHT=1 NORESIZE>
            <FRAME SRC="contents.htm" NAME="Contents" SCROLLING="auto"
                MARGINWIDTH=1 MARGINHEIGHT=1 NORESIZE>
        </FRAMESET>
    </FRAMESET>
</HTML>
```

The outermost FRAMESET element breaks the window into rows; the top
row is given 20 percent of the screen, and the bottom row is given the remainder of the screen. The top row will contain the document welcome.htm. The
bottom row contains a FRAMESET element that divides the row in two columns. The left column gets 20 percent of the row's width and contains
dir.htm. The right column gets the other 80 percent of the row's width and
contains contents.htm.

The next listing is welcome.htm. It displays a single line, "Welcome to
My Frame Document." The line is centered, and the text is green on a
black background.

```
<HTML>
    <HEAD>
        <TITLE>Welcome</TITLE>
    </HEAD>
    <BODY BGCOLOR="000000" TEXT="008000" >
        <P ALIGN=CENTER>Welcome to My Frame Document</P>
    </BODY>
</HTML>
```

Next is dir.htm. It contains a list of topics, with lists nested inside lists.
Like welcome.htm, it uses green letters on a black background.

```
<HTML>
    <HEAD>
        <TITLE>Directory</TITLE>
    </HEAD>
    <BODY BGCOLOR="000000" TEXT="008000" >
        <UL>
            <LI>Multi-Part Documents
            <UL>
                <LI>Reload Part of the Window
                <LI>Interactive Documents
```

```
        </UL>
        <LI>More Control over User Interaction
        <LI>Documents with Memory
        <LI>Live Documents
        <UL>
            <LI>Scrolling Messages
            <LI>Clocks
            <LI>Countdown Timers
            <LI>Self-Updating Documents
        </UL>
    </UL>
    </BODY>
</HTML>
```

Finally, below is contents.htm. It displays one of the topics for this page, and does so in green letters on a black background.

```
<HTML>
    <HEAD>
        <TITLE>Contents</TITLE>
    </HEAD>
    <BODY BGCOLOR="000000" TEXT="008000" >
        <P>
            <B>JavaScript</B> offers you <I>much</I> more expressive
            power than HTML alone. This chapter will touch on a few of
            the things you can do with <B>JavaScript</B>, and is by no
            means exhaustive.
        </P>
    </BODY>
</HTML>
```

RELOADING PART OF THE WINDOW

So what can you do, once you've subdivided the browser window? Well, you can update one frame, loading it with a new document while the other frames remain unchanged. In the document shown in Figure 2.1, the top frame contains information about the overall purpose of the Web site. The lower-left frame contains a directory of pages that pertain to the purpose expressed by the top frame's document. The lower-right frame contains a page that the user has selected from the directory in the lower-left frame. The top and lower-left frames never change, but the user can change pages in the lower-right frame.

CREATING INTERACTIVE DOCUMENTS

You can also write JavaScript code that can rewrite the contents of a frame in response to the user's actions. You can't modify a frame's contents, but you can rewrite the frame contents from scratch. Here are three frame documents that demonstrate this capability:

Here is main2.htm; it simply divides the screen into two rows.

```
<HTML>
    <HEAD>
        <TITLE>Self-Modifying Document</TITLE>
    </HEAD>
    <FRAMESET ROWS="60%,*">
        <FRAME SRC="input.htm" NAME="input" SCROLLING="auto"
            MARGINWIDTH=1 MARGINHEIGHT=1 NORESIZE>
        <FRAMESET ROWS="78%">
            <FRAME SRC="output.htm" NAME="output" SCROLLING="auto"
                MARGINWIDTH=1 MARGINHEIGHT=1 NORESIZE>
        </FRAMESET>
    </FRAMESET>
</HTML>
```

This is input.htm:

```
<HTML>
    <HEAD>
        <TITLE>Input</TITLE>
        <SCRIPT>
<!-- hide script
function sayHello(form)
    {
    parent.output.document.open();
    parent.output.document.open();
    var gt = unescape("%3E");
    parent.output.document.write("<HTML" + gt);
    parent.output.document.write("<BODY BGCOLOR='004000' TEXT='FFFFFF'"
        + gt);
    parent.output.document.write("Hello " + form.firstName.value + " " +
        form.middleName.value + " " + form.lastName.value);
    parent.output.document.write("</BODY" + gt);
    parent.output.document.write("</HTML" + gt);
    parent.output.document.close();
    }
// -->
        </SCRIPT>
    </HEAD>
    <BODY BGCOLOR="004000" TEXT="FFFFFF" >
        <FORM NAME="form">
            <INPUT TYPE=TEXT SIZE=20 NAME="firstName"> First Name
            <BR>
            <INPUT TYPE=TEXT SIZE=20 NAME="middleName"> Middle Name
```

```
        <BR>
        <INPUT TYPE=TEXT SIZE=20 NAME="lastName"> Last Name
        <BR>
        <INPUT TYPE=BUTTON VALUE="Say Hello"
            ONCLICK="sayHello(this.form)">
    </FORM>
  </BODY>
</HTML>
```

input.htm creates a form into which you can write your first name, middle name, and last name. When you're done, you click on the button labeled "Say Hello." When you click on that button, the JavaScript function "sayHello" is called, with a reference to the form as a parameter. The function "sayHello" opens the document in the output frame and creates and displays a new page in the output frame. It uses the form to get the names you entered and incorporates them into the new page. To accomplish this trivial task without JavaScript would require writing a program that runs on a server—a much more difficult task than putting together this little piece of JavaScript.

The following is output.htm:

```
<HTML>
    <BODY BGCOLOR="004000" TEXT="FFFFFF" >
    </BODY>
</HTML>
```

This code does nothing at all except make the background of its frame match the background of the other frame. It doesn't have to do anything else; it's just a placeholder. Figure 2.2 shows the frame document when it's first loaded. Figure 2.3 shows the frame document after data has been entered in the form in the lower-left frame.

More control over user interaction

JavaScript recognizes several events that a user can cause within a document. You can create JavaScript code that reacts to those events, providing interaction with the user.

Within a FORM element, there are SELECT, INPUT, and TEXTAREA elements, which act as input fields. The user can typically move the cursor from one input field to another by using the Tab key or by clicking the pointing device in an input field. When the user moves the cursor from one field (the source) to another (the destination), the destination field is said to have acquired focus; the user can now modify that field's contents. At the same time,

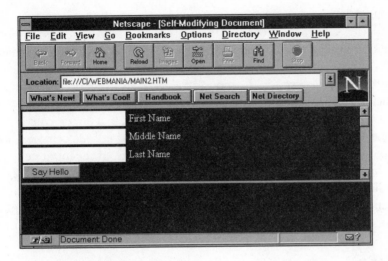

Figure 2.2: Frame before data is entered

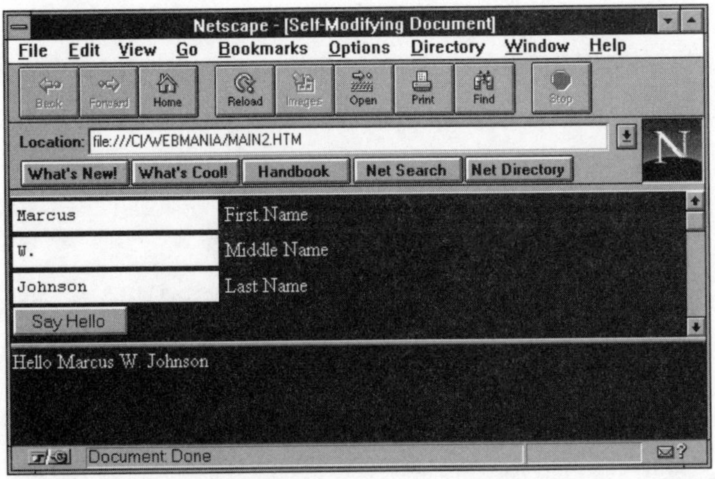

Figure 2.3: Frame after data is entered

the source field has lost focus. In Netscape terminology, the destination field has experienced a focus event and the source field has experienced a blur event.

Another kind of event takes place when the user highlights text in a field; this is called a select event. A change event occurs when text within a field is changed and focus is moved to another field. A click event occurs when certain fields are clicked on with the pointing device.

You can write JavaScript expressions or functions that are executed when any one of these events occurs on a field. The following code demonstrates how these events and their event handlers work. Each of the input fields has event handlers that handle focus, blur, select, change, or click events. Each event handler calls the announce function, passing it the name of the input field and the name of the event. The announce function displays that information in the window's status area.

```
<HTML>
    <HEAD>
        <TITLE>Focus, Blur, Select, Change, Click Test</TITLE>
        <SCRIPT>
<!--
function announce(widgetName, eventType)
    {
    status = "The " + widgetName + " field just experienced a " +
             eventType + " event";
    return true;
    }
//-->
        </SCRIPT>
    </HEAD>
    <BODY >
        <FORM ONSUBMIT="return false">
            <INPUT TYPE=BUTTON NAME="button" VALUE="button"
                ONCLICK="announce('button','click')">
            <INPUT TYPE=CHECKBOX NAME="checkbox"
                ONCLICK="announce('checkbox','click')">A
            <INPUT TYPE=CHECKBOX NAME="checkbox"
                ONCLICK="announce('checkbox','click')">B
            <INPUT TYPE=CHECKBOX NAME="checkbox"
                ONCLICK="announce('checkbox','click')">C
            <INPUT TYPE=RADIO NAME='radio'
                ONCLICK="announce('radio','click')">AM
            <INPUT TYPE=RADIO NAME='radio'
                ONCLICK="announce('radio','click')">FM
            <BR>
            <INPUT TYPE=RESET NAME="reset"
```

```
        ONCLICK="announce('reset','click')">
    <BR>
    <INPUT TYPE=SUBMIT NAME="submit"
        ONCLICK="announce('submit','click')">
    <BR>
    <INPUT TYPE=TEXT NAME="text" SIZE=10
        ONBLUR="announce('text','blur')"
        ONCHANGE="announce('text','change')"
        ONFOCUS="announce('text','focus')"
        ONSELECT="announce('text','select')">
    <BR>
    <TEXTAREA NAME="textArea" COLS="20" ROWS="2"
        ONBLUR="announce('textarea','blur')"
        ONCHANGE="announce('textarea','change')"
        ONFOCUS="announce('textarea','focus')"
        ONSELECT="announce('textarea','select')"
        Sample Text
    </TEXTAREA>
    <BR>
    <SELECT NAME="select"
        ONBLUR="announce('select','blur')"
        ONCHANGE="announce('select','change')"
        ONFOCUS="announce('select','focus')">
        <OPTION>Option 1
        <OPTION>Option 2
        <OPTION>Option 3
    </SELECT>
  </FORM>
 </BODY>
</HTML>
```

A word of caution: You can accidentally force the browser into a loop that
never ends by creating chains of events that repeat themselves. Pop-up windows, created using the alert, confirm, or prompt methods, can interact
badly when created by a focus event handler. As an example, the following
code pops up an alert window when the text field receives focus:

```
<HTML>
    <HEAD>
        <TITLE>Endless Loop</TITLE>
    </HEAD>
    <BODY>
        <FORM>
            <INPUT TYPE=TEXT NAME="text" SIZE=10
                ONFOCUS="alert('Here we go again...')">
        </FORM>
```

```
    </BODY>
</HTML>
```

If the alert window happens to be displayed over the text field, we have a problem. Here's what happens:

1 The text field receives focus.

2 The onFocus event handler begins executing.

3 The alert window pops up, acquiring focus from the text field.

4 The user dismisses the alert window.

5 The alert window is erased. Focus returns to the text field.

6 The onFocus event handler begins executing.

7 The alert window pops up....

And on and on it goes. To avoid this kind of endless loop, place messages in a text input field, on the status area of the window, or in another window or frame altogether.

Within the FORM element, another kind of event, the submit event, occurs when the user clicks on a submit button. Before there was JavaScript, clicking on the submit button sent the form data to a CGI process on a remote server. The CGI process would then process the data and send back a new page of data. With JavaScript, you can write an event handler for the submit event. Within the submit event handler, you can do whatever you like. Most of the input field contents are accessible to your JavaScript code (password fields are the exception); you can modify the data and you can decide not to send it out at all. You can create a document and display it in another frame or window. And you can still send it to a CGI process.

In addition to form and field event handlers, you can write event handlers to be executed when the pointing device moves over certain elements; such an event is called a mouseover event. You can also define event handlers that are executed when the document is loaded (a load event) and when the document is exited (an unload event).

DOCUMENTS WITH MEMORY

Through the use of a feature called a cookie, documents can share information with each other. Cookies are small data objects that reside on the user's machine. You can write JavaScript code to create, modify, and delete cookies.

The power of cookies is that they offer persistence. When the document that created or modified a cookie is no longer loaded, the data in the cookie is still there. Other documents that know about the cookie can access and modify its data, so the data can be shared between documents.

One potential use for cookies is in online catalogs. A store with an extensive inventory would not want to put its entire catalog in a single document. Instead, they would probably break up the catalog into manageable pieces, with each separate document focusing on a particular class of merchandise.

The user of such an online catalog could then select items from several pages. Each page could record the user's selection in a cookie. When the user was finally ready to send in the order, the cookie would be read back into a form for the user to verify. The entire list, containing items from several different documents, would then be submitted to the store.

Using the ability to write frame contents on the fly, you can also use cookies to remember things about the user and to tailor the contents of your document's frames to that user. An example might be a personalized greeting, combined with an indication of how long it has been since the user last loaded the document.

You might want to display some information at the beginning of the day. Using a cookie, your document can remember whether it is being loaded for the first time that day (by a particular user) or a subsequent time. For example, on the first visit of the day you might load a document containing the day's weather forecast, which you probably would not want to see later that same day. You could display a favorite online cartoon; once you've seen that day's cartoon, there's no reason to look at it again and again.

LIVE DOCUMENTS

Live documents are Web pages that change as time passes. You can create timers in your code. When the timer counts down, a JavaScript expression is executed. You can do many things with timers, such as scroll messages on the screen or load a document when the timer counts down.

SCROLLING MESSAGES

You've probably seen those cute little messages that scroll along the status portion of the browser window. They're all done with timers. The basic concept is simple.

You start the message by appending it to some arbitrary number of spaces. (The example that follows uses 200.) The message, with its leading spaces, is then written to the window's status bar. A timer starts that, when timed out, starts the process over again, but with one less space than the previous iteration. When the number of spaces before the message becomes zero, the strategy changes: Instead of appending the message to a string of spaces, a substring of the message is displayed. With each iteration, the starting point of the substring moves one character to the right, making the message appear to move to the left. When the message has disappeared from view, the entire cycle usually starts over.

Here's an example of how to create a scrolling message:

```
<HTML>
    <HEAD>
        <TITLE>Scrolling Message</TITLE>
        <SCRIPT>
<!--
var winLength = 200; // guess at how many spaces wide the status bar is
var speed = 100; // number of milliseconds between updates
function scroll(count)
    {
    var msg = "Hi! This is my scrolling message in the status bar.";
    var out = " ";
    var cmd = "scroll(";

    if (count <= winLength && 0 < count)
        {
        var c = 0;
        for (c = 0 ; c < count ; c++)
            {
            out += " ";
}
        out += msg;
        }
    else if (count <= 0)
        {
        if (-count < msg.length)
            {
            out += msg.substring(-count,msg.length);
}
        else
            {
            count = winLength + 1;
            }
        }
    window.status = out;
    count--;
    cmd += count + ")";
    window.setTimeout(cmd,speed);
    }
//-->
        </SCRIPT>
    </HEAD>
```

```
<BODY ONLOAD="window.setTimeout('scroll(winLength)',speed);">
    </BODY>
</HTML>
```

Scrolling messages don't necessarily have to show up in the status area. You can create a form and place the message in a text field within that form.

CLOCKS

Clocks are really a variation on the scrolling message. They simply stay put and tell the time, like the clock on your VCR (except that it doesn't blink "12:00"—it actually displays the time of day). JavaScript understands dates and times, and creating a simple clock display is quite easy, as you can see from this code and Figure 2.4:

```
<HTML>
    <HEAD>
        <TITLE>Clock</TITLE>
        <SCRIPT>
<!--
function updateTime()
    {
    var now = new Date();
    var time = "" + now.getHours() + ":";
    var minute = now.getMinutes();
    if (minute < 10)
        {
        time += "0";
        }
    time += minute + ":";
    var second = now.getSeconds();
    if (second < 10)
        {
        time += "0";
        }
    time += second;
    window.status = time;
    window.setTimeout("updateTime()",1000);
    }
//-->
        </SCRIPT>
    </HEAD>
    <BODY ONLOAD="window.setTimeout('updateTime()',1000);">
    </BODY>
</HTML>
```

This code gets the current time by creating a new Date object. It extracts the hours, minutes, and seconds and displays them on the status bar. In the case of

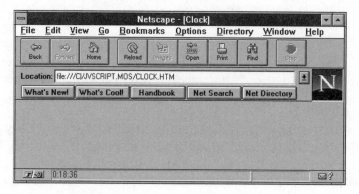

Figure 2.4: A simple clock on the status bar

the minutes and seconds, it also checks whether either value is a single digit. If one of them is, it adds the leading zero (a time of five after twelve would look odd displayed as "12:5:0"). After the time is displayed, a new timer is created that will time out in exactly 1,000 milliseconds. When the timer times out, it displays the time and sets up another timer. And on and on it goes, like sand through an hourglass.

COUNTDOWN TIMERS

Another variation on the theme of timers is a countdown timer—a timer that counts backward. You could use such a timer to let the user know that something is about to happen, and when. Again, it is easy to create countdown timers in JavaScript, as shown here:

```
<HTML>
    <HEAD>
        <TITLE>Count Down</TITLE>
        <SCRIPT>
<!--
function countDown(tick)

    {
    if (tick == Ø)
        {
        window.status = "We have liftoff...";
        return;
        }
    var time = "T minus ";
    var minute = Math.floor(tick / 6Ø);
    if (minute < 1Ø)
        {
```

```
        time += "0";
        }
    time += minute + ":";
    var second = tick % 60;
    if (second < 10)
        {
        time += "0";
        }
    time += second;
    window.status = time;
    --tick;
    var command = "countDown(" + tick + ")";
    window.setTimeout(command,1000);
    }
//-->
        </SCRIPT>
    </HEAD>
    <BODY ONLOAD="window.setTimeout('countDown(120)',1000);">
    </BODY>
</HTML>
```

Here an integer holds the time in seconds. The time is divided by 60 to get the minutes (Math.floor() is used to make sure the quotient is an integer) and the modulus operator is used to get the seconds. The minutes and seconds are displayed in the status bar. At the end of the timer code, a new time-out is created that repeats the code with one less second, one second later. When the seconds get to zero, the status bar is changed and no further time-outs are created.

SELF-UPDATING DOCUMENTS

Finally, a document can update itself. For example, every five minutes a brokerage house might create a GIF image that displays a graph of the rise and fall of the Dow Jones during a five-minute span. You can create a document that includes the GIF file as an inline image, and the document can update itself every five minutes. This document calls history.go(0) every 300 seconds (five minutes). Recall that history.go(0) acts like a press of the reload button.

```
<HTML>
    <HEAD>
        <TITLE>The Dow Jones</TITLE>
    </HEAD>
    <BODY>
        <IMG SRC="http://www.mythical_brokerage_house.com/DJ.GIF"
            ALT="Picture it..." HEIGHT="500" WIDTH="500">
    </BODY ONLOAD="window.setTimeout('history.go(0)',300000)">
</HTML>
```

Style

IMAGE IS EVERYTHING

PROTECTING YOUR DOCUMENT FROM
    ROGUE USERS

DOCUMENT MAINTENANCE

THE LAST RULE

H TML enables you to take plain text and turn it into an attractively laid out document. It also lets you turn the text into an ugly mess that no one would want to read. JavaScript confers an even greater ability to create a spectacular document, and an even greater ability to create a hideous page that no one will want to read. Using JavaScript, you can even crash the browser. This chapter explains how to use JavaScript judiciously so your Web pages both look nice and run smoothly.

IMAGE IS EVERYTHING

Your Web pages are your personal ambassadors to the world. They make a statement about you. Naturally, you can't control everyone's reaction to your pages; some people simply are not going to take an interest in what you have to say. But you can take simple steps in terms of the content of your pages (what you say) and in terms of the presentation of your pages (how you say it) to maximize the impact you want your pages to have.

CONTENT

What you say and how you say it makes a big difference in how readers view your pages. Simple mistakes in the content—particularly the text portions of your page—can lose readers or make a poor impression, and such mistakes are not that difficult to prevent.

Speling "Speling"? That really looks bad, doesn't it? If you're writing the text in your pages in your native language (people tend to cut you some slack otherwise), check your spelling. Misspelled words convey a bad impression, making you look sloppy, careless, ignorant—take your pick. If you make spelling mistakes, the best you can hope for is that your readers don't notice or don't care.

So check the spelling in your pages before you load them onto your server for public consumption. Most word processors have built-in or bundled spell checking capabilities. Most of them can learn to accept and ignore HTML tags. Some online services will check the spelling of your pages within seconds; these services already know to overlook HTML tags.

If you have a lot of JavaScript code in your pages, the spell checker will probably go ballistic over the code. It will not recognize your variable or function names unless you've entered them into the spell checker's dictionary, which is a practice I do not endorse. (It tends to clutter up the dictionary, and unless you're using the spell checker strictly for your Web pages, you've just told the spell checker to ignore what may well be typos in a business letter.) The solution is to make a copy of your page and remove the contents of the <SCRIPT> element before running the copy through a spell checker. Because you'll be making changes by hand, this should be an iterative process (you'll repeat these steps until the text of your page is clean). Of course, you can avoid the iterative process if you have access to software that will merge changes automatically. Here is what you should do:

1 Make a copy of your page

2 Remove the JavaScript code from the copy.

3 Run the copy through a spell checker.

4 If the spell checker reveals spelling errors, fix them in the original page. Otherwise, you're done.

5 Go back to step 1. This will ensure that you've caught all of the mistakes.

Sometimes you may want to deliberately use misspelled words, as in the heading of this section. As long as the typical reader will realize that the word is deliberately misspelled, this is probably not a problem.

You may also use misspelled words in quotations that contain misspellings. To handle this situation, first enclose the quotation within an appropriate element, such as <CITE>, so the reader has a clue that the enclosed text is a quotation. Second, you may want to place the Latin word "sic" in parentheses following the misspelled word. This tells your readers that you are quoting a misspelled word rather than misspelling the word yourself.

Unless you want your readers to instantly consider you an adolescent who finally cracked mommy or daddy's password, avoid misspellings such as "kewl" and "dood" and "warez." Also try to remember the difference between the letter "O" and the number "0." They are not interchangeable.

Grammar   Poor grammar can alienate your readers as much as poor spelling can. Unfortunately, it's a little bit more difficult to check grammar than it is to check spelling. Grammar checking software is less common than spell checking software. Grammar also includes many gray areas, and grammar checking software is more likely than spell checking software to miss errors and falsely label valid text as erroneous. However, few readers will recognize subtle errors, and the rules of grammar often allow for exceptions.

A good approach is to try to catch the big errors. Don't mix up singular and plural in the subject and predicate of a sentence. An old rock standard from the early '60s contains a line, "I knew we was falling in love," that has the same effect on me as fingernails on a chalkboard. Although that particular error may not bother you, it really stands out in print. Don't confuse possessive words with contractions that involve the word "is," especially "its" (which means belonging to or pertaining to "it") and "it's" (which means "it is"). Dust off a copy of Strunk and White's *Elements of Style,* or check it out on the Web.

Adult material   Adults built the World Wide Web for adults. It was never intended to be a medium for children. Nevertheless, it has become a medium that children can and do use.

Does this mean that your pages should be free of content that may not be appropriate for children? Personally, I don't think that's necessary. I don't carry this kind of material in my own pages, primarily because it attracts a lot of hits. I have no compelling reason to degrade my Web space provider's performance or to pay extra for the privilege of doing so.

Still, you may choose to include such material on your page. If you do, it is a common courtesy to have a "gatekeeper" page warning readers that they're about to access material that may not be appropriate for children.

After going through the gatekeeper page, the reader has the protected page's URL. At this point, the reader can bookmark the URL or publish the URL to others, who can then bypass the gatekeeper and go straight to the protected page. JavaScript provides a mechanism for ensuring that readers go through your gatekeeper first: the document object's referrer property.

The referrer property provides you with a read-only string containing the full URL of the page that the reader just came from. When your page is loaded, it can check the referrer property to see if the reader loaded this page from the gatekeeper page and refuse to load the restricted contents. Here's a sample gate-keeper page, referrer.htm:

```
<HTML>
    <HEAD>
        <TITLE>Gatekeeper</TITLE>
    </HEAD>
    <BODY>
        <A HREF="protect.htm">Click here</A>
    </BODY>
</HTML>
```

This very simple page's sole purpose is to provide access to the adult material in protect.htm.

Here's protect.htm:

```
<HTML>
    <HEAD>
        <TITLE>Protected Material</TITLE>
        <SCRIPT>
<!-- beginning of script
if (document.referrer != "file:///C|/JVSCRIPT.MOS/REFERRER.HTM")
        {
        history.back();
        }
else
        {
        // we got here from the correct URL
        }
// end of script -->
        </SCRIPT>
    </HEAD>
    <BODY>
        <!-- protected material goes here -->
    </BODY>
</HTML>
```

This protection is very simple: If the referrer property doesn't match the URL of the gatekeeper page, the browser bounces the reader straight back to where he or she came from. You could enhance this protection scheme by using the alert() method to display a message to the reader, explaining that he or she cannot access this page directly, but must first pass through the gate-keeper page.

To get the URL of the referring page, I originally included code in pro-tect.htm that wrote the contents of the referrer property to the page:

```
document.write(document.referrer);
```

If I placed these pages on my Web space provider, I would comment out the history.back() call and reintroduce the document.write(document.referrer) call. By doing so, I make sure I have the correct format for referrer.htm's URL.

PRESENTATION

The best content in the world is useless if you're the only one who can see it. It's easy to forget that not everyone is using a system exactly like yours. Even if your system presents your page the way you want it to, not everyone else will necessarily see what you want them to see.

Not all browsers support JavaScript   It's a sad but true fact that not all browsers support JavaScript. Readers using popular browsers such as NCSA Mosaic will not benefit from your JavaScript expertise. Unless you want to alienate those readers, you need to be sensitive to the needs of the Netscape-deficient. Two major errors to avoid are littering the screen with JavaScript code and leaving a blank page for the reader to ponder.

Hide your code   The casual reader is probably not interested in your Java-Script code. The reader using a browser that can't interpret JavaScript code is even less likely to be interested in it. Hide your code. Embedding JavaScript within comment tags is an important step in hiding the code. Browsers that don't support JavaScript will display the JavaScript code that lies within the <SCRIPT> element as plain text. If you place this code within comment tags it won't be displayed. Immediately following the <SCRIPT> tag, insert the beginning of an HTML comment (<!--). Netscape will ignore it; other browsers will see that it is the start of a comment.

Just before the </SCRIPT> tag, you need to end the comment. There are two ways you can do this; you can use the method you prefer.

The first way of ending a comment is to place a complete HTML comment at the end of the JavaScript code, like this:

```
<!-- end of script --></SCRIPT>
```

To Netscape, this looks like a new comment followed by the </SCRIPT> end tag. Other browsers ignore the <!-- and see the --> as the end of the comment that was started at the beginning of the <SCRIPT> element.

The other way of ending a comment is to begin a JavaScript one-line com-ment—the kind that starts with // and ends with the end of the source line. Just make sure that the --> is at the end of the comment. As with the first method, browsers that don't support JavaScript will close the comment that was begun after the <SCRIPT> tag when they see the --> at the end of the comment. Netscape sees it as a routine JavaScript comment. The only drawback to this technique is that it forces the </SCRIPT> tag to be on the next source line. If it were on the same line as the one-line comment, it would become part of the comment.

It's easy to hide your JavaScript code. However, your own code could sabotage your efforts to make it invisible. Here are two steps to take to prevent this unwitting sabotage:

First, don't use the decrement operator (--). Some browsers see the double hyphen as the end of the comment; everything following the decrement operator may show up on the reader's screen. Instead, use the -= operator with an operand of 1, like this:

```
x -= 1;
```

Second, avoid using the > character in your script. Some browsers treat the > character as the end of the comment regardless of whether it's preceded by --.

The > symbol will show up in your JavaScript code as the greater than operator and as the end of tags. The first usage is trivial to fix; instead of

```
x > y
```

rewrite your code as:

```
y < x
```

The two expressions are identical in their value: true if x is greater than y and false if x is less than or equal to y.

The second usage is a little harder to fix. Suppose you write a tag like this:

```
document.write("<TITLE>Visible code under some browsers</TITLE>");
```

First, you need to create a string that contains a single > character, like this:

```
var tagEnd = unescape("%3E");
```

Then, in subsequent lines, substitute your string as needed, like this:

```
document.write("<TITLE" + tagEnd + "Invisible code under all browsers</TITLE" +
tagEnd);
```

Try to see your document their way When creating Web pages, it's important to know how they'll look to others. You can download many of the major browsers, such as Mosaic, for your favorite platform and purchase costs are not very high. Get the major browsers and load your pages into them so you can get a sense of how your pages will look to your readers.

Don't forget to use the <NOFRAME> element if your pages use frames. This element allows you to include text that frame-ignorant browsers will display. The text can be as elaborate as a full HTML 2.0 compliant <BODY> element, or it can be as simple as an explanation like this:

```
<NOFRAME>
We are sorry to inform you that you have accessed a page that you need Netscape
2.0 to fully appreciate. You are not using Netscape 2.0; if you were, you
wouldn't see this text. <A HREF="your HTML 2.0 version of this page">Here</A> is
an equivalent page that doesn't require Netscape. Perhaps you should consider
downloading a copy of <A HREF="Netscape's URL for downloading the latest version
of Netscape Navigator">Netscape Navigator</A>.
</NOFRAME>
```

Finally, some browsers, such as lynx, don't know what to do with images. Don't forget to include the ALT attribute in all of your inline images; it lets you define alternate text that can be displayed in lieu of your image.

Not all platforms are created equal, part 1   Not all platforms support 24-bit color in a 1280x1024 screen resolution. If you create a page that relies on having lots of screen real estate and thousands of colors, you will disappoint a lot of readers. Of all the platforms that support the Netscape Navigator, the title of "least forgiving" probably has to go to Windows 3.1, running in 640x480 pixel mode, using 16 colors.

Recall that colors are expressed as a red-green-blue triplet, with 8 bits per component. That's 24 bits. That's wonderful for people with state-of-the-art video, and it's not too bad even for people whose systems can only eke out 8 bits (256 colors). But for video that is restricted to 4 bits for color, it's a challenge. How many colors are you using? Before you answer that, don't forget the colors in your inline GIF and JPEG images. Try out your page on a 16-color system. How does it look? More importantly, can you read it?

Okay, maybe you don't care about those cheapskates who can't be bothered to upgrade their systems with a decent video card and monitor. After all, prices are dropping. What's the problem?

Well, you still need to deal with the 640x480 pixel straightjacket, and that's not necessarily an artifact of a low-end system. The better the screen resolution, the smaller the pixels, and the smaller the pixels, the harder it is to read text. A lot of people suffer from a medical condition called presbyopia. If you're pushing 40 or you've passed that milestone, you probably know what this is. It's why you wear reading glasses, or bifocals, or progressive lenses. You can't focus on small print as you used to. The rest of you whippersnappers out there, heh heh, it's waiting for you.

So what does this mean to you as a page author? It means you want to be careful about creating documents with lots of frames subdividing the canvas. If I, the reader, have to squint to see your frame contents, or scroll madly in all directions, I don't care if you have the plans for world peace in your page. I'm not going to go to the trouble of trying to read it! Bottom line: Keep your pages simple. Keep the clutter to a minimum. To test your pages, here's a very simple page I call "The Bed of Procustes":

```
<HTML>
    <HEAD>
        <TITLE>The Bed of Procustes</TITLE>
        <SCRIPT>
<!-- Hide from primitive browsers
function putToBed(form)
    {
    // get the data from the form...
    var url = form.urlWidget.value;
    var width = form.widthWidget.value;
    var height = form.heightWidget.value;
    // create the command. specifying the url in the command seems to be
    // a problem, so the window is created empty, then loaded
    var command = "window.open('', 'noname',";
    command += " 'toolbar=yes,location=yes,directories=yes,status=yes,";
    command += "menubar=yes,scrollbars=yes,resizable=no,width=" + width;
    command += ",height=" + height + "')";
    // create the window
    var bed = eval(command);
    // do it twice for brain-damaged platforms
    bed = eval(command);
    // load it
    bed.location.href = url;
    // we're not really submitting a form, so return false
    return false;
    }
//-->
        </SCRIPT>
    </HEAD>
    <BODY>
        <FORM ONSUBMIT="putToBed(this)">
            Window Width: <INPUT TYPE=TEXT SIZE=5 NAME="widthWidget">
            Window Height: <INPUT TYPE=TEXT SIZE=5 NAME="heightWidget">
            <BR>
            URL To Be Loaded: <INPUT TYPE=TEXT SIZE=50 NAME="urlWidget">
            <BR>
            <INPUT TYPE=SUBMIT VALUE="Make it so">
        </FORM>
```

```
    </BODY>
</HTML>
```

This page generates a form into which you enter the URL of your page and specify the height and width of the browser. Clicking on the submit button creates a browser window of the specified size. The new browser window has all of the normal buttons and menu items associated with a browser window. After the new window is created, the specified page is loaded into it.

PROTECTING YOUR DOCUMENT FROM ROGUE USERS

This section explains how to write documents defensively. Readers will—sometimes by accident, sometimes maliciously—try to do things with your document that you did not intend them to do. You'd be surprised how many programmers don't follow these principles. (Okay, you've seen enough bugs; maybe you wouldn't be.)

MAKE SURE YOUR FUNCTIONS ARE LOADED

First, you should make sure your functions are loaded, which is easy to do. If you use a function that isn't loaded, your code will malfunction. What's more, it's almost certain to malfunction in a manner that leaves no doubt in the reader's mind that something went wrong—and that it's your fault. If there are JavaScript expressions in the body of your page and those expressions call other JavaScript functions that you wrote, place those JavaScript functions in a <SCRIPT> element within the <HEAD> element. The <HEAD> element is loaded before the <BODY> element; you can depend on the function being there. This approach prevents a user from impatiently clicking on a partially loaded page and invoking a JavaScript function that hasn't been downloaded from the server yet.

VALIDATE INPUT

If you're getting input from the reader, make sure you check it before blindly using it, especially if it's supposed to be a number. Use the parseInt() and parseFloat() functions. If it's supposed to be an integer, check it like this:

```
if (Math.ceil(x) == x)
    {
    // it's an integer
    }
else
    {
```

```
// oops...
}
```

The Math object's ceil() method returns the next higher integer for a floating-point value; for an integer value, it will return the same value. The floor() method will also work.

Finally, if the number is supposed to be within a certain range of values, make sure that it's within the specifications. For example, if it's supposed to be a value from 1 to 10, put something like this in your code:

```
if (x < 1 || 10 < x)
    {
    alert("" + x + "is not between 1 and 10");
    return;
    }
```

BUT SURELY NO ONE WOULD DO THAT!

Sometimes users will input data that they're not supposed to. Some users will be confused about what they're supposed to enter; they won't understand what they're supposed to do. Other users will deliberately try to make your page crash just for fun. Assume that when you ask for a number, someone is going to enter anything except number. "But you're not supposed to do that" is not a valid defense for letting your code malfunction just because you asked for a number but someone entered a phone number or the word "no."

NOT ALL PLATFORMS ARE CREATED EQUAL, PART 2

There are some differences between the implementations of Netscape Navigator for the various supported platforms. You can't expect everyone to use the same platform that you use, and you should write your code to defend against problems tied to specific platforms:

- ▶ Macintosh and Windows browsers can't return NaN (Not a Number) when you call parseInt() or parseFloat() and the argument is not a number. They return 0 instead.

- ▶ random() only works on UNIX platforms.

- ▶ Xwindow platforms have difficulty drawing new browser windows. Even if you specify the parts of the window you want, you're going to get a bare window.

- ▶ When you open a new document, call open() twice. Windows and Macintosh browsers won't open the document unless you call open() twice.

Either use the navigator object's appVersion property to find out what platform your JavaScript code is running on and adjust the runtime behavior of your code accordingly, or include workarounds for known differences between the platforms.

Document maintenance

Nearly all Web pages are living documents. Someone has to maintain them, and there's no guarantee that the person who wrote the original document will always be around to explain how it works. For that matter, there's no guarantee that the original author will remember how it works six months later. Fortunately, there are several simple strategies for making your documents easy to understand and maintain.

COMMENT, COMMENT, COMMENT

Use comments. For every function, explain what the parameters are and what they're used for. Explain what the function does and what it does if the inputs aren't entered correctly. Within the function body, explain what each functional block does, how it does it, and why it does it. Some people use a standard comment block for each function, like this:

```
//
// function name: (name of function)
// author: (author of function)
// revision history: (what was changed, when, and why?)
// parameters: (what are the parameters, what do they
//     represent, what kind of values should they contain?)
// returns: (does the function return a value? What kind
//     of value? What does the value mean?)
// purpose: (what does this function do?)
// global variables used: (useful in debugging to figure
//     out who touched the contents)
//
```

Write down your assumptions. Do certain named objects have to exist for the code to work? Say so!

Using comments to document your code helps you in two ways: First, it helps indicate what you were thinking when you wrote the function. That information will be invaluable later when you need to modify the function or use it in another page.

Second, the act of documenting your code forces you to think about what it does and how it does it. Often, you'll realize that there is a better, faster, more reliable way to do what you're doing, and you'll improve your code.

When modifying code, make sure that your comments are still accurate. There is not much worse than comments that are no longer accurate and that now lead you astray.

CONSISTENT INTERNAL STYLE

There are many ways to write JavaScript. The browser doesn't care what the code looks like, as long as it can tell what you're doing. You need to select a JavaScript style that works for you and that helps you visualize what's going on. Although you have a lot of leeway, it's critical to be consistent.

Here are some general pointers:

▶ Develop a consistent indentation style. I generally prefer to write the start and end tags on separate lines, at the same level of indentation, and I write the contents of the element at a greater indentation level. I also write the start and end tags first, and then go back and insert the contents. I avoid a lot of missing tag errors that way.

▶ Make it easy to differentiate different kinds of text. I prefer to make tags and their attributes uppercase and variables lowercase. I prefer function names made up of a verb followed by a noun, with the verb lowercase and the noun with an initial capital letter (makeWindow, for example).

▶ Use short lines. If your code contains a mistake, Netscape will as often as not tell you about it and it will display the number of the line on which it found the problem. Long lines confuse Netscape, and it will return the favor: Try to guess where the error in your code really is! Also, long lines can be hard to follow; you'll be sorry that you didn't break up your code when you still understood it.

THE LAST RULE

The last rule is to have fun. JavaScript should make it fun to make your pages more exciting and attractive. Don't make it drudgery!

Part 2

The Examples

URL Patch

An Outlined Document

Color Chooser

Form Validation

Form Modification

Games

URL Patch

THE SCENARIO

THE REQUIREMENTS

THE SOLUTION (WITHOUT JAVASCRIPT)

THE SOLUTION (WITH JAVASCRIPT)

MODIFYING THE EXAMPLE FOR
   YOUR OWN USE

N ow you start learning how to put JavaScript to use. In this chapter, you work with an example of redirection. You find out how to build a Web page that redirects the visitor from a soon to be obsolete URL to another, up-to-date one. First you'll try solving the problem without JavaScript. Then you'll do it again with JavaScript, seeing how JavaScript allows you to create a more sophisticated solution.

THE SCENARIO

For one reason or another, you need to move your home page to a new Web server. You've set up your home page on the new server, but now you need to let regular visitors know where the new page is. You still have some time left with the old server, enough time to leave a forwarding address.

THE REQUIREMENTS

The requirements for this document are simple: Create a small Web page that informs visitors to the old URL that your page has moved.

THE SOLUTION (WITHOUT JAVASCRIPT)

This very simple page would no doubt suffice to let visitors know that you've moved your Web page:

```
<HTML>
    <HEAD>
```

```
        <TITLE>We've Moved!</TITLE>
    </HEAD>
    <BODY BGCOLOR="00FFFF" TEXT="000000" LINK="400080" >
        <P ALIGN=CENTER>
            <FONT SIZE="+2">We've moved!</FONT>
        </P>
        <HR>
        <P ALIGN=CENTER>
            The new URL is
            <A HREF="http://www.he.net/~marcj/roadmap.html">
            http://www.he.net/~marcj/roadmap.html</A>
        </P>
        <BR>
        <P ALIGN=CENTER>
            Make a note of it!
        </P>
    </BODY>
</HTML>
```

The result is a screen like the one shown in Figure 4.1. Not bad, but you can do better with JavaScript.

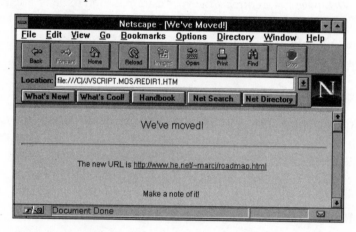

Figure 4.1: Simple redirection page

THE SOLUTION (WITH JAVASCRIPT)

What's wrong with the solution that doesn't use JavaScript? First of all, the viewer might not bother clicking on the link to get to your new home page. You can take him or her there—automatically!

Changing the currently displayed document is simple. The window object has a property called location, which is a location object. Location objects have a property called href, which is a string that contains the currently displayed document's URL. All you have to do is change that property:

```
window.location.href = "http://www.he.net/~marcj/roadmap.html";
```

So how do you execute this expression? Well, the simple way is to make this expression the event handler for the BODY element's load event. The BODY element allows you to specify a JavaScript expression (called an event handler) that will be executed when the document finishes loading (this is called a load event)

```
<BODY ONLOAD="window.location.href =
    'http://www.he.net/~marcj/roadmap.html'">
```

All very well, but now the new URL is not visible on the screen for very long, if at all. Some users like to print the document so they have a reminder to go back and change their links to your home page. Such users will have to be very quick with the print button!

You need to introduce a delay—60 seconds should do it—so your users can write down or print the new URL. Now you can modify the BODY tag, like so:

```
<BODY ONLOAD="setTimeout(window.location.href =
    'http://www.he.net/~marcj/roadmap.html',60000">
```

That, by itself, is much better. Now the user can print the document listing the new URL before the new document is loaded automatically.

But we can add one more twist to it. A page with a long time-out can appear to be loaded and waiting for the user to do something. Let the user know you're not sitting idly by; you can do this by adding a countdown timer to the status part of the window. While you're at it, you might also want to add a screen message telling the user what is going on.

The countdown timer is very straightforward. Start with an arbitrary count of seconds, and once a second, display the time remaining and subtract one second. When the count goes to zero, load the window.location.href property as you saw earlier. The basic structure of the countdown timer looks like this:

```
function countDown(tick)
    {
    if (tick == 0)
        {
        window.location.href="http://www.he.net/~marcj/roadmap.html";
        return;
        }
    // display the time //
```

```
    --tick;
    var command = "countDown(" + tick + ")";
    window.setTimeout(command,1000);
    }
```

You'll note that the timeout value is set to 1000; JavaScript measures time in milliseconds, and one second is 1000 milliseconds.

The display is very simple. Just format the time remaining and write it to the window.status. The format is a little tricky, however. First, you want to convert the time to minutes and seconds. You calculate the minutes like this:

```
var minutes = Math.floor(count / 60);
```

The Math object's floor method is important; if you omit it the minutes will have a decimal portion. The 60 second count will show minute values of 1, 0.98333333, 0.966666666, and so forth. Not what you want!

Then you calculate the seconds using the modulo operator:

```
var seconds = count % 60;
```

The modulo operator returns the remainder left from dividing the left-hand operand (count) by the right-hand operand (60).

The second point in formatting the time is to make sure it looks right. Minutes and seconds are usually displayed with two digits. However, JavaScript formats minutes and seconds values of less than 10 as single digits. To get around this, check whether minutes is less than 10; if it is, add a leading zero to the display string. You do the same thing for the seconds.

This is all a little too involved to place in an ONLOAD event handler as a set of expressions; instead you can make it into a function and call the function as the BODY element's ONLOAD event handler.

Here's the document you have now:

```
<HTML>
    <HEAD>
        <TITLE>We've Moved!</TITLE>
        <SCRIPT LANG="JavaScript">
<!--
function countDown(tick)
    {
    if (tick == 0)
        {
        window.location.href="http://www.he.net/~marcj/roadmap.html";
        return;
        }
    var time = "Transfer in ";
    var minute = Math.floor(tick / 60);
```

```
        if (minute < 10)
            {
            time += "0";
            }
        time += minute + ":";
        var second = tick % 60;
        if (second < 10)
            {
            time += "0";
            }
        time += second;
        window.status = time;
        --tick;
        var command = "countDown(" + tick + ")";
        window.setTimeout(command,1000);
        }
//-->
        </SCRIPT>
    </HEAD>
    <BODY ONLOAD="window.setTimeout('countDown(60)',1000);"
        BGCOLOR="00FFFF" TEXT="000000" LINK="400080">
        <P ALIGN=CENTER>
            <FONT SIZE="+2">We've moved!</FONT>
        </P>
        <HR>
        <P ALIGN=CENTER>
            The new URL is
            <A HREF="http://www.he.net/~marcj/roadmap.html">
            http://www.he.net/~marcj/roadmap.html</A>
        </P>
        <BR>
        <P ALIGN=CENTER>
            Make a note of it!
        </P>
        <BR>
        <P ALIGN=CENTER>
            Go ahead and transfer, or, if you're using <B>Netscape</B>,
            relax, and leave the driving to us! We'll be leaving in
            about a minute....
        </P>
    </BODY>
</HTML>
```

Figure 4.2 shows what this document looks like.

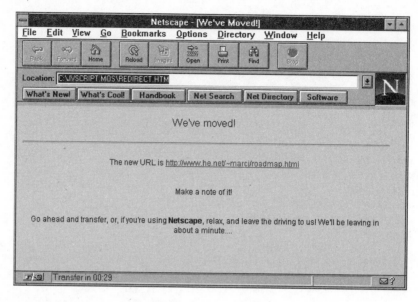

Figure 4.2: Redirection with JavaScript

MODIFYING THE EXAMPLE FOR YOUR OWN USE

You can use this example by simply changing the URL used; it shows up three times, and it's a simple find-and-replace operation for your text editor. You can also change the length of the countdown timer by changing the 60 in the BODY element to a different value. You can change the text that appears in the status bar. Don't be afraid to experiment with it!

An Outlined Document

The scenario

The requirements

The solution (without JavaScript)

The solution (with JavaScript)

Improving the solution

Modifying the example for
  your own use

5

In this chapter, you learn how to create an outlined document, a document that includes an outline describing its logical structure. You can use such an outline both to get an overview of the document and to skip quickly to various parts of the document. This chapter shows you how to create an outlined document on the World Wide Web. First you create a simple outlined document without JavaScript. Then you use JavaScript to build a much more sophisticated outlined document that is always visible on screen and that you can collapse or expand to see in less or greater detail.

THE SCENARIO

You want to put a document on the World Wide Web; the document includes an outline describing its logical structure. The ideal candidate for an outlined document is one that has a logical structure that fits into an outline. You should also be able to read the document piecemeal, and possibly in random order; the outline will help you jump directly to the portion of the document you want to read. Examples include Frequently Asked Questions (FAQs), legal documents, and directories. The example in this chapter is a well-organized set of bookmarks to other Web sites, based on my own bookmark collections.

THE REQUIREMENTS

There are five requirements for putting together your outline.

- ▸ The outline must be able to accommodate a document that is divided into several Web pages.

- ▸ The user must be able to access the document outline easily from any point on any of the constituent Web pages.

- ▸ The document outline must help the user navigate the constituent Web pages.

- ▸ The user must be able to quickly navigate the document outline, regardless of its length.

- ▸ The design of the document outline should be reusable. In particular, it must not set arbitrary limits, such as the maximum number of links in the outline or how deeply nested the outline can be, that might hinder the reuse of the design. The design of the outline must be extensible to handle arbitrarily complex documents.

THE SOLUTION (WITHOUT JAVASCRIPT)

A conventional approach to the problem would be to create a single document that contains the document outline. The document outline would consist of links to the Web pages that make up the document. The links would be arranged as items in a list, as shown in Listing 5.1.

Listing 5.1: A document outline without JavaScript

```
<HTML>
    <HEAD>
        <TITLE>Marc Johnson's Roadmap</TITLE>
    </HEAD>
    <BODY>
        <H1>Marc Johnson's Roadmap</H1>
        <UL>
            <LI><A HREF="index.html">My home page</A>
            <LI><A HREF="amusement.html">Amusements</A>
            <UL>
                <LI><A HREF="amusement.html#Comics">Comics</A>
                <LI><A HREF="amusement.html#Funnies">Funnies</A>
                <LI><A HREF="amusement.html#Games">Games</A>
                <LI><A HREF="amusement.html#Media">Media</A>
                <LI><A HREF="amusement.html#Travel">Travel</A>
            </UL>
            <LI><A HREF="business.html">Business</A>
            <UL>
                <LI><A HREF="business.html#Book Stores">Book Stores</A>
                <LI><A HREF="business.html#Other">Other</A>
            </UL>
            <LI><A HREF="internet.html">Internet</A>
```

Listing 5.1: A document outline without JavaScript (Continued)

```
            <UL>
                <LI><A HREF="internet.html#Providers">Providers</A>
                <LI><A HREF="internet.html#Resources">Resources</A>
                <LI><A HREF="internet.html#Surfing">Surfing</A>
                <LI><A HREF="internet.html#Web Pages">Web Pages</A>
                <UL>
                    <LI><A HREF="internet.html#Graphics">Graphics</A>
                    <LI><A HREF="internet.html#HTML">HTML</A>
                    <LI><A HREF="internet.html#Icons">Icons</A>
                    <LI><A HREF="internet.html#Pages">Pages</A>
                    <LI><A HREF="internet.html#Tools">Tools</A>
                </UL>
            </UL>
            <LI><A HREF="reference.html">Reference Materials</A>
            <UL>
                <LI><A HREF="reference.html#Books">Books</A>
                <LI><A HREF="reference.html#Documents">Documents</A>
                <LI><A HREF="reference.html#Education">Education</A>
                <LI><A HREF="reference.html#Government">Government</A>
                <LI><A HREF="reference.html#Jobs">Jobs</A>
                <LI><A HREF="reference.html#Reference
                    Servers">Reference Servers</A>
            </UL>
            <LI><A HREF="sf.html">Science Fiction</A>
            <UL>
                <LI><A HREF="sf.html#Books">Books</A>
                <LI><A HREF="sf.html#Miscellaneous
                    Television">Miscellaneous Television</A>
                <LI><A HREF="sf.html#Star Trek">Star Trek</A>
                <LI><A HREF="sf.html#World Designs">World Designs</A>
            </UL>
            <LI><A HREF="software.html">Software</A>
            <UL>
                <LI><A HREF="software.html#Academia">Academia</A>
                <LI><A HREF="software.html#AandD">Analysis and
                    Design</A>
                <LI><A HREF="software.html#Linux">Linux</A>
                <LI><A HREF="software.html#Programming">Programming</A>
                <LI><A HREF="software.html#Shareware">Shareware</A>
                <LI><A HREF="software.html#Vendors">Vendors</A>
            </UL>
            <LI><A HREF="weather.html">Weather</A>
            <UL>
                <LI><A HREF="weather.html#Images">Images</A>
                <LI><A HREF="weather.html#NWS Bulletins">NWS
                    Bulletins</A>
                <LI><A HREF="weather.html#Weather Servers">Weather
                    Servers</A>
            </UL>
        </UL>
        <HR>
    </BODY>
</HTML>
```

Figure 5.1 shows (partially) what the HTML code in Listing 5.1 produces. This document meets requirement 3. That is, it helps users navigate the various Web pages the document consists of; they can do this simply by clicking on links in the outline. It also meets requirement 4—in other words, it lets you quickly navigate the document outline. Scrolling through the outline looking for the right link is much faster than scrolling through the document itself and following links and waiting for them to load. There is no specific limit to how deeply you can nest UL elements, so the design of this document meets requirement 5; it is extensible and reusable. The fact that the document will probably be divided into several Web pages is also not a problem. This is the kind of thing that conventional Web pages can easily handle with ordinary links—so the document meets requirement 1.

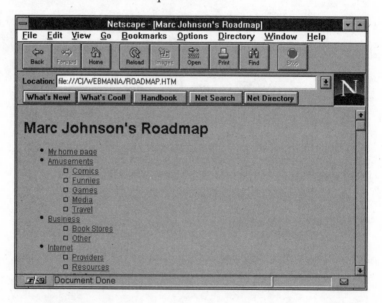

Figure 5.1: A document outline

There is still requirement 2 remaining—this is the requirement that the user can access the document outline easily from any point on any of the constituent Web pages. If you're not using JavaScript, there's not a very good solution here. About the best you can do is to insert links back to the document outline page. You have to insert links into each Web page in the document, which can be a problem if you don't have direct control over all of the constituent Web pages. Alternatively, you can simply assume that the user can use the browser's back button to return to the outline. This solution is a maintenance headache and highly dependent on user cooperation.

THE SOLUTION (WITH JAVASCRIPT)

Although you can create a workable outline document without JavaScript, JavaScript can improve upon the solution, if you put in a little work. With JavaScript, you can keep the outline visible while the user reads the document, and you can make the outline much easier to navigate.

FRAME IN THE OUTLINE

You will better meet requirement 2—the requirement that users can access the document outline easily from any point on any of the constituent Web pages— if the document outline is always visible. You can do this by creating a frame document, splitting the window in two. While this does steal some room from the document pages themselves, the loss is minimal, as most Web pages don't fit within the browser window anyway. The following code puts the document outline on the left and the current document page on the right:

```
<HTML>
    <HEAD>
        <TITLE>Marc's List of Great Web Pages</TITLE>
    </HEAD>
    <FRAMESET COLS="30%,*">
        <FRAME NAME="outline" SRC="outline.htm">
        <FRAME NAME="contents" SRC="main.htm">
    </FRAMESET>
</HTML>
```

Now the document outline is next to the current page of the document, as you can see in Figure 5.2. You don't have to insert links to the document outline into each document Web page. The document outline is much easier to get to than in the non-JavaScript solution. You don't have to hunt around to find it—it's always there on display.

MAKE THE DOCUMENT OUTLINE SMARTER

Using JavaScript, you can also make it easier for the user to quickly navigate the document outline. You can allow the user to hide irrelevant portions of the outline, leaving only the portions that are important to him or her. You can do this by making the outline a dynamic document created on the fly instead of a static document loaded from the server.

You can visualize the document outline shown in Figure 5.1 as a tree structure. With JavaScript, you can create a new-and-improved tree structure whose branches can be collapsed so that the subordinate branches and leaves are out of the way. This approach allows the user to "prune" the tree on the fly,

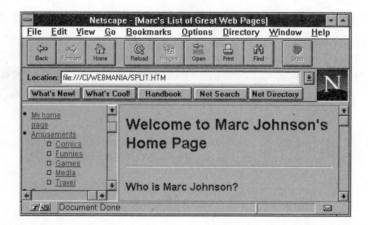

Figure 5.2: A frame document

leaving a shorter outline that's easier to navigate. Naturally, you should be able to bring back the subordinate branches and leaves at any time. As an example, Figure 5.3 shows a full outline; Figure 5.4 shows the same outline with the Web Pages branch collapsed.

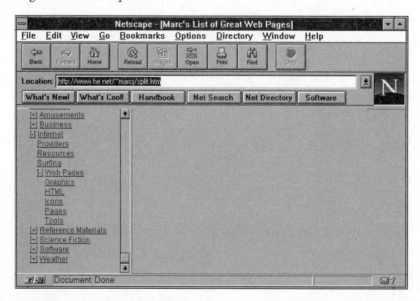

Figure 5.3: The Web Pages branch is open.

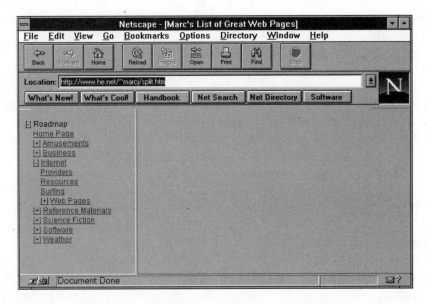

Figure 5.4: The Web Pages branch has been collapsed and is closed.

Creating a collapsible tree structure   First you'll create a simple tree structure consisting of two kinds of objects: branch objects and leaf objects. Branch objects have zero or more subordinate leaf objects and zero or more subordinate branch objects. Leaf objects have no constituent objects.

A branch object has a title property; this is the text that will be displayed in the document outline. It also has a flags property that, if set, indicates that its constituent branch and leaf objects are to be displayed. If the flags property is clear, its constituent objects are not to be displayed. A branch object also has a url property, which is the URL of a document that describes the branch and its constituent objects—a summary, perhaps. The url property may be empty if there is no document logically associated with the branch and its constituent objects.

A leaf object also has a title property and a url property. The url property should not be empty; the leaf should point to a document. As with the branch object, you can use the title and url properties to create a link (<A HREF="...">...</A>) element.

The branch and leaf objects are similar enough that you can effectively combine them into a single kind of object, called a *node object*. The entire document outline can then be represented as a list of node objects, which greatly simplifies the tasks of initializing and displaying the outline.

You also need some way to indicate, within the list of nodes, that you've listed all of the constituent objects of a given branch. One way is to mark the last constituent node object with a special flag. There are two problems with this approach. First, when you add new branches and leaves to the tree, you may accidentally place the new nodes after the end-of-branch flag. If you do, the new nodes will appear to be a constituent of the wrong branch, or may not even appear to belong to another branch. Second, there is a problem when a node object is the last object in more than one branch, such as the internet.html#Tools link in Listing 5.1. You either have to somehow represent the fact that a node marked as end-of-branch may terminate more than one branch (and indicate which ones) or mark the node's branch as the termination of its parent branch by applying an end-of-branch marker to it. Either way, it's needlessly messy and not very intuitive to the person maintaining the document outline.

The solution I chose was to create a special empty node object that follows the last node of a branch, similar to the </UL> tag that terminates a <UL> list element—it's a little harder to overlook an explicitly defined node than a node that happens to be a leaf or branch (like most of the nodes) and also the end of a branch.

So now you have a node object. It has a flags property, which is used to contain the information about whether the node is a branch, a leaf, or an empty node. The flags property can also indicate whether the branch is open (constituent objects displayable) or closed (constituent objects suppressed). It has a title property, which empty node objects don't use. It has a url property, which is also used only by leaf and branch nodes. There is also one more property, the index property, which contains the index of the node object into the array of node objects. You'll use this property later to close and open branch objects.

There's one more thing you need for your node object: a method for it to display itself. This way, you can display the document outline by iterating over an array of node objects. So you'll add a drawNode method. When you create a new node object, you'll set the drawNode method to a function designed to draw a branch node, a leaf node, or an empty node. Here's what the function that creates a new node object looks like:

```
function node(flags, title, url)
    {
    this.index = nodeCtr;
    this.flags = flags;
    if (flags == __leaf__ || ((flags & __branch__) == __branch__))
        {
        this.title = title;
        if (flags == __leaf__)
```

```
        {
        this.url = url;
        this.drawNode = drawLeaf;
        }
    else
        {
        if (node.arguments.length >= 3)
            {
            this.url = url;
            }
        else
            {
            this.url = "";
            }
        this.drawNode = drawBranch;
        }
    }
else
    {
    this.drawNode = drawEmptyNode;
    }
}
```

In plain English, here's what happens in the node function:

First, the node's index property is set to the value of a variable called nodeCtr; this variable is explained in the section "Creating Arrays of Depth and Node Objects" later in this chapter.

Next, the node's flags property is set to the value of the flags parameter. The flags value is a bitmap, which is a number made up of individual binary digits, as you can see in Figure 5.5. Bitmaps are useful for expressing sets of Boolean (yes/no, true/false) values without using a lot of different variables.

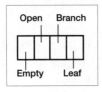

Figure 5.5: The bitmap structure

Then the flags value is tested. If the flags value indicates that the node is a leaf or a branch, one block of code is executed; otherwise, the node must be an empty node. Note that the test for the node being a branch is different from the test for it being a leaf—a branch node's flags value also indicates whether it's open. Rather than test for leaf or open branch or closed branch, you test for leaf, or "has branch bit set."

Once it's determined that the node is either a leaf or a branch, the title property is set to the value of the title parameter. Then the code further differentiates between a leaf or a branch.

If the node is a leaf, the node's url property is set to the value of the url parameter and the drawNode method is set to the drawLeaf function.

If the node is not a leaf (and is therefore a branch), the code checks how many parameters were passed. If there are at least three arguments (node.arguments.length >= 3), a url was passed and the node's url property is set to the url parameter's value. Otherwise, the url property is set to an empty string. The node's drawNode method is set to the drawBranch function.

The empty node initialization is simple: The node's drawNode method is set to the drawEmptyNode function.

How deep is the tree? And where are we, anyway?   You need something else to make the tree display work: something to keep track of how deep into the tree you are. As you traverse the tree, you may be going up and down branches. To remember whether, at a given depth, you're supposed to display a node's contents, you need an object that stores, at a given depth, whether or not you're supposed to display objects.

I call this object a depth object. It has two properties: saved and value. The value property contains a zero value if the objects at or below this depth are not to be displayed and a nonzero value if the objects are to be displayed. The saved property keeps track of the previous value of the value property.

There are two methods: open() and close(). The open() method is called when a branch object is encountered in the list of nodes. It copies the depth object's value property to its saved property and sets the depth object's value property to a value corresponding to the __open__ bit in the branch object's flags property. The close() method is called when an empty object is encountered in the list of nodes. It simply restores the depth object's value property from its saved property. The depth function that defines a new depth object sets the saved and value properties to zero (not displayed), the open method to the depthOpen function, and the close method to the depthClose function. The depth functions look like this:

```
function depthOpen(newValue)
    {
    this.saved = this.value;
    this.value = newValue;
    }
```

```
function depthClose()
    {
    this.value = this.saved;
    }
function depth()
    {
    this.saved = 0;
    this.value = 0;
    this.open = depthOpen;
    this.close = depthClose;
    }
```

Creating arrays of depth and node objects You need an array of depth objects to keep track, at each level of the outline, of whether objects are to be displayed; its length is the depth of the deepest branch node in the nodes array. In the example shown here, you can go three branches deep, so there need to be three depth objects. To create the array, you will use a function described in Netscape's online documentation (see the Quick Reference), MakeArray:

```
function MakeArray(n)
    {
    this.length = n;
    for (var i = 1; i <= n; I++)
        {
        this[ i ] = 0;
        }
    return this;
    }
```

You then create the depthList and nodeList variables:

```
var depthList = new MakeArray(3);
var nodeList = new MakeArray(53);
```

You need to initialized the depth and node objects after creating the arrays. For the depth objects, this is very straightforward:

```
for (var n = 1; n <= 3; n++)
    {
    depthList[ n ] = new depth();
    }
```

For the nodeList objects, the process is a bit more involved. To make it a little easier, I created a counter variable, which you saw earlier in the node object constructor function:

```
var nodeCtr = 0;
nodeCtr++; nodeList[ nodeCtr ] = new node(...);
```

```
nodeCtr++; nodeList[ nodeCtr ] = new node(...);
    .
    .
    .
```

If you use this strategy, it's harder to miss a node or to initialize a node twice. At the end of the initialization sequence, you can also check your work. The following code, which is executed after the last node is created, verifies that nodeCtr agrees with the nodeList array's length property. If the two values disagree, construct a string that describes the error and put it on the screen in an alert box:

```
if (nodeCtr != nodeList.length)
    {
    alert("Node counter (" + nodeCtr + ") does not match nodeList.length (" +
nodeList.length + ")");
    }
```

You can remove or, better, comment out this check after you've tested the pages and verified that you did not see this alert window.

In initializing the nodeList, it's also a good idea to indent objects when you encounter a branch object, like so:

```
nodeList[ nodeCtr ] = new node(__branch__, ...
    nodeList[ nodeCtr ] = new node(__leaf__, ...
    nodeList[ nodeCtr ] = new node(__leaf__, ...
nodeList[ nodeCtr ] = new node(__empty__, ...
```

This way, you have a visual check that you've balanced the branch and empty nodes correctly, and that branch node and empty node pairs contain the correct objects. You'll also perform a check when you draw the tree, as you'll see later in this chapter.

Drawing the nodes So now you have your new objects fairly well defined, except for the drawNode functions (drawBranch, drawLeaf, and drawEmptyNode). Let's take a look at them.

Drawing empty nodes The drawEmptyNode function is called when the node is empty. The empty node draw method is simple:

```
function drawEmptyNode()
    {
    depthList[ parent.toc.level ].close();
    parent.toc.level--;
    }
```

Now where did parent.toc.level come from? Well, the actual document that will display the document outline does not change, nor does the function used in it to draw the tree. The function used to draw the tree needs to keep track of how many levels deep it is. Therefore, it's logical for the variable that maintains the depth to be kept in that document. You can access a global variable in another document by including its parentage—parent.toc in this case. This tells you that the level variable is maintained in the document that is displayed in the frame named toc, and that the frame toc is subordinate to this frame's parent window or frame.

Drawing leaf nodes   The drawLeaf function, which is called when the node is a branch, is a little more complicated than the drawEmptyNode function:

```
function drawLeaf()
    {
    for (var j = 0; j < parent.toc.level; j++)
        {
        if (depthList[ j + 1 ].value == 0)
            {
            return;
            }
        }
    for (var k = 0; k < parent.toc.level; k++)
        {
        parent.toc.document.write("    ");
        }
    parent.toc.document.write("<A
        HREF=\"javascript:parent.outlineData.setContents('" + this.url +
        "');\"" + gt + this.title + "</A" + gt);
    drawLineBreak();
    }
```

This code first checks the depth objects that dictate whether objects at this level or above are to be displayed. If any of the depth objects indicate that the objects at or below their level are not to be displayed, the code simply returns—there's nothing to do.

Once it's established that you will be drawing something, you write four nonbreaking space characters to the toc frame's document, and you do this for each level that we need to indent. Nonbreaking spaces are treated specially by the browser, which does not collapse them into a single space as it does normal space and tab characters.

Finally, you create a link for the leaf. You can't use the leaf's url property itself as the HREF parameter; you need to make the document appear in the other window. To do that, the setContents function takes the url property as an argument and sets the location of the contents frame with it:

```
function setContents(url)
    {
    parent.contents.location = url;
    }
```

And where is this outlineData frame? You can't see it, but it's used to contain the data to be displayed in the document outline, and it contains the node and depth functions. This keeps the data away from view and encapsulates it so that it can be modified or swapped out without changing the rest of the documents.

To make the outlineData frame invisible, you modify the main document slightly:

```
<HTML>
    <HEAD>
        <TITLE>Marc's List of Great Web Pages</TITLE>
    </HEAD>
    <FRAMESET ROWS="100%,*">
        <FRAMESET COLS="30%,*">
            <FRAME NAME="toc" SRC="empty.htm">
            <FRAME NAME="contents" SRC="empty.htm">
        </FRAMESET>
        <FRAME NAME="outlineData" SRC="data.htm">
    </FRAMESET>
</HTML>
```

The outer FRAMESET element allocates 100 percent of the window to the inner FRAMESET. The remaining space (even though there isn't any) is allocated to the outlineData frame, which is invisible. You also use the empty.htm url now for the contents of the toc frame. You're going to redraw the outline on the fly, so you only need a placeholder until you first draw the document outline.

Finally, you may have noticed the gt variable used in the creation of the link. This is a variable that contains a > character, hiding it from ignorant browsers:

```
var gt = unescape("%3E");
```

Finally, drawLeaf calls drawLineBreak, which looks like this:

```
function drawLineBreak()
    {
    parent.toc.document.write("<BR" + gt);
    }
```

This forces a new line for the next node.

The final result of drawLeaf looks like this:

```
<A HREF="javascript:parent.outlineData.setContents('index.html')">Home Page</A>
```

Drawing branch nodes   The drawBranch function, which is called when the node is a branch, is a little more complicated than the drawLeaf function:

```
function drawBranch()
    {
    for (var j = 0; j < parent.toc.level; j++)
        {
        if (depthList[ j + 1 ].value == 0)
            {
            parent.toc.level++;
            return;
            }
        }
    for (var k = 0; k < parent.toc.level; k++)
        {
        parent.toc.document.write("    ");
        }
    parent.toc.document.write("<A NAME=\"line" + this.index + "\"
    HREF="javascript:parent.outlineData.clickOnBranch(" + this.index + ")\"" + gt);
    if (this.flags & __open__) == 0)
        {
        parent.toc.document.write("[+]");
        depthList[ parent.toc.level + 1 ].open(0);
        }
    else
        {
        parent.toc.document.write("[-]");
        depthList[ parent.toc.level + 1 ].open(0);
        }
    parent.toc.document.write("</A" + gt + " ");
    if (this.url.length == 0)
        {
        parent.toc.document.write(this.title);
        }
    else
        {
        parent.toc.document.write("<A
            HREF=\"javascript:parent.outlineData.setContents('" +
            this.url + "');\"" + gt + this.title + "</A" + gt);
    drawLineBreak();
    parent.toc.level++;
    }
```

Like the drawLeaf method, drawBranch checks the depthList array to see if there's anything to draw. If there isn't, it increments parent.toc.level anyway, so that you can continue to keep track of how far deep you are in the tree.

This function then draws the sequence of nonbreaking spaces, just as drawLeaf does. Then it creates a special anchor element that has a NAME attribute as well as a HREF attribute. The NAME attribute consists of a string, "line," followed by the index of the branch object in the array.

The HREF attribute consists of another function, javascript:parent.outlineData.clickOnBranch(), which takes the branch object's index as its argument. The link displayed to the user consists of either [+] indicating that the branch can be opened or [−] indicating that the branch can be closed or collapsed.

Following the anchor that handles closing or opening the branch, the function also draws the link itself, if any. If there is no URL for the branch, it simply draws the title. Otherwise, it sets up a call to setContents, as in the drawLeaf function.

Finally, it calls drawLineBreak and increments parent.toc.level.

The clickOnBranch function, which the drawBranch function sets up to be the onClick event handler for the [+] or [−] links, is fairly simple:

```
function clickOnBranch(index)
    {
    nodeList[ index ].flags = nodeList[ index ].flags ^ __open__;
    var command = "parent.toc.location = 'treeview.htm#line" + index + "'";
    setTimeout(command, 100);
    }
```

First, the exclusive-or operator, ^, toggles the branch object's open state. Then, the code creates a command to set the toc frame's location to treeview.htm at the branch's point. This ensures that when the outline is redrawn, the user will see the branch that was just clicked on.

Finally, the command is executed 100 milliseconds later, by using the window's setTimeout method. The command is executed with a delay because, under Netscape 2.01, executing it immediately causes a "recursive interrupt" error.

Exporting knowledge of nodes   There are two other functions defined in outline.htm's SCRIPT element:

```
function nodeCount()
    {
    return nodeList.length;
    }
and
```

```
function writeNode(k)
    {
    nodeList[ k ].drawNode();
    }
```

The purpose of these functions is to export some of the node functionality to code that doesn't know anything about nodes. The drawTree function needs to know how many nodes there are but it doesn't know about the nodeList object so it doesn't know that nodeList has a length property. Similarly, it doesn't know about nodes and it certainly doesn't know that they have a drawNode method. But the code in data.htm knows these things and can export the necessary knowledge to the outside world.

Loading the outline   You've seen all the code in the data.htm file's SCRIPT element. There is one additional piece of JavaScript code in data.htm: the BODY element contains an ONLOAD handler:

```
ONLOAD="parent.toc.location = 'treeview.htm'"
```

This forces the loading of treeview.htm into the toc frame after the data is loaded.

Listing 5.2 shows the entire data.htm file.

Listing 5.2: The data.htm file

```
<HTML>
    <HEAD>
        <SCRIPT>
<!--
var __leaf__   = 1;
var __branch__ = 2;
var __open__   = 4;
var __empty__  = 8;

function depthOpen(newValue)
    {
    this.saved = this.value;
    this.value = newValue;
    }

function depthClose()
    {
    this.value = this.saved;
    }

function drawEmptyNode()
    {
```

Listing 5.2: The data.htm file (Continued)

```
        depthList[ parent.toc.level ].close();
        parent.toc.level--;
        }

var gt = unescape("%3E");

function drawLineBreak()
    {
    parent.toc.document.write("<BR" + gt);
    }

function setContents(url)
    {
    parent.contents.location = url;
    }

function drawLeaf()
    {
    for (var j = 0; j < parent.toc.level; j++)
        {
        if (depthList[ j + 1 ].value == 0)
            {
            return;
            }
        }
    for (var k = 0; k < parent.toc.level; k++)
        {
        parent.toc.document.write("    ");
        }
    parent.toc.document.write(
        "<A HREF=\"javaScript:parent.outlineData.setContents('" +
        this.url + "');\"" + gt + this.title + "</A" + gt);
    drawLineBreak();
    }

function clickOnBranch(index)
    {
    confirm("toggled");
    nodeList[ index ].flags = nodeList[ index ].flags ^ __open__;
    var command = "parent.toc.location = 'treeview.htm#line" + index +
        "'";
    setTimeout(command, 100);
    }

function drawBranch()
```

Listing 5.2: The data.htm file (Continued)

```javascript
    {
    for (var j = Ø; j < parent.toc.level; j++)
        {
        if (depthList[ j + 1 ].value == Ø)
            {
            parent.toc.level++;
            return;
            }
        }
    for (var k = Ø; k < parent.toc.level; k++)
        {
        parent.toc.document.write("    ");
        }
    parent.toc.document.write("<A NAME=\"line" + this.index +
        "\" HREF=\"javascript:parent.outlineData.clickOnBranch(" +
        this.index + ")\"" + gt);
    if ((this.flags & __open__) == Ø)
        {
        parent.toc.document.write("[+]");
        depthList[ parent.toc.level + 1 ].open(Ø);
        }
    else
        {
        parent.toc.document.write("[-]");
        depthList[ parent.toc.level + 1 ].open(1);
        }
    parent.toc.document.write("</A" + gt + " ");
    if (this.url.length == Ø)
        {
        parent.toc.document.write(this.title);
        }
    else
        {
        parent.toc.document.write(
            "<A HREF=\"javascript:parent.outlineData.setContents('" +
            this.url + "')\"" + gt + this.title + "</A" + gt);
        }
    drawLineBreak();
    parent.toc.level++;
    }

function node(flags, title, url)
    {
    this.index = nodeCtr;
    this.flags = flags;
```

Listing 5.2: The data.htm file (Continued)

```
    if (flags == __leaf__ || ((flags & __branch__) == __branch__))
        {
        this.title = title;
        if (flags == __leaf__)
            {
            this.url = url;
            this.drawNode = drawLeaf;
            }
        else
            {
            if (node.arguments.length >= 3)
                {
                this.url = url;
                }
            else
                {
                this.url = "";
                }
            this.drawNode = drawBranch;
            }
        }
    else
        {
        this.drawNode = drawEmptyNode;
        }
    }

function depth()
    {
    this.saved = Ø;
    this.value = Ø;
    this.open = depthOpen;
    this.close = depthClose;
    }

function MakeArray(n)
    {
    this.length = n;
    for (var i = 1; i <= n; i++)
        {
        this[ i ] = Ø;
        }
    return this;
    }
```

Listing 5.2: The data.htm file (Continued)

```
var depthList = new MakeArray(3);

for (var n = 1; n <= 3; n++)
    {
    depthList[ n ] = new depth();
    }

var nodeList = new MakeArray(53);

var nodeCtr = 0;

nodeCtr++; nodeList[ nodeCtr ] = new node(__branch__ + __open__,
"Roadmap");
nodeCtr++;      nodeList[ nodeCtr ] = new node(__leaf__, "Home Page",
"index.html");
nodeCtr++;      nodeList[ nodeCtr ] = new node(__branch__,
"Amusements", "amusement.html");
nodeCtr++;          nodeList[ nodeCtr ] = new node(__leaf__, "Comics",
"amusement.html#Comics");
nodeCtr++;          nodeList[ nodeCtr ] = new node(__leaf__, "Funnies",
"amusement.html#Funnies");
nodeCtr++;          nodeList[ nodeCtr ] = new node(__leaf__, "Games",
"amusement.html#Games");
nodeCtr++;          nodeList[ nodeCtr ] = new node(__leaf__, "Media",
"amusement.html#Media");
nodeCtr++;          nodeList[ nodeCtr ] = new node(__leaf__, "Travel",
"amusement.html#Travel");
nodeCtr++;      nodeList[ nodeCtr ] = new node(__empty__);
nodeCtr++;      nodeList[ nodeCtr ] = new node(__branch__, "Business",
"business.html");
nodeCtr++;          nodeList[ nodeCtr ] = new node(__leaf__, "Book
Stores", "business.html#Book Stores");
nodeCtr++;          nodeList[ nodeCtr ] = new node(__leaf__, "Other",
"business.html#Other");
nodeCtr++;      nodeList[ nodeCtr ] = new node(__empty__);
nodeCtr++;      nodeList[ nodeCtr ] = new node(__branch__, "Internet",
"internet.html");
nodeCtr++;          nodeList[ nodeCtr ] = new node(__leaf__,
"Providers", "internet.html#Providers");
nodeCtr++;          nodeList[ nodeCtr ] = new node(__leaf__,
"Resources", "internet.html#Resources");
nodeCtr++;          nodeList[ nodeCtr ] = new node(__leaf__, "Surfing",
"internet.html#Surfing");
nodeCtr++;          nodeList[ nodeCtr ] = new node(__branch__, "Web
Pages", "internet.html#Web Pages");
```

Listing 5.2: The data.htm file (Continued)

```
nodeCtr++;              nodeList[ nodeCtr ] = new node(__leaf__,
"Graphics", "internet.html#Graphics");
nodeCtr++;              nodeList[ nodeCtr ] = new node(__leaf__,
"HTML", "internet.html#HTML");
nodeCtr++;              nodeList[ nodeCtr ] = new node(__leaf__,
"Icons", "internet.html#Icons");
nodeCtr++;              nodeList[ nodeCtr ] = new node(__leaf__,
"Pages", "internet.html#Pages");
nodeCtr++;              nodeList[ nodeCtr ] = new node(__leaf__,
"Tools", "internet.html#Tools");
nodeCtr++;          nodeList[ nodeCtr ] = new node(__empty__);
nodeCtr++;       nodeList[ nodeCtr ] = new node(__empty__);
nodeCtr++;       nodeList[ nodeCtr ] = new node(__branch__, "Reference
Materials", "reference.html");
nodeCtr++;              nodeList[ nodeCtr ] = new node(__leaf__, "Books",
"reference.html#Books");
nodeCtr++;              nodeList[ nodeCtr ] = new node(__leaf__,
"Documents", "reference.html#Documents");
nodeCtr++;              nodeList[ nodeCtr ] = new node(__leaf__,
"Education", "reference.html#Education");
nodeCtr++;              nodeList[ nodeCtr ] = new node(__leaf__,
"Government", "reference.html#Government");
nodeCtr++;              nodeList[ nodeCtr ] = new node(__leaf__, "Jobs",
"reference.html#Jobs");
nodeCtr++;              nodeList[ nodeCtr ] = new node(__leaf__, "Reference
Servers", "reference.html#Reference Servers");
nodeCtr++;       nodeList[ nodeCtr ] = new node(__empty__);
nodeCtr++;       nodeList[ nodeCtr ] = new node(__branch__, "Science
Fiction", "sf.html");
nodeCtr++;              nodeList[ nodeCtr ] = new node(__leaf__, "Books",
"sf.html#Books");
nodeCtr++;              nodeList[ nodeCtr ] = new node(__leaf__,
"Miscellaneous Television", "sf.html#Miscellaneous Television");
nodeCtr++;              nodeList[ nodeCtr ] = new node(__leaf__, "Star
Trek", "sf.html#Star Trek");
nodeCtr++;              nodeList[ nodeCtr ] = new node(__leaf__, "World
Designs", "sf.html#World Designs");
nodeCtr++;       nodeList[ nodeCtr ] = new node(__empty__);
nodeCtr++;       nodeList[ nodeCtr ] = new node(__branch__, "Software",
"software.html");
nodeCtr++;              nodeList[ nodeCtr ] = new node(__leaf__,
"Academia", "software.html#Academia");
nodeCtr++;              nodeList[ nodeCtr ] = new node(__leaf__, "Analysis
and Design", "software.html#AandD");
```

Listing 5.2: The data.htm file (Continued)

```
nodeCtr++;          nodeList[ nodeCtr ] = new node(__leaf__, "Linux",
"software.html#Linux");
nodeCtr++;          nodeList[ nodeCtr ] = new node(__leaf__,
"Programming", "software.html#Programming");
nodeCtr++;          nodeList[ nodeCtr ] = new node(__leaf__,
"Shareware", "software.html#Shareware");
nodeCtr++;          nodeList[ nodeCtr ] = new node(__leaf__, "Vendors",
"software.html#Vendors");
nodeCtr++;      nodeList[ nodeCtr ] = new node(__empty__);
nodeCtr++;      nodeList[ nodeCtr ] = new node(__branch__, "Weather",
"weather.html");
nodeCtr++;          nodeList[ nodeCtr ] = new node(__leaf__, "Images",
"weather.html#Images");
nodeCtr++;          nodeList[ nodeCtr ] = new node(__leaf__, "NWS
Bulletins", "weather.html#NWS Bulletins");
nodeCtr++;          nodeList[ nodeCtr ] = new node(__leaf__, "Weather
Servers", "weather.html#Weather Servers");
nodeCtr++;      nodeList[ nodeCtr ] = new node(__empty__);
nodeCtr++; nodeList[ nodeCtr ] = new node(__empty__);

if (nodeCtr != nodeList.length)
    {
    alert("Node counter (" + nodeCtr + ") does not match
nodeList.length (" + nodeList.length + ")");
    }

function nodeCount()
    {
    return nodeList.length;
    }

function writeNode(k)
    {
    nodeList[ k ].drawNode();
    }
//-->
      </SCRIPT>
   </HEAD>
   <BODY ONLOAD="parent.toc.location = 'treeview.htm'">
   </BODY>
</HTML>
```

Drawing the tree The treeview.htm file is fairly simple. It provides a place to draw the tree and it holds the code for drawing the entire tree. Because of how the nodes were designed, the code for drawing the tree may never need to change.

```
<HTML>
    <HEAD>
    <BASE HREF="http://www.he.net/~marcj/">
        <SCRIPT LANGUAGE="JavaScript">
<!--

var level = 0;

function drawTree()
    {
    var depth = parent.outlineData.nodeCount();

    for (var k = 1; k <= depth; k++)
        {
        parent.outlineData.writeNode(k);
        if (level < 0)
            {
            alert("Too many empty nodes, index = " + k);
            level = 0;
            break;
            }
        }
    if (level != 0)
        {
        alert("Too few empty nodes, level = " + level);
        }
    }

drawTree();

//-->
        </SCRIPT>
    </HEAD>
    <BODY>
    </BODY>
</HTML>
```

The global variable, level, is initialized to 0. Then the drawTree function is defined.

The code first finds out how deep the tree is—how many nodes are in the tree. It uses the nodeCount function you saw in the data.htm file. This code has no knowledge of the nodeList object so it cannot access its length attribute directly.

Then, for each node, you call writeNode. Again, because the code in tree-view.htm has no knowledge of node objects, it cannot call the drawNode method directly. After each call to writeNode, you make sure the tree is balanced—that there aren't more empty nodes than branch nodes. If the level drops below zero, you've encountered one more empty node than there are branch nodes. You issue an alert in this case, indicating the node where you found the problem.

After all of the nodes are drawn, level should be zero again. If it isn't, there weren't enough empty nodes in the list of nodes. Again, you display an alert window indicating the problem and how many empty nodes are missing.

After the function is defined, you call it. At this point, you're still loading the HEAD element, so everything you're writing to the document object will be displayed. There is no conflict with what you've written so far, because you haven't written anything yet.

Figures 5.6 and 5.7 show typical pictures of your new document. Figure 5.6 shows the document when first loaded. Figure 5.7 shows the document after a previously closed branch has been opened and one of the leaves displayed.

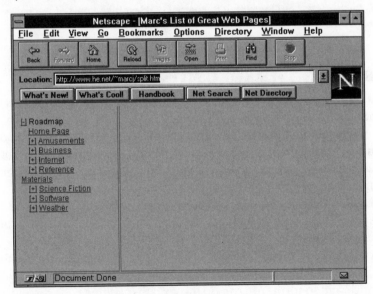

Figure 5.6: JavaScript outline when first loaded

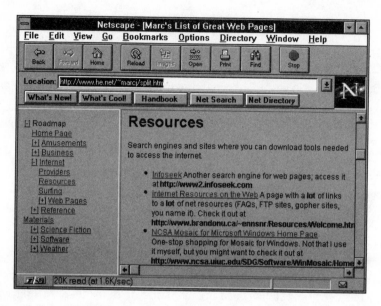

Figure 5.7: JavaScript outline with a document displayed and part of the outline expanded

IMPROVING THE SOLUTION

There is no program that cannot, in some way, be improved upon. So it is with the JavaScript outline presented in this chapter. There are some inefficiencies in the code, although they pertain mostly to the file length of data.htm. You could encapsulate calls to parent.toc.document.write in a single function, for example. This really won't help much, as the length of time it takes to load data.htm is really a function of how long and complex your outline is.

You could modify the node constructor function to keep track of the depth of the nodes. This would make it easy to further automate the construction of the depthList array.

You can add additional HTML to be written before and after the document outline, adding information about the document, your corporate logo, a copyright notice, and so forth. You can do this by either adding code directly to the drawTree function or by creating functions (perhaps drawHead and draw-Foot) in the data.htm file that can be called from drawTree.

It's also fairly easy to replace [+] and [–] with images, such as open and closed file folders (don't forget to specify the HEIGHT and WIDTH attributes!) or with more descriptive text. Just don't forget to keep the images or text small. You don't want to crowd the frame!

MODIFYING THE EXAMPLE FOR YOUR OWN USE

Modifying this example to suit your own needs is simply a matter of replacing the nodeList and depthList initialization sequences with sequences of your own liking. Change the BASE element in treeview.htm's to point to your own pages' location.

Color Chooser

THE SCENARIO

THE REQUIREMENTS

THE SOLUTION (WITHOUT JAVASCRIPT)

THE SOLUTION (WITH JAVASCRIPT)

IMPROVING THE SOLUTION

MODIFYING THE EXAMPLE
FOR YOUR OWN USE

I n this chapter, you learn how to create a color chooser, a tool that lets you try combinations of colors on a Web page without having to edit and re-edit the page.

You can specify five global colors in a Web page's <BODY> tag. The five colors stipulate which colors the browser will use when it displays the Web page, and you specify them in attributes of the Web page's <BODY> tag. The BG-COLOR attribute specifies the color of the page's background. The TEXT attribute specifies the default color of the text in the page. The LINK attribute specifies the color of the text and border of link elements the user has not yet visited. The ALINK attribute specifies the color of the active link, which is the link element that the user has just clicked on. Finally, the VLINK attribute specifies the color of the text of link elements that the user has visited.

All colors are specified as 24-bit values—8 bits for the red component, 8 bits for the green component, and 8 bits for the blue component. The three colors are always specified in that order—red, green, blue—and the overall color is an *RGB* (red, green, blue) value. Not all video systems can directly support 24-bit colors; for such systems, applications such as Netscape must either use approximations of the 24-bit value or must dither the color. *Dithering* involves mixing pixels of different colors to fool the eye into seeing the illusion of a 24-bit color. Either way, two colors that are technically different may appear to be identical on some systems.

You can specify the color values you use in your Web page by using RGB values. An RGB value is a string consisting of a pound sign (#) followed by a two-digit hexadecimal (base 16) value for the red component, a two-digit hexadecimal value for the green component, and a two-digit hexadecimal value for the blue component. For example, a value of #1E90FFdescribes a color whose red component is 1E, whose green component is 90, and whose blue component is FF. It is very blue, with a good bit of green to it, and a little bit of red. Netscape calls this color "dodgerblue."

Including dodgerblue, Netscape has named 140 colors. Instead of using RGB values, you can use one of the named colors, and you can use a named color anywhere you can use an RGB value.

Note: Hexadecimal numbers are number written in base 16. They use the ten digits you're familiar with, plus the first six letters (A through F) to represent 10 through 15. By convention, the letters are usually written as capitals. In the two-digit color values, the digit on the left is multiplied by 16 and the digit on the right is added to that product to get a decimal number. Thus, 1E is 1 multiplied by 16, plus 14 (E = 14), for a value of 30; 90 is 9 multiplied by 16, plus 0, for a value of 144; and FF is 15 multiplied by 16 (F = 15), plus 15, for a value of 255. To translate larger numbers from hexadecimal to decimal, start with the leftmost number. If it's a letter, translate it to its decimal value (A = 10, B = 11, and so on). This starts your running total. For each digit to the right, multiply the running total by 16, translate the digit to decimal, and add the digit's value to the running total.

The scenario

A color chooser allows the user to specify colors for the five <BODY> color attributes. Such a tool lets you try out combinations of colors to see what they look like together. Perhaps two colors are too similar and you can't tell one from the other, or maybe one of the colors cannot be distinguished from the background color. You'll be able to pick out these problems when you use a color chooser. The color chooser lets you experiment without showing your failures to the world.

The requirements

What should a color chooser do? For starters, it should let you use Netscape's named colors, such as dodgerblue or floralwhite. It should also let you use RGB values—after all, the 140 named colors only represent a tiny fraction of the nearly seventeen million colors that you can define with RGB values. The color chooser should let you fine-tune the colors, making a given color just a little more red, or maybe a little less green. It must let you specify colors for each of the five <BODY> color attributes. It has to let you see a sample page with the colors you've specified. And it should show you what the <BODY> tag looks like with the colors you've selected, so you can use the tag in a Web page.

THE SOLUTION (WITHOUT JAVASCRIPT)

Because you need to be able to specify colors for each of the five <BODY> color attributes, you need a form with five input fields. These fields should be text fields, so you can enter either an RGB value or a named field. Each field needs to be large enough to hold the longest named color (20 characters, for lightgoldenrodyellow). The form needs a submit button; it should also have a reset button—that's just good form etiquette. Listing 6.1 shows the HTML for the color chooser Web page and Figure 6.1 shows you the form that you'll use.

Listing 6.1: A simple color chooser

```
<HTML>
    <HEAD>
        <TITLE>Color Chooser</TITLE>
    </HEAD>
    <BODY>
        <CENTER><H1>Color Selector</H1></CENTER>
        <FORM ACTION="http://cgi.server " METHOD=POST>
            <INPUT TYPE="text" NAME="fgcolor" SIZE="20"> Foreground Color
            <BR>
            <INPUT TYPE="text" NAME="text" SIZE="20"> Test Color
            <BR>
            <INPUT TYPE="text" NAME="link" SIZE="20"> Link Color
            <BR>
            <INPUT TYPE="text" NAME="alink" SIZE="20"> Active Link Color
            <BR>
            <INPUT TYPE="text" NAME="vlink" SIZE="20"> Visited Link Color
            <HR>
            <INPUT TYPE="submit" VALUE="See Result">
            <INPUT TYPE="reset" VALUE="Ugh! Start Over!">
        </FORM>
    </BODY>
</HTML>
```

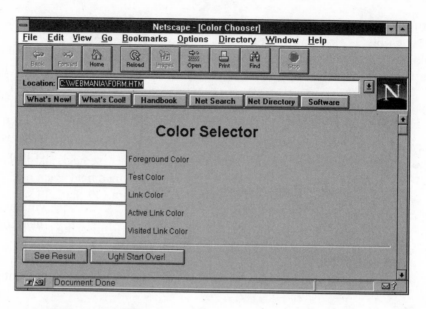

Figure 6.1: A simple color chooser

How good a solution is this? Let's measure it against the requirements. Can you use named colors? Yes, although you run the risk of making typos. Can you use RGB values? Again, yes, with the risk of mistyping them. Can you fine-tune colors? Yes, if they're RGB values. To fine-tune named colors, you need the documentation in front of you to get the RGB value of the named color. Can you set each of the <BODY> tag's five color attributes? Yes, you can. Can you see what the colors look like together?

Whoops.

No, not with just the code in Listing 6.1. You also need a CGI (Common Gateway Interface) program back on the server. The CGI program has to get the string generated when you press the submit button, parse it into the colors for each of the attributes, construct a valid HTML page that uses the five attributes, and send that page back as a response. It should also handle the last requirement, by including the <BODY> tag attributes in the displayed text.

You can't solve this problem with HTML alone, without JavaScript. You must have the CGI program as well. Unfortunately, some Web servers won't let you write your own CGI programs and run them from their system. The language you use is determined by what your Web server supports, and if you decide to change Web servers, you may have to start over from scratch—the new server may not support your CGI program.

THE SOLUTION (WITH JAVASCRIPT)

In addition to the problems intrinsic to writing CGI (the server may not allow CGI programs, CGI programs are not necessarily portable from one server to another, a CGI program on a slow, bogged-down server may be very slow), there are bandwidth considerations. Every time you press the See Result button, your selections are passed through the network back to the server. Then the server sends back a new page. This is a waste of bandwidth, and makes you vulnerable to the rising amount of traffic on the Internet: The browser may well time out before it gets the result from the server.

With JavaScript, you can do much better.

You can eliminate the need for the CGI program by breaking the window into two frames. You place the form in one frame and use the form's field contents to draw a new document in the second frame. This eliminates the repeated, and unnecessary, traffic between the users' browsers and the server.

You need three documents now. The first document is a frame document that splits the window into frames, as shown here:

```
<HTML>
    <HEAD>
        <TITLE>Color Chooser</TITLE>
    </HEAD>
    <FRAMESET ROWS="*,15%">
        <FRAME SRC="selector.htm" NAME="Selector">
        <FRAME SRC="blank.htm" NAME="ViewScreen">
    </FRAMESET>
</HTML>
```

You also need a blank document to load into the ViewScreen frame. Here is such a document:

```
<HTML>
    <HEAD>
    </HEAD>
    <BODY>
    </BODY>
</HTML>
```

Finally, you need the document that creates the form and processes the data in the form. This document is described in the next section.

THE FORM

Using JavaScript, you can make the form much easier to use and make it impossible for the user to enter an illegal color value.

First, let's divide the top frame into three parts. In the first part, the user specifies a color. In the second part, the user applies the selected color to one or more of the <BODY> tag's five color attributes. In the third part are the See Result and Ugh! Start Over! buttons. Figure 6.2 shows how the three parts of the frame will be laid out.

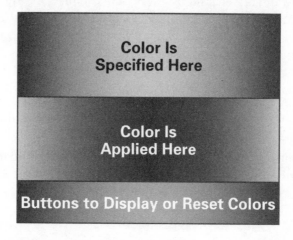

Figure 6.2: Layout of the color chooser form

Selecting a color   In the top part of the page, let's use a table to lay out the fields for selecting a color. The table is divided into separate sections: one for the red component, one for the blue component, and one for the green component. There's also one more section for entering a named color. Figure 6.3 shows the high-level layout of the color selection table.

Figure 6.3: Color selection table (high-level)

Within each of the "Define Color Component" blocks in Figure 6.3, you can add fields. A text field for setting the color level makes sense, and you can add buttons to increment and decrement the color level—that should suffice for fine-tuning. The text field should be used for entering a hexadecimal value for the color's component of the RGB color value, but let's add another text field. Some computer systems express colors in RGB format but do so by using decimal values separated by commas, as in 255,0,255 (equivalent to #FF00FF). Let's use the other text field to handle decimal values. You'll also need some text to let the user know which set of fields are for which color, and you'll need some table headings to let the user know what to do with the text fields and buttons. Figure 6.4 shows what you need.

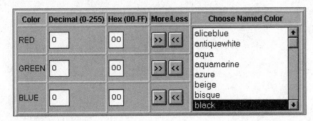

Figure 6.4: Color selection table (detailed)

To create the table shown in Figure 6.4, you need to create a TABLE element using the HTML code in Listing 6.2.

Listing 6.2: Creating the color selection table

```
<TABLE BORDER="2" CELLSPACING="2">
   <TR>
      <TH>Color</TH>
      <TH>Decimal (0-255)</TH>
      <TH>Hex (00-FF)</TH>
      <TH>More/Less</TH>
      <TH>Choose Named Color</TH>
   </TR>
   <TR>
      <TD>RED</TD>
      <TD><INPUT TYPE=TEXT SIZE=3 VALUE="0"></TD>
      <TD><INPUT TYPE=TEXT SIZE=2 VALUE="00"></TD>
      <TD>
         <INPUT TYPE=BUTTON VALUE=">>">
         <INPUT TYPE=BUTTON VALUE="<<">
      </TD>
      <TD ROWSPAN=3>
         <SELECT SIZE=8>
            <OPTION VALUE="F0F8FF">aliceblue
            <OPTION VALUE="FAEBD7">antiquewhite
            <OPTION VALUE="00FFFF">aqua
            <OPTION VALUE="7FFFD4">aquamarine
            <OPTION VALUE="F0FFFF">azure
            <OPTION VALUE="F5F5DC">beige
            <OPTION VALUE="FFE4C4">bisque
```

Listing 6.2: Creating the color selection table (Continued)

```
           <OPTION VALUE="000000" SELECTED>black
           <OPTION VALUE="FFEBCD">blanchedalmond
           <OPTION VALUE="0000FF">blue
           <OPTION VALUE="8A2BE2">blueviolet
           <OPTION VALUE="A52A2A">brown
           <OPTION VALUE="DEB887">burlywood
           <OPTION VALUE="5F9EA0">cadetblue
           <OPTION VALUE="7FFF00">chartreuse
           <OPTION VALUE="D2691E">chocolate
           <OPTION VALUE="FF7F50">coral
           <OPTION VALUE="6495ED">cornflowerblue
           <OPTION VALUE="FFF8DC">cornsilk
           <OPTION VALUE="DC143C">crimson
           <OPTION VALUE="00FFFF">cyan
           <OPTION VALUE="00008B">darkblue
           <OPTION VALUE="008B8B">darkcyan
           <OPTION VALUE="B8860B">darkgoldenrod
           <OPTION VALUE="A9A9A9">darkgray
           <OPTION VALUE="006400">darkgreen
           <OPTION VALUE="BDB76B">darkkhaki
           <OPTION VALUE="8B008B">darkmagenta
           <OPTION VALUE="556B2F">darkolivegreen
           <OPTION VALUE="FF8C00">darkorange
           <OPTION VALUE="9932CC">darkorchid
           <OPTION VALUE="8B0000">darkred
           <OPTION VALUE="E9967A">darksalmon
           <OPTION VALUE="8FBC8F">darkseagreen
           <OPTION VALUE="483D8B">darkslateblue
           <OPTION VALUE="2F4F4F">darkslategray
           <OPTION VALUE="00CED1">darkturquoise
           <OPTION VALUE="9400D3">darkviolet
           <OPTION VALUE="FF1493">deeppink
           <OPTION VALUE="00BFFF">deepskyblue
           <OPTION VALUE="696969">dimgray
           <OPTION VALUE="1E90FF">dodgerblue
           <OPTION VALUE="B22222">firebrick
           <OPTION VALUE="FFFAF0">floralwhite
           <OPTION VALUE="228B22">forestgreen
           <OPTION VALUE="FF00FF">fuchsia
           <OPTION VALUE="DCDCDC">gainsboro
           <OPTION VALUE="F8F8FF">ghostwhite
           <OPTION VALUE="FFD700">gold
           <OPTION VALUE="DAA520">goldenrod
           <OPTION VALUE="808080">gray
           <OPTION VALUE="008000">green
           <OPTION VALUE="ADFF2F">greenyellow
           <OPTION VALUE="F0FFF0">honeydew
           <OPTION VALUE="FF69B4">hotpink
           <OPTION VALUE="CD5C5C">indianred
```

Listing 6.2: Creating the color selection table (Continued)

```
<OPTION VALUE="4B0082">indigo
<OPTION VALUE="FFFFF0">ivory
<OPTION VALUE="F0E68C">khaki
<OPTION VALUE="E6E6FA">lavender
<OPTION VALUE="FFF0F5">lavenderblush
<OPTION VALUE="7CFC00">lawngreen
<OPTION VALUE="FFFACD">lemonchiffon
<OPTION VALUE="ADD8E6">lightblue
<OPTION VALUE="F08080">lightcoral
<OPTION VALUE="E0FFFF">lightcyan
<OPTION VALUE="FAFAD2">lightgoldenrodyellow
<OPTION VALUE="90EE90">lightgreen
<OPTION VALUE="D3D3D3">lightgray
<OPTION VALUE="FFB6C1">lightpink
<OPTION VALUE="FFA07A">lightsalmon
<OPTION VALUE="20B2AA">lightseagreen
<OPTION VALUE="87CEFA">lightskyblue
<OPTION VALUE="778899">lightslategray
<OPTION VALUE="B0C4DE">lightsteelblue
<OPTION VALUE="FFFFE0">lightyellow
<OPTION VALUE="00FF00">lime
<OPTION VALUE="32CD32">limegreen
<OPTION VALUE="FAF0E6">linen
<OPTION VALUE="FF00FF">magenta
<OPTION VALUE="800000">maroon
<OPTION VALUE="66CDAA">mediumaquamarine
<OPTION VALUE="0000CD">mediumblue
<OPTION VALUE="BA55D3">mediumorchid
<OPTION VALUE="9370DB">mediumpurple
<OPTION VALUE="3CB371">mediumseagreen
<OPTION VALUE="7B68EE">mediumslateblue
<OPTION VALUE="00FA9A">mediumspringgreen
<OPTION VALUE="48D1CC">mediumturquoise
<OPTION VALUE="C71585">mediumvioletred
<OPTION VALUE="191970">midnightblue
<OPTION VALUE="F5FFFA">mintcream
<OPTION VALUE="FFE4E1">mistyrose
<OPTION VALUE="FFE4B5">moccasin
<OPTION VALUE="FFDEAD">navajowhite
<OPTION VALUE="000080">navy
<OPTION VALUE="FDF5E6">oldlace
<OPTION VALUE="808000">olive
<OPTION VALUE="6B8E23">olivedrab
<OPTION VALUE="FFA500">orange
<OPTION VALUE="FF4500">orangered
<OPTION VALUE="DA70D6">orchid
<OPTION VALUE="EEE8AA">palegoldenrod
<OPTION VALUE="98FB98">palegreen
<OPTION VALUE="AFEEEE">paleturquoise
```

Listing 6.2: Creating the color selection table (Continued)

```
            <OPTION VALUE="DB7093">palevioletred
            <OPTION VALUE="FFEFD5">papayawhip
            <OPTION VALUE="FFDAB9">peachpuff
            <OPTION VALUE="CD853F">peru
            <OPTION VALUE="FFC0CB">pink
            <OPTION VALUE="DDA0DD">plum
            <OPTION VALUE="B0E0E6">powderblue
            <OPTION VALUE="800080">purple
            <OPTION VALUE="FF0000">red
            <OPTION VALUE="BC8F8F">rosybrown
            <OPTION VALUE="4169E1">royalblue
            <OPTION VALUE="8B4513">saddlebrown
            <OPTION VALUE="FA8072">salmon
            <OPTION VALUE="F4A460">sandybrown
            <OPTION VALUE="2E8B57">seagreen
            <OPTION VALUE="FFF5EE">seashell
            <OPTION VALUE="A0522D">sienna
            <OPTION VALUE="C0C0C0">silver
            <OPTION VALUE="87CEEB">skyblue
            <OPTION VALUE="6A5ACD">slateblue
            <OPTION VALUE="708090">slategray
            <OPTION VALUE="FFFAFA">snow
            <OPTION VALUE="00FF7F">springgreen
            <OPTION VALUE="4682B4">steelblue
            <OPTION VALUE="D2B48C">tan
            <OPTION VALUE="008080">teal
            <OPTION VALUE="D8BFD8">thistle
            <OPTION VALUE="FF6347">tomato
            <OPTION VALUE="40E0D0">turquoise
            <OPTION VALUE="EE82EE">violet
            <OPTION VALUE="F5DEB3">wheat
            <OPTION VALUE="FFFFFF">white
            <OPTION VALUE="F5F5F5">whitesmoke
            <OPTION VALUE="FFFF00">yellow
            <OPTION VALUE="9ACD32">yellowgreen
        </SELECT>
    </TD>
</TR>
<TR>
    <TD>GREEN</TD>
    <TD><INPUT TYPE=TEXT SIZE=3 VALUE="0"></TD>
    <TD><INPUT TYPE=TEXT SIZE=2 VALUE="00"></TD>
    <TD>
        <INPUT TYPE=BUTTON VALUE=">>">
        <INPUT TYPE=BUTTON VALUE="<<">
    </TD>
</TR>
<TR>
    <TD>BLUE</TD>
```

Listing 6.2: Creating the color selection table (Continued)

```
        <TD><INPUT TYPE=TEXT SIZE=3 VALUE="0"></TD>
        <TD><INPUT TYPE=TEXT SIZE=2 VALUE="00"></TD>
        <TD>
            <INPUT TYPE=BUTTON VALUE=">>">
            <INPUT TYPE=BUTTON VALUE="<<">
        </TD>
    </TR>
</TABLE>
```

The input fields in this table need some event handlers so that, when the user does something with each field, you can do something useful with the input. You need ONCHANGE event handlers for the TEXT fields; they'll be called when the user enters a new value in the TEXT field and moves focus to another field. You need ONCLICK event handlers for the BUTTON fields; they are called when the user clicks on a button. And, finally, you need an ON-CHANGE event handler for the SELECT field; it is called when the user selects a new value and moves focus to another field.

There are six TEXT fields, six BUTTON fields, and a SELECT field, so you'll need a total of 13 event handler functions. Wrong! You need five event handler functions. Why? Think about it: What's the difference between the event handler that handles a change in the red decimal field and the event handler that handles a change in the green decimal field? Very little; they have to do the same thing, except that one pertains to the red component and one pertains to the green component. The code doesn't have to be different.

To create an RGB color one color at a time, you need to store each of the three components separately. To do that, let's create three global variables for them:

```
var redness = 0;
var greenness = 0;
var blueness = 0;
```

Now let's give each of the TEXT and BUTTON fields names. The names will be based on which color they deal with and what they do with it, so the six TEXTfieldsarenamed"redDec,""redHex,""greenDec,""greenHex,""blueDec," and "blueHex." The six BUTTON fields are named "redPlus," "redMinus," "greenPlus," "greenMinus," "bluePlus," and "blueMinus."

Giving the fields names tied to their colors allows you to combine similar event handlers. Here is the handler for the change event on the decimal TEXT fields:

```
function readDecimal(text)
    {
    var suffixLength = 3;
    var nameLength = text.name.length;
    var colorName = text.name.substring(0, nameLength - suffixLength);
    var colorValue = parseInt(text.value);
    if (255 < colorValue || colorValue < 0)
        {
        alert("Illegal hex value entered for " + colorName);
        return;
        }
    setColor(colorName, colorValue)
    }
```

The readDecimal function is specified in the <INPUT> tag as

```
ONCHANGE="readDecimal(this)"
```

passing a reference to the TEXT field as the single parameter. The TEXT field's name is available as its name property. You want the color part, which is the part of the name preceding the suffix Dec. To get the color portion, you use the substring method to extract the substring from the first character of the string to the first character of the Dec suffix. Having the color name (red, green, or blue), you now need the value. You get the color by using the built-in function parseInt() on the TEXT field's value, which is obtained by using its value property. If the color is out of range—less than 0 or greater than 255—an alert window is displayed, telling the user that the value entered is rejected, and the function returns. Otherwise, a new function, setColor(), is called with the name and value of the color.

Similarly, you need a function to handle the change event on the hexadecimal TEXT fields. Listing 6.3 shows the readHex()function, which serves that purpose.

Notice that this function is exactly like readDecimal, except for one difference: The value is appended to the string "0x" in the call to parseInt(). This forces parseInt() to interpret the characters in the value as hexadecimal characters.

Finally, let's look at the event handlers for the plus (>>) and minus (<<) BUTTON fields. Listing 6.4 shows the event handler for the plus buttons.

Listing 6.3: readHex() ONCHANGE event handler

```
function readHex(text)
    {
    var suffixLength = 3;
    var nameLength = text.name.length;
    var colorName = text.name.substring(0, nameLength - suffixLength);
    var colorValue = parseInt("0x" + text.value);
    if (255 < colorValue || colorValue < 0)
        {
        alert("Illegal hex value entered for " + colorName);
        return;
        }
    setColor(colorName, colorValue);
    }
```

Listing 6.4: plus() ONCLICK event handler

```
function plus(text)
    {
    var suffixLength = 4;
    var nameLength = text.name.length;
    var colorName = text.name.substring(0, nameLength - suffixLength);
    var colorValue = 1 + eval("" + colorName + "ness");
    if (255 < colorValue || colorValue < 0)
        {
        alert("Sorry, can't go any higher on " + colorName);
        return;
        }
    setColor(colorName, colorValue);
    }
```

This function is also similar to the readDecimal() and readHex() functions.
The difference is in how it acquires the color value. It creates a string containing the color name and the string "ness" (the leading quotes force Netscape to
create a string value) and calls the built-in function eval(), using the string as
its parameter. Notice that the string built is going to be either "redness,"
"greenness," or "blueness"—one of the global variables you're using to hold
the three color components. The eval() function returns the value contained
in the specified variable. The color value is set to 1 plus that value (placing the
1 first forces Netscape to create an integer value).

Finally, the function for handling the click event of the minus (<<) buttons
is shown in Listing 6.5.

Listing 6.5: minus() ONCLICK event handler

```
function minus(text)
    {
    var suffixLength = 5;
    var nameLength = text.name.length;
    var colorName = text.name.substring(0, nameLength - suffixLength);
    var colorValue = -1 + eval("" + colorName + "ness");
    if (255 < colorValue || colorValue < 0)
        {
        alert("Sorry, can't go any lower on " + colorName);
        return;
        }
    setColor(colorName, colorValue);
    }
```

The only difference between the plus() and minus() functions is that the minus() function adds −1 instead of 1 to the color value.

So now let's see the setColor() function, which is shown in Listing 6.6.

Listing 6.6: setColor() function

```
function setColor(colorName, colorValue)
    {
    eval("" + colorName + "ness = " + colorValue);
    setDec(colorName);
    setHex(colorName);
    }
```

This time, a string is constructed that looks like what you'd write to set the appropriate color variable. If this function is called with "red" and 100, for instance, a string "redness = 100" is created. The eval() function is called with this string as its argument and the new value is written to the appropriate variable. Then the functions setDec() and setHex() are called, with the name of the color as a parameter.

The setDec() function updates the decimal TEXT field and the setHex() function updates the hexadecimal TEXT field. The setDec() function is shown in Listing 6.7.

Listing 6.7: setDec() function

```
function setDec(color)
    {
    eval("document.chooserForm." + color + "Dec.value = " + color + "ness");
    }
```

This is a very simple function. It creates a string setting the appropriate field from the appropriate variable and then uses the eval() function to execute the string. If called with a string of "green," for instance, the string that gets executed is "document.chooserForm.greenDec.value = greenness." The chooserForm part is the name of the FORM element that contains all of the fields in the page; the FORM tag is <FORM name="chooserForm">.

The setHex() function is a little more complicated. Strangely, while parseInt() knows how to read hexadecimal values, there is no built-in function to create a hexadecimal string. The setHex() function is shown in Listing 6.8.

Listing 6.8: setHex() function

```
function setHex(color)
   {
   var value = eval("" + color + "ness");
   var command = "document.chooserForm." + color + "Hex.value = '";
   command += toHex2(value);
   command += "'";
   eval(command);
   }
```

Again, a string is created that is then executed by eval(). This time, the actual value of the color variable has to be extracted and converted to a hexadecimal string. That's the function of toHex2(), seen in Listing 6.9.

Listing 6.9: toHex2() function

```
function toHex2(value)
   {
   var val = "" + toHex(Math.floor(value / 16));
   val += toHex(value & 15);
   return val;
   }
```

The function toHex2() creates a string consisting of two hexadecimal digits. The first digit is created by the function toHex() (seen in Listing 6.10), called with the value divided by 16. (Recall that using Math.floor() on the result of a divide gives the integer quotient.) The second digit is also created by the function toHex(), called with the value logically ANDed with 15. This is equivalent to using the modulus operator with a second operand of 16 (try it and see!).

Listing 6.10: toHex() function

```
function toHex(value)
    {
    if (value <= 9)
        {
        return value;
        }
    else
        {
        if (value == 10) return "A";
        if (value == 11) return "B";
        if (value == 12) return "C";
        if (value == 13) return "D";
        if (value == 14) return "E";
        if (value == 15) return "F";
        return "??" + value + "??";
        }
    }
```

If the value passed to toHex() is less than or equal to 9, the value is returned as is. Otherwise, the values of 10 to 15 are "translated" to "A," "B," "C," "D," "E," and "F," respectively. If this function were to be used in a library, which is a good possibility, it would need to be a little more robust; hence the final

```
return "??" + value + "??"
```

which handles values that are out of range.

So far, you have gotten data from the table's decimal, hexadecimal, plus, and minus input fields; set the appropriate variable; and updated the decimal and hexadecimal field values. It was relatively easy, and there wasn't a lot of code (discounting the 140 OPTION elements in the SELECT element). This partic-ular technique, by the way, is an example of a powerful object-oriented para-digm called "model-view-controller," or MVC for short. The controller objects (the TEXT and BUTTON fields) update the model objects (the redness, green-ness, and blueness variables); the model objects, in turn, update their views (the TEXT field values).

Now let's tie in the SELECT field. Listing 6.11 shows the SELECT field's ON-CHANGE event handler, readSelector().

The readSelector() function gets the index of the selected field from the select object's selectedIndex property. Clicking on an already selected OPTION field re-sults in "unselection" of that OPTION. When that happens, the selectedIndex property is set to –1, indicating no selection. In that case, readSelector() simply returns. Otherwise, the selected option's value is retrieved (selector[index

Listing 6.11: readSelector() ONCHANGE event handler

```
function readSelector(selector)
    {
    var index = selector.selectedIndex;
    if (index == -1)
        {
        return; // handle case when nothing is selected...
        }
    var value = parseInt("0x" + selector[ index ].value);
    with Math
        {
        setColor("red", floor(value / 65536));
        value = value & 65535;
        setColor("green", floor(value / 256));
        setColor("blue", value & 255);
        }
    }
```

].value), appended to a "0x" string as in the readHex() function in Listing 6.3, and passed to parseInt(). The result is divided by 65536 (0x010000), yielding the red component. The remainder is obtained by ANDing with 65535 (0x00FFFF). The remaining value is divided by 256, yielding the green component, and ANDed with 255 (0x0000FF) to yield the blue component. The setColor() function is called for each color. As a result, when a named color is selected from the list, its red, green, and blue components show up in the text fields. The user can then fine-tune the named color, adding to and subtracting from the red, green, and blue components to his or her liking.

Assigning a color to a <BODY> attribute   Although the top part of the page is devoted to selecting a color, the middle part is devoted to assigning the currently selected color to one of the five <BODY> attributes. As with the color selection, let's use a table to neatly arrange the attributes. Figure 6.5 shows the table we'll use.

Background	Foreground	Link	Visited Link	Active Link
#FFFFFF	#000000	#0000FF	#FF0000	#00FF00

Figure 6.5: Attribute table

Listing 6.12 shows the HTML used to generate this table.

Listing 6.12: Attribute table HTML

```
<TABLE BORDER="2" CELLSPACING="2">
    <TR>
        <TH ALIGN=CENTER>Background</TH>
        <TH ALIGN=CENTER>Foreground</TH>
        <TH ALIGN=CENTER>Link</TH>
        <TH ALIGN=CENTER>Visited Link</TH>
        <TH ALIGN=CENTER>Active Link</TH>
    </TR>
    <TR>
        <TD ALIGN=CENTER><INPUT TYPE=TEXT SIZE=7 NAME="BGCOLOR"></TD>
        <TD ALIGN=CENTER><INPUT TYPE=TEXT SIZE=7 NAME="TEXT"></TD>
        <TD ALIGN=CENTER><INPUT TYPE=TEXT SIZE=7 NAME="LINK"></TD>
        <TD ALIGN=CENTER><INPUT TYPE=TEXT SIZE=7 NAME="VLINK"></TD>
        <TD ALIGN=CENTER><INPUT TYPE=TEXT SIZE=7 NAME="ALINK"></TD>
    </TR>
</TABLE>
```

As with the color selection discussed earlier, let's put the model-view-controller paradigm to work. The model consists of five global variables that contain the current color values for each of the <BODY> attributes:

```
var newBGCOLOR = "#FFFFFF";
var newTEXT = "#000000";
var newLINK = "#0000FF";
var newVLINK = "#FF0000";
var newALINK = "#00FF00";
```

These colors are arbitrary, by the way; it's a serviceable combination—white background, black text, blue links, red visited links, and green active links.

You already have the views—the TEXT fields in the table seen in Listing 6.12. You need the controller shown in Listing 6.13.

Listing 6.13: A selector for attribute selection

```
Apply This Color To Which Attribute?
<SELECT ONCHANGE="attributeSelector(this)">
    <OPTION VALUE="BGCOLOR">Background
    <OPTION VALUE="TEXT" SELECTED>Foreground
    <OPTION VALUE="LINK">Link
    <OPTION VALUE="VLINK">Visited Link
    <OPTION VALUE="ALINK">Active Link
</SELECT>
```

Now you'll need some code to tie it all together. The attributeSelector() function, which you can see set as the SELECT field's ONCHANGE event handler in Listing 6.13, is a good start. Listing 6.14 shows the function.

Listing 6.14: attributeSelector() ONCHANGE event handler

```
function attributeSelector(selector)
    {
    var index = selector.selectedIndex;
    if (index == -1)
        {
        return; // handle case when nothing is selected...
        }
    setAttribute(selector[ index ].value);
    }
```

As with readSelector() in Listing 6.11, take care to guard against the possibility that the user has clicked on the currently selected option, leaving no option selected. If there is a valid selection, its value is passed to the setAttribute() function shown in Listing 6.15.

Listing 6.15: setAttribute() function

```
function setAttribute(attributeName)
    {
    var color = "#" + toHex2(redness) + toHex2(greenness) + toHex2(blueness);
    eval("new" + attributeName + " = \"" + color + "\"");
    eval("document.chooserForm." + attributeName + ".value = \"" + color + "\"");
    }
```

The setAttribute() function creates a color string consisting of a # character followed by the current values of the redness, greenness, and blueness variables. The values are run through toHex2() (see Listing 6.9) and a string is created to set the attribute variable and then executed. (In the case of the ALINK attribute, for example, the string would look like newALINK = "#rrggbb", where "rr," "gg," and "bb" are the current redness, greenness, and blueness values.) The attribute view in the table (see Listing 6.12) is then updated by creating a string and executing it. (In the case of the ALINK attribute, for example, the string would look like document.chooserForm.ALINK.value = "#rrggbb".)

You need one more function to protect the field values from being overwritten. The fields are TEXT fields, because you can easily write to them using JavaScript code, as does setAttribute(). This also means that the user can place text in them. You need a function to restore the fields, such as restoreAttribute(), shown in Listing 6.16.

Listing 6.16: restoreAttribute() function

```
function restoreAttribute(attribute)
    {
    eval("document.chooserForm." + attribute.name + ".value = new" +
attribute.name);
    }
```

The restoreAttribute() function is set up as the ONCHANGE event handler for all five attribute input fields. The function creates and executes a string to restore the field's contents from the appropriate variable. The string created and executed for the BGCOLOR field, for example, would be

```
document.chooserForm.BGCOLOR.value = newBGCOLOR
```

Submit and Reset   The top part of the page selects the color. The middle part of the page assigns the selected color to an attribute. The bottom part of the page lets the user see the attribute combination or to reset the combination. The non-JavaScript solution used SUBMIT and RESET input fields. Because this isn't a form that will be submitted to a server, ordinary BUTTON fields will do nicely, as seen in Listing 6.17.

Listing 6.17: SUBMIT and RESET buttons (not!)

```
<INPUT TYPE=BUTTON NAME="Apply" VALUE="Let Me See What This Looks Like!"
ONCLICK="resetViewScreen()">
<INPUT TYPE=BUTTON VALUE="Ycch! Start Over!" ONCLICK="setDefaults()">
```

The buttons have ONCLICK event handlers—resetViewScreen() and setDefaults(). Listing 6.18 shows the simpler setDefaults() function.

The setDefaults() function uses setColor() (Listing 6.6) to initialize the redness, greenness, and blueness variables to 0; the setColor() calls will initialize the color selection fields. The attribute color variables are reset to the default colors and the attribute fields are set to the same colors.

Listing 6.19 shows the rather busier resetViewScreen() function.

Listing 6.18: setDefaults() function

```
function setDefaults()
    {
    setColor("red", 0);
    setColor("green", 0);
    setColor("blue", 0);
    newBGCOLOR = "#FFFFFF";
    newTEXT = "#000000";
    newLINK = "#0000FF";
    newVLINK = "#FF0000";
    newALINK = "#00FF00";
    document.chooserForm.BGCOLOR.value = "#FFFFFF";
    document.chooserForm.TEXT.value = "#000000";
    document.chooserForm.LINK.value = "#0000FF";
    document.chooserForm.VLINK.value = "#FF0000";
    document.chooserForm.ALINK.value = "#00FF00";
    }
```

Listing 6.19: resetViewScreen() function

```
function resetViewScreen()
    {
    parent.ViewScreen.document.close();
    parent.ViewScreen.document.open();
    parent.ViewScreen.document.open();
    drawLine("<HTML" + gt);
        drawLine("<HEAD" + gt);
        drawLine("</HEAD" + gt);
        drawLine("<BODY BGCOLOR=" + newBGCOLOR + " TEXT=" + newTEXT + " LINK=" +
newLINK + " VLINK=" + newVLINK + " ALINK=" + newALINK + gt);
            drawLine("<P" + gt + "Foreground text ");
            drawLine("<FONT COLOR=\"" + newLINK + "\"" + gt + "Link</FONT" + gt +
" ");
            drawLine("<FONT COLOR=\"" + newVLINK + "\"" + gt + "Visited
Link</FONT" + gt + " ");
            drawLine("<FONT COLOR=\"" + newALINK + "\"" + gt + "Active
Link</FONT" + gt);
            drawLineBreak();
            drawLine("If you like this combination, you need to incorporate this
into your HTML:");
            drawLineBreak();
            drawLine("&lt;BODY BGCOLOR=\"" + newBGCOLOR + "\" TEXT=\"" + newTEXT
+ "\" LINK=\"" + newLINK + "\" VLINK=\"" + newVLINK + "\" ALINK=\"" + newALINK +
"\"&gt;");
            drawLine("</P" + gt);
        drawLine("</BODY" + gt);
    drawLine("</HTML" + gt);
    }
```

The resetViewScreen() function draws the frame in the bottom of the window. It uses the functions drawLine() and drawLineBreak() to draw the frame, which you can see in Figure 6.6.

Foreground text Link Visited Link Active Link
If you like this combination, you need to incorporate this into your HTML:
<BODY BGCOLOR="#FFFFFF" TEXT="#000000" LINK="#0000FF" VLINK="#FF0000" ALINK="#00FF00">

Figure 6.6: Output frame

The drawLine() and drawBreak() functions are simple functions for writing a line of text and a <BR> element, respectively, to the ViewScreen frame:

```
function drawLine(s)
    {
    parent.ViewScreen.document.writeln("" + s);
    }

function drawLineBreak()
    {
    drawLine("<BR" + gt);
    }
```

IMPROVING THE SOLUTION

You can improve upon the JavaScript solution in several ways. There are other ways to select colors, such as using percentage values for the red, green, and blue components. You could create a client-side image map and generate an RGB color based on where the user clicks on the map.

The solution prevents the user from entering data into the attribute fields. Why not allow the user to enter a standard RGB color value in #rrggbb format?

It would be useful to reload the color selection table from one of the attribute fields. For example, you might try out a color combination and decide that it would be better if you could adjust one of the attributes a little bit. It would be easier to be able to click on a button and reload the red, green, and blue values directly from the attribute instead of loading the values by hand.

You could use cookies to save a color solution, and even let the user supply a name for the solution. When you brought up the color chooser the next time, you could reload the color table from one of the user's cookies.

MODIFYING THE EXAMPLE FOR YOUR OWN USE

This is not the kind of page that needs to be modified so that you can use it; it's a complete application in its own right, and it is not tied to anyone's URLs. Feel free to try some of the modifications suggested in the previous section. Modify the visible text and button names. Do not alter the field names, however; the code requires the field names to tie into the data they control.

Form Validation

THE SCENARIO

THE REQUIREMENTS

THE SOLUTION (WITHOUT JAVASCRIPT)

THE SOLUTION (WITH JAVASCRIPT)

IMPROVING THE SOLUTION

MODIFYING THE EXAMPLE
FOR YOUR OWN USE

W hen a user enters data into the fields of a form in your Web page, it's entirely possible that the data might not make sense. The user may enter a numeric value that is too low or too high. The user may enter text where you expect a number, or vice versa. The user may misspell text. The user may skip a required field. There are probably as many ways to enter invalid data as there are ways to write forms.

It should not come as a surprise, then, that an important step in creating a form is making sure that what the user entered makes sense. That step is called *form validation.*

Creating a form that validates input—regardless of whether you use JavaScript—requires a CGI (Common Gateway Interface) program on the server. The Web page is only a front end to the server.

THE SCENARIO

Suppose your boss has asked you to create a Web page from which customers can order computer equipment. You need to collect the customer's name, address, phone number, age, credit card information, and what the customer wants to order.

THE REQUIREMENTS

The customer must have a first and last name; a middle initial is optional. The customer must have a street address. The customer must reside in the United

States and must provide either a 5-digit zip code or a 5+4 zip code. The customer must supply a daytime phone number, including area code. The customer must provide his or her age, and must be at least 18. The customer must supply a credit card number, credit card type (Visa or MasterCard), and date of expiration.

The customer may order any of the following: HAL-470 computer ($2,000), Banana9000 computer ($3,000), high-resolution monitor ($800), low-resolution monitor ($50), deluxe keyboard ($250), regular keyboard ($40), laser printer ($2,000), inkjet printer ($600), dot-matrix printer ($200), mouse ($100), trackball ($125), or scanner ($500). The customer may not order more than $5,000 worth of equipment.

The solution (without JavaScript)

To create a Web page form, you must first choose the kinds of input fields you need. To capture the customer's name, INPUT TEXT elements are the obvious choice. Let's make the first and last names 20 characters each and the middle initial 1 character.

The address is next. A TEXTAREA element, 2 rows of 30 characters each, will suffice for the street address, and INPUT TEXT elements will work for the city, state, and zip codes—20 characters for the city, 2 characters for the state, and 10 for the zip code.

For the customer's daytime phone number, use three INPUT TYPE elements—three characters for the area code, three characters for the office code, and four characters for the remainder of the phone number.

A three-character INPUT TEXT element will suffice for the customer's age—we could get an order from someone older than 99.

The credit card information is easy: Four INPUT TEXT elements for the credit card number, four characters each; an INPUT RADIO element to select between Visa and MasterCard; and two INPUT TEXT elements for the expiration date, two characters each.

You'll need a SELECT element for the merchandise, and it has to allow for multiple selections.

Finally, you'll need an INPUT SUBMIT element to send the data to the server, and an INPUT RESET element to allow the customer to start over.

Putting it all together, you have a Web page. Listing 7.1 shows the HTML and Figure 7.1 shows you what the form looks like on the screen.

Listing 7.1: Non-JavaScript solution

```html
<HTML>
    <HEAD>
        <TITLE>ComputoRama Order Form</TITLE>
    </HEAD>
    <BODY>
        <FORM ACTION="mailto:mailhost@computoRama.usa.com" METHOD=POST>
            <TABLE BORDER="2" CELLPADDING="1">
                <TR>
                    <TD ROWSPAN="2">Who Are You?</TD>
                    <TD><INPUT TYPE="text" NAME="FirstName" SIZE=20></TD>
                    <TD><INPUT TYPE="text" NAME="MiddleInitial" SIZE=1></TD>
                    <TD><INPUT TYPE="text" NAME="LastName" SIZE=20></TD>
                    <TD><INPUT TYPE="text" NAME="Age" SIZE=3></TD>
                </TR>
                <TR>
                    <TD><FONT SIZE="-2">First Name</FONT></TD>
                    <TD><FONT SIZE="-2">MI</FONT></TD>
                    <TD><FONT SIZE="-2">Last Name></TD>
                    <TD><FONT SIZE="-2">Age></TD>
                </TR>
                <TR>
                    <TD ROWSPAN="3">How Do We Contact You?</TD>
                    <TD COLSPAN="4" VALIGN="TOP">Street Address: <TEXTAREA
                    name="StreetAddress" rows=2 cols=30></TEXTAREA></TD>
                </TR>
                <TR>
                    <TD COLSPAN="2">City: <INPUT TYPE="text" NAME="City"
                    SIZE=20></TD>
                    <TD COLSPAN="2">State: <INPUT TYPE="text" NAME= "State"
                    SIZE=2></TD>
                </TR>
                <TR>
                    <TD COLSPAN="2">ZIP Code: <INPUT TYPE="text" NAME="ZIPCode"
                    SIZE=10></TD>
                    <TD COLSPAN="2">Daytime Phone
                        (<INPUT TYPE="text" NAME="Phone1" SIZE=3>)
                        <INPUT TYPE="text" NAME="Phone2" SIZE=3>-
                        <INPUT TYPE="text" NAME="Phone3" SIZE=4></TD>
                </TR>
                <TR>
                    <TD>Credit Card
                        <INPUT TYPE="radio" NAME="CreditCardType" VALUE="Visa"
                        CHECKED>Visa
                        <INPUT TYPE="radio" NAME="CreditCardType"
                        VALUE="MasterCard">M/C</TD>
                    <TD COLSPAN="2" ALIGN="CENTER">
                        <INPUT TYPE="text" NAME="CreditCardNumber1" SIZE=4>
                        <INPUT TYPE="text" NAME="CreditCardNumber2" SIZE=4>
```

Listing 7.1: Non-JavaScript solution (Continued)

```
                    <INPUT TYPE="text" NAME="CreditCardNumber3" SIZE=4>
                    <INPUT TYPE="text" NAME="CreditCardNumber4" SIZE=4></TD>
                <TD COLSPAN="2">Expiration Date:
                    <INPUT TYPE="text" NAME="ExpirationMonth" SIZE=2>/
                    <INPUT TYPE="text" NAME="ExpirationYear" SIZE=2></TD>
            </TR>
            <TR>
                <TD>Merchandise</TD>
                <TD COLSPAN=4><SELECT MULTIPLE NAME="Merchandise" SIZE=1>
                    <OPTION SELECTED> HAL-470 <OPTION> Banana9000
                    <OPTION> High Res Monitor <OPTION> Low Res Monitor
                    <OPTION> Deluxe Keyboard <OPTION> Regular Keyboard
                    <OPTION> Laser Printer <OPTION> Inkjet Printer <OPTION>
                    Dot Matrix Printer
                    <OPTION> Mouse <OPTION> Trackball
                    <OPTION> Scanner
                    </SELECT></TD>
            </TR>
            <TR>
                <TD ALIGN=CENTER COLSPAN="5">
                    <H1>Thank You For Your Order!</H1>
                </TD>
            </TR>
        </TABLE>
        <CENTER>
        <INPUT TYPE="submit" VALUE="Ship It!"> <INPUT TYPE="reset"
        VALUE="Clear Entries">
        </CENTER>
    </FORM>
  </BODY>
</HTML>
```

The rest of the solution resides on the server, and is beyond the scope of this book. There will be a CGI (Common Gateway Interface) program on the server that will process the results when the customer presses the Ship It! button. That program will have to perform form validation and return an error to the customer if mandatory fields are omitted or mistyped. That is in addition to whatever work must be performed to process a valid order.

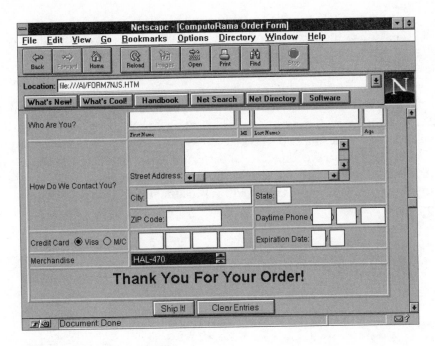

Figure 7.1: Non-JavaScript solution

THE SOLUTION (WITH JAVASCRIPT)

Using JavaScript, you can enhance the form shown in Figure 7.1 to perform much of the form validation on the customer's browser. The advantages of doing so are

▶ Better performance for the customer. Data entry errors will be caught much more quickly by the JavaScript code than by the CGI program on the server. (It takes time to transmit the data to the server, and CGI programs are not, as a rule, any faster than JavaScript programs.) Feedback to the customer is nearly instantaneous. If there are no errors, the CGI program, which now has less error-checking to do, will process the order more quickly.

▶ Better performance for the server. Because more errors are caught locally, there is less traffic to and from the server. The CGI program does not have to be as complicated and should execute more quickly, which decreases the load on the server. The system can handle more orders than it could when the server CGI program had to proofread the forms.

So what can you do to add form validation to this Web page? Plenty.

First, get rid of the SUBMIT button. You can write an event handler to catch the submit event, and that event handler can prevent submission of the form. However, whether the customer's data is transmitted or not, the page will be cleared. If you make the SUBMIT button an ordinary BUTTON INPUT element and give it an ONCLICK event handler, you'll have better control over the screen. All the ONCLICK event handler has to do is perform the form validation and, if all the customer data is acceptable, call document.forms[0].submit().

Having created an event handler to perform forms validation, let's start with the customer's name. Recall that the customer must supply a first and last name. To verify this, you simply need to check that the fields have a nonzero length, like this:

```
function nameOK()
    {
    if (document.forms[ 0 ].FirstName.value.length == 0)
        {
        alert("I need a first name, please");
        return false;
        }
    if (document.forms[ 0 ].LastName.value.length == 0)
        {
        alert("I need a last name, please");
        return false;
        }
    return true;
    }
```

Then, in your "submit" button event handler, call the function:

```
function checkForm()
    {
    if (nameOK() == false)
        {
        return;
        }
    // other tests...
    document.forms[ 0 ].submit();
    }
```

The age field has to be filled in, and the age must be a number greater than or equal to 18. First, verify that the customer has entered anything. Then verify that the customer has entered a number: Use the substring method to get the first character in the field and verify that it is a digit. For that, you need a little routine:

```
function isDigit(c)
   {
   var test = "" + c;
   if (test == "0" || test == "1" || test == "2" || test == "3" || test == "4"
   || test == "5" || test == "6" || test == "7" || test == "8" || test == "9")
      {
      return true;
      }
   return false;
   }
```

Finally, having verified that the customer entered something that starts with a digit, use the built-in function parseInt() to convert the customer's input and verify that the value is at least 18. Putting these steps together, you have something like this:

```
function ageOK()
   {
   if (document.forms[ 0 ].Age.value.length == 0)
      {
      alert("Sorry, you have failed to enter an age");
      return false;
      }
   var c = document.forms[ 0 ].Age.value.substring(0, 1);
   if (isDigit(c) == false)
      {
      alert("Sorry, you have failed to enter an appropriate age");
      return false;
      }
   var result = parseInt(document.forms[ 0 ].Age.value, 10);
   if (result < 18)
      {
      alert("Sorry, you have failed to enter an appropriate age");
      return false;
      }
   return true;
   }
```

As with NameOK(), you then add this to the checkForm() function:

```
function checkForm()
   {
   if (nameOK() == false)
      {
```

```
    return;
    }
if (AgeOK() == false)
    {
    return;
    }
// other tests...
document.forms[ 0 ].submit();
}
```

Now that the customer's name and age have been verified as present and acceptable, it's time to verify the address. Verifying the presence of the street address, city, and state fields is exactly like verifying the presence of the first and last name fields: Just check for a nonzero length of the field's value property. The zip code is a little more interesting, however. Recall that the zip code must be either a five-digit code or ZIP+4—5 digits, a hyphen, and four digits.

Because this is something you're going to do more than once, let's write a function to verify that a given string is composed entirely of digits. It should simply extract the characters from the string one by one and verify that each one is a digit:

```
function isAllDigits(s)
    {
    var test = "" + s;
    for (var k = 0; k < test.length; k++)
        {
        var c = test.substring(k, k+1);
        if (isDigit(c) == false)
            {
            return false;
            }
        }
    return true;
    }
```

Then checking the zip code field is easy. First, check the length of the field value—it should be either 5 or 10. If the length is 5, call isAllDigits() for the value. If it's 10 digits, use the substring method to get the first 5 characters and verify that they're all digits. If they are, check the next character—it should be a hyphen—and then use the substring method to get the last four characters. Check that they're all digits as well. The function should look like this:

```
function zipOK()
    {
    var zip = document.forms[ 0 ].ZIPCode.value;
```

```
  if (zip.length == 5)
      {
      var result = isAllDigits(zip);
      if (result == false)
          {
          alert("Invalid character in zip code");
          }
      return result;
      }
  else if (zip.length == 10)
      {
      var result = isAllDigits(zip.substring(0,5));
      if (result == true)
          {
          if (zip.substring(5,6) != "-")
              {
              result = false;
              }
          else
              {
              result = isAllDigits(zip.substring(6,10));
              }
          }
      if (result == false)
          {
          alert("Invalid character in zip code");
          }
      return result;
      }
  else
      {
      alert("Invalid zip code; please re-enter it");
      return false;
      }
  }
```

Checking the phone number is now very easy. You simply verify that all three fields are filled in and that they're all digits.

Checking the credit card numbers is also easy; just verify that there are four digits in each of the four fields. But you can take it a step further. Most credit card numbers can be validated by using a rule called MOD 10, and for a given company, there is usually a fixed prefix or range of prefixes for the card number. All Visa card numbers begin with 4, and all MasterCard card numbers begin with 51, 52, 53, 54, or 55, and both numbers can be validated with the MOD 10 rule.

The MOD 10 rule says to scan the card number from right to left. Starting with the digit on the right, double every other digit as you move to the left. For the number 49927398716, this means you wind up with these numbers: 4 (9+9) 9 (2+2) 7 (3+3) 9 (8+8) 7 (1+1) 6, or 4 18 9 4 7 6 9 16 7 2 6. Doubled numbers that become 2-digit values are then replaced with the sum of the digits: 4 (1+8) 9 4 7 6 9 7 (1+6) 2 6, or 4 9 9 4 7 6 9 7 7 2 6. These digits are then added up; the sum should be evenly divisible by 10 (in this case, they add up to 70—the number passes).

Applying the MOD 10 rule to our credit card numbers means that the first and third digits of each set of four digits needs to be doubled. Rather than manipulate the digits of the result, you can write a function to get the doubled and digit-summed value of a given digit:

```
function doubleForMod10(c)
    {
    var d = 0 + c;
    if (d == 0) return 0;
    if (d == 1) return 2;
    if (d == 2) return 4;
    if (d == 3) return 6;
    if (d == 4) return 8;
    if (d == 5) return 1; // 5+5 = 10; 1+0 = 1
    if (d == 6) return 3; // 6+6 = 12; 1+2 = 3
    if (d == 7) return 5; // 7+7 = 14; 1+4 = 5
    if (d == 8) return 7; // 8+8 = 16; 1+6 = 7
    return 9; // (digit must be 9) 9+9 = 18; 1+8 = 9
    }
```

Then, for the entire four digits, obtain the sum:

```
function sumForMod10(s)
    {
    var v = parseInt(s, 10); // get the value
    var result = doubleForMod10(Math.floor(v / 1000));
    v = v % 1000;
    result += Math.floor(v / 100);
    v = v % 100;
    result += doubleForMod10(Math.floor(v / 10));
    v = v % 10;
    result += v;
    return result;
    }
```

Putting all this together, let's validate the credit card number using the code shown in Listing 7.2.

Listing 7.2: The validateCreditCardNumber() function

```
function validateCreditCardNumber()
    {
    if (document.forms[ 0 ].CreditCardNumber1.value.length != 4)
        {
        alert("The credit card number is not completely filled out");
        return false;
        }
    if (document.forms[ 0 ].CreditCardNumber2.value.length != 4)
        {
        alert("The credit card number is not completely filled out");
        return false;
        }
    if (document.forms[ 0 ].CreditCardNumber3.value.length != 4)
        {
        alert("The credit card number is not completely filled out");
        return false;
        }
    if (document.forms[ 0 ].CreditCardNumber4.value.length != 4)
        {
        alert("The credit card number is not completely filled out");
        return false;
        }
    if (isAllDigits(document.forms[ 0 ].CreditCardNumber1.value) == false)
        {
        alert("The credit card number contains invalid characters");
        return false;
        }
    if (isAllDigits(document.forms[ 0 ].CreditCardNumber2.value) == false)
        {
        alert("The credit card number contains invalid characters");
        return false;
        }
    if (isAllDigits(document.forms[ 0 ].CreditCardNumber3.value) == false)
        {
        alert("The credit card number contains invalid characters");
        return false;
        }
    if (isAllDigits(document.forms[ 0 ].CreditCardNumber4.value) == false)
        {
        alert("The credit card number contains invalid characters");
        return false;
        }
    if (document.forms[ 0 ].CreditCardType[ 1 ].checked == true) // Visa
        {
        if (document.forms[ 0 ].CreditCardNumber1.value.substring(0,1) != "4")
            {
            alert("The credit card number is not valid; please re-enter it");
            return false;
            }
```

Listing 7.2: The validateCreditCardNumber() function (Continued)

```
        }
    else // must be MasterCard
        {
        var prefix =
        parseInt(document.forms[0].CreditCardNumber1.value.substring(0,2));
        if (prefix < 51 || 55 < prefix)
            {
            alert("The credit card number is not valid; please re-enter it");
            return false;
            }
        }
    var sum = sumForMod10(document.forms[ 0 ].CreditCardNumber1.value);
    sum += sumForMod10(document.forms[ 0 ].CreditCardNumber2.value);
    sum += sumForMod10(document.forms[ 0 ].CreditCardNumber3.value);
    sum += sumForMod10(document.forms[ 0 ].CreditCardNumber4.value);
    if (sum % 10 != 0)
        {
        alert("The credit card number is not valid; please re-enter it");
        return false;
        }
    return true;
    }
```

Verifying the expiration date is straightforward. Make sure the month and year fields are filled in (make sure they have nonzero lengths). Make sure month is a value from 1 to 12. Make sure month and year are at least a month in the future. Listing 7.3 shows how it works.

Listing 7.3: The dateOK() function

```
function dateOK()
    {
    if (document.forms[ 0 ].ExpirationMonth.value.length == 0)
        {
        alert("You must fill in the expiration date");
        return false;
        }
    if (isDigit(document.forms[ 0 ].ExpirationMonth.value.substring(0,1)) ==
    false)
        {
        alert("Expiration date should be numeric");
        return false;
        }
    var eMonth = parseInt(document.forms[ 0 ].ExpirationMonth.value, 10);
    if (eMonth < 1 || 12 < eMonth)
        {
```

Listing 7.3: The dateOK() function (Continued)

```javascript
      alert("Expiration date is out of range");
      }
if (document.forms[ 0 ].ExpirationYear.value.length == 0)
    {
    alert("You must fill in the expiration date");
    return false;
    }
if (isDigit(document.forms[ 0 ].ExpirationYear.value.substring(0,1)) == false)
    {
    alert("Expiration date should be numeric");
    return false;
    }
var eYear = parseInt(document.forms[ 0 ].ExpirationYear.value, 10);
if (eYear < 50)
    {
    eYear += 2000;
    }
else
    {
    eYear += 1900;
    }
var today = new Date(); // get today's date
var thisYear = 1900 + today.getYear();
var thisMonth = 1 + today.getMonth();
if (eYear < thisYear)
    {
    alert("Your credit card seems to have expired");
    return false;
    }
if (thisYear < eYear)
    {
    return true;
    }
if (eMonth < thisMonth)
    {
    alert("Your credit card seems to have expired");
    return false;
    }
if (thisMonth < eMonth)
    {
    return true;
    }
alert("Your credit card has expired or is about to expire");
return false;
}
```

Finally, the last item: the merchandise selected. You'll need to make one minor modification to the OPTION elements and give them values so you can add them up. Then it's simply a matter of walking the list of options and tallying up the result. While you're checking for a result in excess of $5,000, you should also say something if the customer didn't order anything:

```
function merchandiseOK()
    {
    var tally = 0;
    var optionCount = document.forms[ 0 ].Merchandise.options.length;
    for (var k = 0; k < optionCount; k++)
        {
        if (document.forms[ 0 ].Merchandise.options[ k ].selected == true)
            {
            tally += parseInt(document.forms[ 0 ].Merchandise.options[ k ].value,
            10);
            if (5000 < tally)
                {
                alert("Sorry, we cannot handle a transaction in excess of
                $5,000.00");
                return false;
                }
            }
        }
    if (tally == 0)
        {
        alert("Sorry, you don't seem to have ordered anything");
        return false;
        }
    return true;
    }
```

Listing 7.4 shows the entire solution, using JavaScript. There is no separate figure for the JavaScript solution, because as far as the screen is concerned, there are no differences.

Listing 7.4: JavaScript solution for form validation

```
<HTML>
    <HEAD>
        <TITLE>ComputoRama Order Form</TITLE>
        <SCRIPT LANGUAGE="JavaScript">
<!-- hide the code!
function nameOK()
    {
    if (document.forms[ 0 ].FirstName.value.length == 0)
```

Listing 7.4: JavaScript solution for form validation (Continued)

```
        {
        alert("I need a first name, please");
        return false;
        }
    if (document.forms[ 0 ].LastName.value.length == 0)
        {
        alert("I need a last name, please");
        return false;
        }
    return true;
    }

function isDigit(c)
    {
    var test = "" + c;
    if (test == "0" || test == "1" || test == "2" || test == "3" || test == "4"
    || test == "5" || test == "6" || test == "7" || test == "8" || test == "9")
        {
        return true;
        }
    return false;
    }

function ageOK()
    {
    if (document.forms[ 0 ].Age.value.length == 0)
        {
        alert("Sorry, you have failed to enter an age");
        return false;
        }
    var c = document.forms[ 0 ].Age.value.substring(0, 1);
    if (isDigit(c) == false)
        {
        alert("Sorry, you have failed to enter an appropriate age");
        return false;
        }
    var result = parseInt(document.forms[ 0 ].Age.value, 10);
    if (result < 18)
        {
        alert("Sorry, you have failed to enter an appropriate age");
        return false;
        }
    return true;
    }

function isAllDigits(s)
    {
    var test = "" + s;
    for (var k = 0; k < test.length; k++)
```

Listing 7.4: JavaScript solution for form validation (Continued)

```
        {
        var c = test.substring(k, k+1);
        if (isDigit(c) == false)
            {
            return false;
            }
        }
    return true;
    }

function addressOK()
    {
    if (document.forms[ 0 ].StreetAddress.value.length == 0)
        {
        alert("We need a street address");
        return false;
        }
    if (document.forms[ 0 ].City.value.length == 0)
        {
        alert("We need a city");
        return false;
        }
    if (document.forms[ 0 ].State.value.length != 2)
        {
        alert("We need a 2-letter state abbreviation");
        return false;
        }
    return true;
    }

function zipOK()
    {
    var zip = document.forms[ 0 ].ZIPCode.value;
    if (zip.length == 5)
        {
        var result = isAllDigits(zip);
        if (result == false)
            {
            alert("Invalid character in zip code");
            }
        return result;
        }
    else if (zip.length == 10)
        {
        var result = isAllDigits(zip.substring(0,5));
        if (result == true)
            {
            if (zip.substring(5,6) != "-")
                {
```

Listing 7.4: JavaScript solution for form validation (Continued)

```
                result = false;
                }
           else
                {
                result = isAllDigits(zip.substring(6,10));
                }
           }
       if (result == false)
           {
           alert("Invalid character in zip code");
           }
       return result;
       }
   else
       {
       alert("Invalid zip code; please re-enter it");
       return false;
       }
    }

function phoneOK()
    {
    if (document.forms[ 0 ].Phone1.value.length != 3)
        {
        alert("We need a phone number, including area code");
        return false;
        }
    if (document.forms[ 0 ].Phone2.value.length != 3)
        {
        alert("We need a phone number, including area code");
        return false;
        }
    if (document.forms[ 0 ].Phone3.value.length != 4)
        {
        alert("We need a phone number, including area code");
        return false;
        }
    if (isAllDigits(document.forms[ 0 ].Phone1.value) == false)
        {
        alert("Bad character in phone number");
        return false;
        }
    if (isAllDigits(document.forms[ 0 ].Phone2.value) == false)
        {
        alert("Bad character in phone number");
        return false;
        }
    if (isAllDigits(document.forms[ 0 ].Phone3.value) == false)
        {
```

Listing 7.4: JavaScript solution for form validation (Continued)

```
        alert("Bad character in phone number");
        return false;
        }
    return true;
    }

function doubleForMod10(c)
    {
    var d = 0 + c;
    if (d == 0) return 0;
    if (d == 1) return 2;
    if (d == 2) return 4;
    if (d == 3) return 6;
    if (d == 4) return 8;
    if (d == 5) return 1; // 5+5 = 10; 1+0 = 1
    if (d == 6) return 3; // 6+6 = 12; 1+2 = 3
    if (d == 7) return 5; // 7+7 = 14; 1+4 = 5
    if (d == 8) return 7; // 8+8 = 16; 1+6 = 7
    return 9; // (digit must be 9) 9+9 = 18; 1+8 = 9
    }

function sumForMod10(s)
    {
    var v = parseInt(s, 10); // get the value
    var result = doubleForMod10(Math.floor(v / 1000));
    v = v % 1000;
    result += Math.floor(v / 100);
    v = v % 100;
    result += doubleForMod10(Math.floor(v / 10));
    v = v % 10;
    result += v;
    return result;
    }

function validateCreditCardNumber()
    {
    if (document.forms[ 0 ].CreditCardNumber1.value.length != 4)
        {
        alert("The credit card number is not completely filled out");
        return false;
        }
    if (document.forms[ 0 ].CreditCardNumber2.value.length != 4)
        {
        alert("The credit card number is not completely filled out");
        return false;
        }
    if (document.forms[ 0 ].CreditCardNumber3.value.length != 4)
        {
        alert("The credit card number is not completely filled out");
```

Listing 7.4: JavaScript solution for form validation (Continued)

```
      return false;
      }
  if (document.forms[ 0 ].CreditCardNumber4.value.length != 4)
      {
      alert("The credit card number is not completely filled out");
      return false;
      }
  if (isAllDigits(document.forms[ 0 ].CreditCardNumber1.value) == false)
      {
      alert("The credit card number contains invalid characters");
      return false;
      }
  if (isAllDigits(document.forms[ 0 ].CreditCardNumber2.value) == false)
      {
      alert("The credit card number contains invalid characters");
      return false;
      }
  if (isAllDigits(document.forms[ 0 ].CreditCardNumber3.value) == false)
      {
      alert("The credit card number contains invalid characters");
      return false;
      }
  if (isAllDigits(document.forms[ 0 ].CreditCardNumber4.value) == false)
      {
      alert("The credit card number contains invalid characters");
      return false;
      }
  if (document.forms[ 0 ].CreditCardType[ 1 ].checked == true) // Visa
      {
      if (document.forms[ 0 ].CreditCardNumber1.value.substring(0,1) != "4")
          {
          alert("The credit card number is not valid; please re-enter it");
          return false;
          }
      }
  else // must be MasterCard
      {
      var prefix =
      parseInt(document.forms[0].CreditCardNumber1.value.substring(0,2));
      if (prefix < 51 || 55 < prefix)
          {
          alert("The credit card number is not valid; please re-enter it");
          return false;
          }
      }
  var sum = sumForMod10(document.forms[ 0 ].CreditCardNumber1.value);
  sum += sumForMod10(document.forms[ 0 ].CreditCardNumber2.value);
  sum += sumForMod10(document.forms[ 0 ].CreditCardNumber3.value);
  sum += sumForMod10(document.forms[ 0 ].CreditCardNumber4.value);
```

Listing 7.4: JavaScript solution for form validation (Continued)

```
    if (sum % 10 != 0)
        {
        alert("The credit card number is not valid; please re-enter it");
        return false;
        }
    return true;
    }

function dateOK()
    {
    if (document.forms[ 0 ].ExpirationMonth.value.length == 0)
        {
        alert("You must fill in the expiration date");
        return false;
        }
    if (isDigit(document.forms[ 0 ].ExpirationMonth.value.substring(0,1)) ==
false)
        {
        alert("Expiration date should be numeric");
        return false;
        }
    var eMonth = parseInt(document.forms[ 0 ].ExpirationMonth.value, 10);
    if (eMonth < 1 || 12 < eMonth)
        {
        alert("Expiration date is out of range");
        }
    if (document.forms[ 0 ].ExpirationYear.value.length == 0)
        {
        alert("You must fill in the expiration date");
        return false;
        }
    if (isDigit(document.forms[ 0 ].ExpirationYear.value.substring(0,1)) == false)
        {
        alert("Expiration date should be numeric");
        return false;
        }
    var eYear = parseInt(document.forms[ 0 ].ExpirationYear.value, 10);
    if (eYear < 50)
        {
        eYear += 2000;
        }
    else
        {
        eYear += 1900;
        }
    var today = new Date(); // get today's date
    var thisYear = 1900 + today.getYear();
    var thisMonth = 1 + today.getMonth();
    if (eYear < thisYear)
```

Listing 7.4: JavaScript solution for form validation (Continued)

```
            {
        alert("Your credit card seems to have expired");
        return false;
            }
    if (thisYear < eYear)
            {
        return true;
            }
    if (eMonth < thisMonth)
            {
        alert("Your credit card seems to have expired");
        return false;
            }
    if (thisMonth < eMonth)
            {
        return true;
            }
    alert("Your credit card has expired or is about to expire");
    return false;
            }

function merchandiseOK()
    {
    var tally = 0;
    var optionCount = document.forms[ 0 ].Merchandise.options.length;
    for (var k = 0; k < optionCount; k++)
        {
        if (document.forms[ 0 ].Merchandise.options[ k ].selected == true)
            {
            tally += parseInt(document.forms[ 0 ].Merchandise.options[ k ].value);
            if (5000 < tally)
                {
                alert("Sorry, we cannot handle a transaction in excess of
                $5,000.00");
                return false;
                }
            }
        }
    if (tally == 0)
        {
        alert("Sorry, you don't seem to have ordered anything");
        return false;
        }
    return true;
    }

function checkForm()
    {
    if (nameOK() == false)
```

Listing 7.4: JavaScript solution for form validation (Continued)

```
          {
          return;
          }
      if (ageOK() == false)
          {
          return;
          }
      if (addressOK() == false)
          {
          return;
          }
      if (zipOK() == false)
          {
          return;
          }
      if (phoneOK() == false)
          {
          return;
          }
      if (validateCreditCardNumber() == false)
          {
          return;
          }
      if (dateOK() == false)
          {
          return;
          }
      if (merchandiseOK() == false)
          {
          return;
          }
      document.forms[ 0 ].submit();
      }
// end of code -->
      </SCRIPT>
   </HEAD>
   <BODY>
      <FORM ACTION="mailto:mailhost@computoRama.usa.com" METHOD=POST>
         <TABLE BORDER="2" CELLPADDING="1">
            <TR>
               <TD ROWSPAN="2">Who Are You?</TD>
               <TD><INPUT TYPE="text" NAME="FirstName" SIZE=20></TD>
               <TD><INPUT TYPE="text" NAME="MiddleInitial" SIZE=1></TD>
               <TD><INPUT TYPE="text" NAME="LastName" SIZE=20></TD>
               <TD><INPUT TYPE="text" NAME="Age" SIZE=3></TD>
            </TR>
            <TR>
               <TD><FONT SIZE="-2">First Name</FONT></TD>
               <TD><FONT SIZE="-2">MI</FONT></TD>
```

Listing 7.4: JavaScript solution for form validation (Continued)

```
            <TD><FONT SIZE="-2">Last Name></TD>
            <TD><FONT SIZE="-2">Age</TD>
    </TR>
    <TR>
        <TD ROWSPAN="3">How Do We Contact You?</TD>
        <TD COLSPAN="4" VALIGN="TOP">Street Address: <TEXTAREA
        name="StreetAddress" rows=2 cols=30></TEXTAREA></TD>
    </TR>
    <TR>
        <TD COLSPAN="2">City: <INPUT TYPE="text" NAME="City"
        SIZE=20></TD>
        <TD COLSPAN="2">State: <INPUT TYPE="text" NAME="State"
        SIZE=2></TD>
    </TR>
    <TR>
        <TD COLSPAN="2">ZIP Code: <INPUT TYPE="text" NAME="ZIPCode"
        SIZE=10></TD>
        <TD COLSPAN="2">Daytime Phone
            (<INPUT TYPE="text" NAME="Phone1" SIZE=3>)
            <INPUT TYPE="text" NAME="Phone2" SIZE=3>-
            <INPUT TYPE="text" NAME="Phone3" SIZE=4></TD>
    </TR>
    <TR>
        <TD>Credit Card
            <INPUT TYPE="radio" NAME="CreditCardType" VALUE="Visa"
            CHECKED>Visa
            <INPUT TYPE="radio" NAME="CreditCardType"
            VALUE="MasterCard">M/C</TD>
        <TD COLSPAN="2" ALIGN="CENTER">
            <INPUT TYPE="text" NAME="CreditCardNumber1" SIZE=4>
            <INPUT TYPE="text" NAME="CreditCardNumber2" SIZE=4>
            <INPUT TYPE="text" NAME="CreditCardNumber3" SIZE=4>
            <INPUT TYPE="text" NAME="CreditCardNumber4" SIZE=4></TD>
        <TD COLSPAN="2">Expiration Date:
            <INPUT TYPE="text" NAME="ExpirationMonth" SIZE=2>/
            <INPUT TYPE="text" NAME="ExpirationYear" SIZE=2></TD>
    </TR>
    <TR>
        <TD>Merchandise</TD>
        <TD COLSPAN=4><SELECT MULTIPLE NAME="Merchandise" SIZE=1>
            <OPTION SELECTED VALUE="2000"> HAL-470 <OPTION
            VALUE="3000"> Banana9000
            <OPTION VALUE="800"> High Res Monitor <OPTION VALUE="50">
            Low Res Monitor
            <OPTION VALUE="250"> Deluxe Keyboard <OPTION VALUE="40">
            Regular Keyboard
            <OPTION VALUE="2000"> Laser Printer <OPTION VALUE="600">
            Inkjet Printer <OPTION VALUE="200"> Dot Matrix Printer
```

Listing 7.4: JavaScript solution for form validation (Continued)

```
                          <OPTION VALUE="100"> Mouse <OPTION VALUE="125"> Trackball
                          <OPTION VALUE="500"> Scanner
                          </SELECT></TD>
              </TR>
              <TR>
                  <TD ALIGN=CENTER COLSPAN="5">
                      <H1>Thank You For Your Order!</H1>
                  </TD>
              </TR>
          </TABLE>
          <CENTER>
              <INPUT TYPE="button" VALUE="Ship It!" ONCLICK="checkForm()">
              <INPUT TYPE="reset" VALUE="Clear Entries">
          </CENTER>
      </FORM>
    </BODY>
</HTML>
```

IMPROVING THE SOLUTION

You can further improve the JavaScript solution. You could perform additional checking for post office box addresses (hint: make a copy of the street address and convert the copy to uppercase), because only the United States Postal Service can deliver to a post office box. You could verify that the state is a valid post office abbreviation (convert it to uppercase). If you're really ambitious, you can try tying the state, zip code, and area code together to see if they work (an address in Georgia with a zip code that starts with 8 and an area code of 919 would be a bad address, for example). A confirmation box announcing what customers have purchased and how much they're about to spend would be a very nice touch. If the customer clicks on CANCEL, no harm done. While you have the customer there, why not scroll additional advertising along the status bar?

MODIFYING THE EXAMPLE FOR YOUR OWN USE

Although this is a fictitious example, the techniques used here do carry over to real-world applications. In particular, some of the functions used in the Java-Script solution—in particular isDigit() and isAllDigits()—are quite useful for checking numeric output, such as the phone number and credit card number validation in this chapter, or driver's license and social security numbers. The MOD 10 algorithm is in fact used by most major credit cards, and I've tested it against all of my bank cards—it really works.

Form
Modification

THE SCENARIO

THE REQUIREMENTS

THE SOLUTION (WITHOUT JAVASCRIPT)

THE SOLUTION (WITH JAVASCRIPT)

IMPROVING THE SOLUTION

MODIFYING THE EXAMPLE
  FOR YOUR OWN USE

F orm modification is the process by which data entered by a user is translated into another format before being submitted to the form's server. When data from a form is submitted to its server, the data has to be formatted in a way that the server can understand. The format is usually in the form

```
<url>?<field1=value>?<field2=value>...
```

where <field1>, <field2>, and so forth are the NAME attributes of the INPUT, SELECT, and TEXTAREA elements of the form. The values are, with minor translations made by the browser, the VALUE attributes of those elements.

So why would you need to go to the trouble of form modification? Because the format of the values and the fields are not necessarily very user friendly. If you have to create a Web page to interface to such a server and you have no control over the server's input requirements, you can use form modification to create a superior, easier-to-use Web page.

THE SCENARIO

The United States Department of Commerce Bureau of the Census operates the Tiger Map Service. The Tiger Map Service defines a URL, http://tiger.census.gov/cgi-bin/mapgen, and a set of field-value pairs that can be specified. The server responds with a GIF file that displays a made-to-order map specified by the field-value pairs.

The interface defines a very rich set of field-value pairs. One of these actually allows you to shorten the data sent to the server by defining a URL that contains additional field-value pairs. The critical set of pairs, however, define the area that the map will display. These are

- lon=*number*
- lat=*number*
- wid=*number*
- ht=*number*

These four field-value pairs define the longitude (east-west coordinate), the latitude (north-south coordinate), and the width and height of the area displayed by the map. The values are specified in decimal degrees; you would specify a latitude of 38 degrees, 45 minutes to the server as 38.75 degrees, for example.

Naturally, this scenario requires a Web page with a form for creating a map GIF file.

THE REQUIREMENTS

The typical user will want to look at famous U.S. landmarks or at his or her hometown. The typical user will also have, at best, a vague idea of the coordinates of the location he or she wants to see. (You can check a map to get a general idea of the coordinates you need.) The user will usually have no idea at all how to set the width and height to capture the desired level of detail. The greater the values of the wid and ht fields, the larger the area displayed in the map and the less detail displayed. But how small should these field values be to get the desired level of detail? Most users won't know and will need to experiment to get the desired results.

For these reasons, the Web page should let users enter the coordinates and height and width fields as easily as possible, and should make it easy for them to change the fields and try again.

THE SOLUTION (WITHOUT JAVASCRIPT)

To capture the required fields, you need four INPUT elements with NAME attributes of lat, lon, wid, and ht. To give the user a reasonable map size, let's add iht and iwd fields. These fields describe the image height and image width; both values are specified in pixels. You can make them HIDDEN type INPUT elements, and give them fixed values. Let's use an image area 320 pixels wide and 200 pixels high.

The rest of the Web page has the standard HTML/HEAD/BODY structure, with the fields contained in a FORM element. The FORM ACTION attribute needs to be specified as "http://tiger.census.gov/cgi-bin/mapgen" and the METHOD attribute should be "GET." Listing 8.1 contains the code for this Web page.

Listing 8.1: HTML for non-JavaScript solution

```
<HTML>
    <HEAD>
        <TITLE>Map Service</TITLE>
    </HEAD>
    <BODY>
        <PRE>
            <FORM ACTION="http://tiger.census.gov/cgi-bin/mapgen"
            METHOD="GET">
Longitude:      <INPUT NAME="lon" TYPE="text" SIZE=10>
Latitude:       <INPUT NAME="lat" TYPE="text" SIZE=10>
Width:          <INPUT NAME="wid" TYPE="text" SIZE=10>
Height:         <INPUT NAME="ht"  TYPE="text" SIZE=10>
<INPUT NAME="iwd" TYPE="hidden" VALUE="320">
<INPUT NAME="iht" TYPE="hidden" VALUE="200">
<INPUT TYPE="submit"><INPUT TYPE="reset">
            </FORM>
        </PRE>
    </BODY>
</HTML>
```

Figure 8.1 shows the form with some sample values entered, and Figure 8.2 shows the map GIF file that the server returned as a result.

THE SOLUTION (WITH JAVASCRIPT)

One problem with the Tiger Map Service interface is that it uses decimal degrees. Unfortunately, that doesn't tie in very well with most sources of map data, which usually specify locations in terms of degrees, minutes, and seconds.

Even worse is the fact that most people have no idea how much real estate is covered by one degree of latitude or longitude, or one minute, or one second. How is the average user going to know what to specify for the height and width of the area?

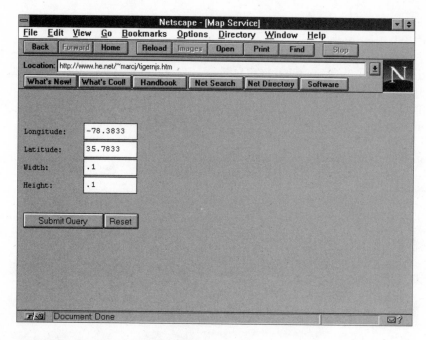

Figure 8.1: Non-JavaScript form with sample values

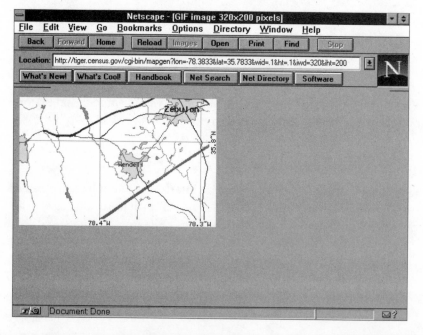

Figure 8.2: Result of submitting data from Figure 8.1

You need a more intuitive interface than the server allows.

First, the user has to be able to specify the latitude and longitude in conventional terms of degrees, minutes, and seconds. Second, you need a more intuitive way to manage the area's height and width. Given that one of the requirements of this page is to make it easy to change these values, let's start with an arbitrary height and width of one degree, and let the user modify the height and width by zooming in and out. Zooming in will be defined as cutting the height and width in half, which places one quarter the area (more or less) in the same image size. Zooming out will be defined as doubling the height and width, placing four times the area in the same image size.

Finally, you can add buttons to allow the user to fine-tune the center coordinates. That will further meet the requirement of allowing the user to easily make quick changes to the map.

You do all this by creating two FORM elements. The first FORM element is very similar to the FORM element in Listing 8.1. There is one big difference: The INPUT elements are HIDDEN type instead of TEXT, and the descriptive text is removed, making the form invisible.

The second FORM element is the form the user will see. It has two BUTTON INPUT elements, one to execute the zoom in and one to execute the zoom out. There is also a TEXT INPUT element for displaying the current magnification factor. This element is useful because the server sometimes cannot meet the request and a "Sorry, Busy" GIF image appears instead of the requested map. Once users have more or less zeroed in on the area of choice, they tend to keep zooming in, and may not recall how far they have zoomed in. Displaying the magnification factor helps them keep track of how far they have zoomed in. This visual feedback helps if the user zooms in but doesn't get a map because the server is busy. There is at least a clue that maybe the user should press the GO! button instead of pressing the Zoom In button again.

In addition to the zoom controls, there are three TEXT INPUT elements for the latitude (one for degrees, one for minutes, and one for seconds) and three for the longitude. There are also four BUTTON INPUT elements that allow the user to make small adjustments to the map, moving it to the west, north, east, or south.

Finally, there is a BUTTON INPUT element to act as a submit button and a RESET INPUT element. You don't want a real SUBMIT INPUT element, because the data in this FORM element is not going to be sent to a server.

LAYING OUT THE CONTROLS

There are a lot of controls for this Web page: seven BUTTON INPUT elements, seven TEXT INPUT elements, and a RESET INPUT element. If you put them in a TABLE element, you can manage them better.

Let's start with one TABLE element. It, in turn, will contain three TABLE elements—one for the zoom controls, one for the location controls, and one for the submit and reset controls. The TABLE element will be inside the FORM element, and the TABLE HTML will look something like this:

```
<FORM>
    <TABLE>
        <TR>
            <TD>
                <TABLE>
                </TABLE>          .
            </TD>
            <TD>
                <TABLE>
                </TABLE>
            </TD>
            <TD>
                <TABLE>
                </TABLE>
            </TD>
        </TR>
    </TABLE>
</FORM>
```

This code describes a TABLE element with a single TABLE ROW (TR) element. The TABLE ROW element contains three TABLE DATA (TD) elements. Each TABLE DATA element contains a TABLE element. This produces an effect of three TABLE elements lined up side by side, as shown in Figure 8.3.

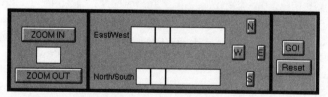

Figure 8.3: Gross table structure

The first TABLE element will contain the zoom controls. It looks like this:

```
<TABLE>
    <TR>
        <TD>
            <INPUT TYPE="button" VALUE="ZOOM IN">
        </TD>
    </TR>
    <TR>
        <TD>
            <INPUT TYPE="text" NAME="mag" SIZE=4>
        </TD>
    </TR>
    <TR>
        <TD>
            <INPUT TYPE="button" VALUE="ZOOM OUT">
        </TD>
    </TR>
</TABLE>
```

This code creates three rows, with one data cell each. The top cell contains the ZOOM IN button, the middle cell contains the magnification factor display, and the bottom cell contains the ZOOM OUT button, as you can see in Figure 8.4.

Figure 8.4: Zoom controls

The second table contains the location controls. The layout of the table is like this:

```
<TABLE>
    <TR>
        <TD>
            East/West <INPUT TYPE="text" NAME="londeg" SIZE=4><INPUT TYPE="text"
            NAME="lonmin" SIZE=2><INPUT TYPE="text" NAME="lonsec" SIZE=10>
        </TD>
        <TD ROWSPAN="2">
            <TABLE>
            </TABLE>
```

```
        </TD>
    </TR>
    <TR>
        <TD>
        North/South <INPUT TYPE="text" NAME="latdeg" SIZE=2><INPUT TYPE="text"
        NAME="latmin" SIZE=2><INPUT TYPE="text" NAME="latsec" SIZE=10>
        </TD>
    </TR>
</TABLE>
```

This code creates three cells in two rows—two cells on the left (one top cell and one bottom cell) and a third cell on the right that's the height of the other two cells combined as shown in Figure 8.5.

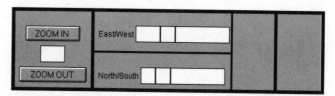

Figure 8.5: Location controls

The two left-hand cells provide the TEXT INPUT elements for entering the longitude (east-west coordinate) and the latitude (north-south coordinate). The large cell on the right contains another TABLE element that will contain the east-north-west-south adjustment buttons.

The adjustment controls TABLE is laid out like this:

```
<TABLE>
    <TR>
        <TD>
        </TD>
        <TD>
            <INPUT TYPE="button" VALUE="N">
        </TD>
        <TD>
        </TD>
    </TR>
    <TR>
        <TD>
            <INPUT TYPE="button" VALUE="W">
        </TD>
        <TD>
        </TD>
```

```
        <TD>
            <INPUT TYPE="button" VALUE="E">
        </TD>
    </TR>
    <TR>
        <TD>
        </TD>
        <TD>
            <INPUT TYPE="button" VALUE="S">
        </TD>
        <TD>
        </TD>
    </TR>
</TABLE>
```

This layout produces a simple compass star, as shown in Figure 8.6.

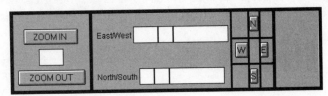

Figure 8.6: Compass controls

Finally, the third table contains the submit and reset controls, as laid out here:

```
<TABLE BORDER="0" CELLPADDING="2">
    <TR>
        <TD>
            <INPUT TYPE="button" VALUE="GO!">
        </TD>
    </TR>
    <TR>
        <TD>
            <INPUT TYPE="RESET">
        </TD>
    </TR>
</TABLE>
```

You can see these controls in Figure 8.7.

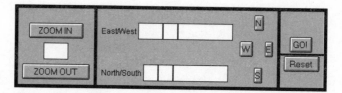

Figure 8.7: The map controls

LAYING OUT THE WINDOW

Having organized the new FORM element's contents for the screen, you need to give some thought to the setup of the overall screen. One of the problems with the non-JavaScript implementation is that the map replaces the form on the screen; to return to the form data, the user has to use the BACK button. At no time can the user see the data and the map together. You can fix this shortcoming by using frames:

```
<HTML>
    <HEAD>
        <TITLE>Tiger Map Service</TITLE>
    </HEAD>
    <FRAMESET ROWS="220, *">
        <FRAMESET COLS="*,350,*">
            <FRAME NAME="leftBorder" SRC="wall.htm">
            <FRAME NAME="viewer" SRC="view.htm">
            <FRAME NAME="rightBorder" SRC="wall.htm">
        </FRAMESET>
        <FRAME NAME="control" SRC="mapctrl.htm">
        </FRAME>
    </FRAMESET>
</HTML>
```

This frame document divides the screen vertically into an upper frame 220 pixels high and a lower frame that occupies the remainder of the screen. The FORM elements will be in the lower frame. The 220 pixel height of the top frame allows most browsers to display the 200 pixel high image without a scroll bar. The top frame is then subdivided vertically into a 350 pixel wide frame flanked by two frames on either side. The 350 pixel width of the viewer frame allows most browsers to display the 320 pixel wide image without a scroll bar. Figure 8.8 shows the resulting screen.

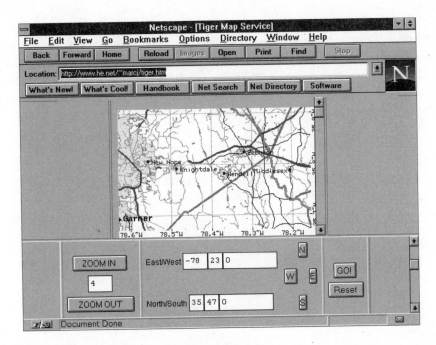

Figure 8.8: JavaScript solution with map displayed

With this frame solution, there is one other minor modification to be made to the hidden form. The hidden form needs a TARGET attribute:

```
<FORM NAME="realForm" ACTION="http://tiger.census.gov/cgi-bin/mapgen"
      METHOD="GET" TARGET="viewer">
```

The TARGET attribute tells the browser to display the submission results in the viewer frame. Without that, the results would replace the contents of the control frame, and the user would lose his or her view of the data.

ADDING FUNCTIONALITY TO THE CONTROLS

With the two FORM elements defined, the data entered into the second FORM element has to wind up, in modified format, in the first FORM element. This will require event handlers for some of the INPUT elements in the second FORM element.

BUTTON type elements are the easiest INPUT elements to use. The ON-CLICK event is very understandable to users, much more so than ONCHANGE, ONFOCUS, and ONBLUR events, which have subtle differences in their behavior from one platform to another. A mouse click behaves pretty much the same on all platforms.

The jobs of the ONCLICK event handlers depend on the BUTTON elements they work on. The GO! and ZOOM controls should display a new map. The compass controls should modify the contents of the longitude or latitude fields, but should not display a new map. The user may want to use more than one compass control to move the image further east and further north, for example, and will not want to wait between adjustments for the wrong area to be displayed.

The E and W buttons can share a function; they both adjust the longitude, just in opposite directions. Similarly, the N and S buttons can share a function. Let's call these functions changeLongitude() and changeLatitude(). Called with a negative value, changeLongitude() moves the center of the picture west and changeLatitude() moves the center of the picture south. Called with a positive value, changeLongitude() moves the center of the picture east and changeLatitude() moves the center of the picture north.

The two functions are nearly identical; this is changeLongitude():

```
function changeLongitude(dir)
    {
    var delta = 0.1 / getMagnification();
    var longitude = getLongitude();
    if (dir < 0)
        {
        longitude -= delta;
        }
    else
        {
        longitude += delta;
        }
    setLongitude(longitude);
    }
```

The current magnification factor is obtained by a call to getMagnification() and a value of one-tenth of a degree is divided by the magnification factor. Because the image spans a degree divided by the magnification factor, this is a delta of one tenth of the image. The longitude is then obtained by a call to getLongitude(). The delta is either subtracted from it or added to it. The new longitude is written back out with setLongitude().

The changeLatitude() function is identical except that it deals with latitude instead of longitude.

The getMagnification() function obtains the value from the TEXT INPUT element named "mag":

```
function getMagnification()
    {
    var magnification = 1;
    if (document.showForm.mag.value.length != 0)
        {
        magnification =
            Math.abs(parseFloat(document.showForm.mag.value));
        if (magnification == 0)
            {
            magnification = 1;
            }
        }
    return magnification;
    }
```

The return value is set to 1 as a default. If anything is entered on screen, parseFloat() is called to evaluate the contents. The absolute value of the result is taken—a negative magnification factor doesn't make sense. If the result is 0, the value is replaced with the default value of 1.

The getLongitude() function calculates a decimal longitude from the three TEXT INPUT elements in which the user has entered the longitude in degrees, minutes, and seconds:

```
function getLongitude()
    {
    var londeg = 0;
    if (document.showForm.londeg.value.length != 0)
        {
        londeg = Math.abs(parseInt(document.showForm.londeg.value));
        }
    var lonmin = 0;
    if (document.showForm.lonmin.value.length != 0)
        {
        lonmin = Math.abs(parseInt(document.showForm.lonmin.value));
        }
    var lonsec = 0;
    if (document.showForm.lonsec.value.length != 0)
        {
        lonsec = Math.abs(parseFloat(document.showForm.lonsec.value));
        }
    var lon = -(londeg + ((lonmin + (lonsec / 60)) / 60));
    return lon;
    }
```

As with the magnification value calculated in getMagnification(), values are calculated for the three fields, with 0 as the default value for each field. Because the degrees and minutes fields are assumed to be integer values, parseInt() rather than parseFloat() is used to evaluate their values.

The calculation of the result from the degrees, minutes, and seconds values is straightforward, with one interesting quirk: The value has to be negative. The Tiger Map Service delivers maps for the continental United States, and longitudes are, by convention, negative west of the Prime Meridian.

There is an equivalent function to evaluate the latitude fields, getLatitude(). It is identical to the getLongitude() function except that the return value is positive. (Again, by convention, latitudes in the northern hemisphere are positive values.)

The setLongitude() function translates the decimal longitude back into degrees, minutes, and seconds and writes the values back to the TEXT INPUT elements:

```
function setLongitude(longitude)
    {
    longitude = Math.abs(longitude);
    var degrees = Math.floor(longitude);
    longitude = longitude - Math.floor(longitude);
    longitude *= 60;
    var minutes = Math.floor(longitude)
    // complicated math to eliminate eensy teensy fractions of seconds
    var seconds = 60 * (longitude - Math.floor(longitude))
    seconds *= 1000;
    seconds = Math.round(seconds);
    seconds /= 1000;
    if (seconds >= 60)
        {
        seconds -= 60;
        minutes++;
        }
    if (minutes >= 60)
        {
        minutes -=60;
        degrees++;
        }
    document.showForm.londeg.value = -degrees;
    document.showForm.lonmin.value = minutes;
    document.showForm.lonsec.value = seconds;
    }
```

The longitude value is made positive by a call to Math.abs( ). The integer portion is extracted using Math.floor( ); this is the degrees part of the value. The remaining fractional part is obtained and multiplied by 60, and the integer portion of the result is taken with Math.floor( ); this is the minutes part of the value. The remaining fractional part is obtained and multiplied by 60; this is the seconds part of the value, which is allowed to have a fractional part.

You might think that that's enough, but from the standpoint of user interaction, it isn't. The seconds field on the form is defined as displaying ten digits, but Netscape's math functions result in a value with more than ten digits of precision. Furthermore, the act of translating the three input fields into decimal degrees and then translating that result back into degrees, minutes, and seconds may introduce a tiny discrepancy into the result. This is due to the limitations inherent in representing fractions such as one third in the computer's binary memory: There is no value expressible in a finite set of powers of 2 that exactly equals one third.

So the seconds value is multiplied by 1,000, rounded off with Math.round( ), and divided by 1,000. This gives a precision of 1/1,000 of a second. At the equator, where one degree of longitude is widest, 1/1,000 of a second is approximately an inch and a quarter, or about three centimeters. That should be good enough.

Because of rounding, the seconds value may now equal 60, which is one minute. This scenario has to be handled, and the carry effect may propagate to the degrees, as would happen if the initial calculation of minutes and seconds arrived at values of 59 and 59.99999.

Finally, after you have calculated acceptable values for degrees, minutes, and seconds, the values are written to the appropriate TEXT INPUT elements. The degrees are written as a negative value.

As with getLongitude( ) and getLatitude( ), setLongitude( ) has a matching function, setLatitude( ). The calculations are identical, and the difference is that the degrees latitude are written back as a positive value.

So that's how the compass point buttons work. Let's look at the zoom buttons next.

The zoom buttons cause two things to occur: First, they change the current magnification factor. Second, they update the hidden form—the one that contains the fields that the Tiger Map Service needs—and submit the data to the server. This function does the work for both buttons:

```
function zoom(dir)
    {
    var magnification = getMagnification();
    if (dir < 0)
```

```
        {
    magnification /= 2;
        }
    else
        {
    magnification *= 2;
        }
    display(magnification);
    }
```

If the parameter dir is negative, the user is zooming out; if dir is positive, the user is zooming in. So, the magnification factor is obtained by a call to get-Magnification and either halved or doubled. The new magnification factor is then passed to display(), which is shown here:

```
function display(magnification)
    {
    document.showForm.mag.value = magnification;
    var lon = getLongitude();
    setLongitude(lon);
    document.realForm.lon.value = lon;
    document.realForm.wid.value = 1 / magnification ;
    var lat = getLatitude();
    setLatitude(lat);
    document.realForm.lat.value = lat;
    document.realForm.ht.value = 1 / magnification;
    document.realForm.submit();
    }
```

First, the new magnification factor is written back to the TEXT INPUT field. Then the decimal longitude is obtained, the display is updated, and the decimal longitude is written to the hidden form's lon field. The hidden form's wid field is set to the inverse of the magnification factor. Remember, the higher the factor, the smaller of an area you're looking at.

The analogous calls are then made to set the hidden form's lat and ht values, and the hidden form's submit method is called, sending the request to the server.

Finally, the Go button's ONCLICK event handler is extremely simple: It just calls getMagnification() and sends the result to display(), like this:

```
display(getMagnification())
```

PUTTING EVERYTHING TOGETHER

Listing 8.2 shows the finished mapctrl.htm file.

Listing 8.2: HTML for the JavaScript solution

```
<HTML>
    <HEAD>
        <TITLE>Map Service</TITLE>
        <SCRIPT LANGUAGE="JavaScript">
<!--

function getMagnification()
    {
    var magnification = 1;
    if (document.showForm.mag.value.length != 0)
        {
        magnification = Math.abs(parseFloat(document.showForm.mag.value));
        if (magnification == 0)
            {
            magnification = 1;
            }
        }
    return magnification;
    }

function setLongitude(longitude)
    {
    longitude = Math.abs(longitude);
    var degrees = Math.floor(longitude);
    longitude = longitude - Math.floor(longitude);
    longitude *= 60;
    var minutes = Math.floor(longitude)
    // complicated math to eliminate eensy teensy fractions of seconds
    var seconds = 60 * (longitude - Math.floor(longitude))
    seconds *= 1000;
    seconds = Math.round(seconds);
    seconds /= 1000;
    if (seconds >= 60)
        {
        seconds -= 60;
        minutes++;
        }
    if (minutes >= 60)
        {
        minutes -=60;
        degrees++;
        }
    document.showForm.londeg.value = -degrees;
    document.showForm.lonmin.value = minutes;
    document.showForm.lonsec.value = seconds;
    }

function setLatitude(latitude)
    {
```

Listing 8.2: HTML for the JavaScript solution (Continued)

```
        latitude = Math.abs(latitude);
        var degrees = Math.floor(latitude);
        latitude = latitude - Math.floor(latitude);
        latitude *= 60;
        var minutes = Math.floor(latitude)
        // complicated math to eliminate eensy teensy fractions of seconds
        var seconds = 60 * (latitude - Math.floor(latitude))
        seconds *= 1000;
        seconds = Math.round(seconds);
        seconds /= 1000;
        if (seconds >= 60)
            {
            seconds -= 60;
            minutes++;
            }
        if (minutes >= 60)
            {
            minutes -=60;
            degrees++;
            }
        document.showForm.latdeg.value = degrees;
        document.showForm.latmin.value = minutes;
        document.showForm.latsec.value = seconds;
        }

function getLongitude()
    {
    var londeg = 0;
    if (document.showForm.londeg.value.length != 0)
        {
        londeg = Math.abs(parseInt(document.showForm.londeg.value));
        }
    var lonmin = 0;
    if (document.showForm.lonmin.value.length != 0)
        {
        lonmin = Math.abs(parseInt(document.showForm.lonmin.value));
        }
    var lonsec = 0;
    if (document.showForm.lonsec.value.length != 0)
        {
        lonsec = Math.abs(parseFloat(document.showForm.lonsec.value));
        }
    var lon = -(londeg + ((lonmin + (lonsec / 60)) / 60));
    return lon;
    }

function getLatitude()
    {
    var latdeg = 0;
```

Listing 8.2: HTML for the JavaScript solution (Continued)

```
    if (document.showForm.latdeg.value.length != 0)
        {
        latdeg = Math.abs(parseInt(document.showForm.latdeg.value));
        }
    var latmin = 0;
    if (document.showForm.latmin.value.length != 0)
        {
        latmin = Math.abs(parseInt(document.showForm.latmin.value));
        }
    var latsec = 0;
    if (document.showForm.latsec.value.length != 0)
        {
        latsec = Math.abs(parseFloat(document.showForm.latsec.value));
        }
    var lat = latdeg + ((latmin + (latsec / 60)) / 60);
    return lat;
    }

function display(magnification)
    {
    document.showForm.mag.value = magnification;
    var lon = getLongitude();
    setLongitude(lon);
    document.realForm.lon.value = lon;
    document.realForm.wid.value = 1 / magnification ;
    var lat = getLatitude();
    setLatitude(lat);
    document.realForm.lat.value = lat;
    document.realForm.ht.value = 1 / magnification;
    document.realForm.submit();
    }

function zoom(dir)
    {
    var magnification = getMagnification();
    if (dir < 0)
        {
        magnification /= 2;
        }
    else
        {
        magnification *= 2;
        }
    display(magnification);
    }

function changeLongitude(dir)
    {
    var delta = 0.1 / getMagnification();
```

Listing 8.2: HTML for the JavaScript solution (Continued)

```
    var longitude = getLongitude();
    if (dir < 0)
        {
        longitude -= delta;
        }
    else
        {
        longitude += delta;
        }
    setLongitude(longitude);
    }

function changeLatitude(dir)
    {
    var delta = 0.1 / getMagnification();
    var latitude = getLatitude();
    if (dir < 0)
        {
        latitude -= delta;
        }
    else
        {
        latitude += delta;
        }
    setLatitude(latitude);
    }

//-->
    </SCRIPT>
    </HEAD>
    <BODY BGCOLOR="#000000" TEXT="#FF0000">
        <FORM NAME="realForm"
            ACTION="http://tiger.census.gov/cgi-bin/mapgen"
            METHOD="GET" TARGET="viewer">
            <INPUT NAME="lon" TYPE="hidden" SIZE=10>
            <INPUT NAME="lat" TYPE="hidden" SIZE=10>
            <INPUT NAME="wid" TYPE="hidden" SIZE=10>
            <INPUT NAME="ht"  TYPE="hidden" SIZE=10>
            <INPUT NAME="iwd" TYPE="hidden" SIZE=10 VALUE="320">
            <INPUT NAME="iht" TYPE="hidden" SIZE=10 VALUE="200">
        </FORM>
        <CENTER>
        <FORM NAME="showForm">
            <TABLE BORDER="2" CELLPADDING="2">
            <TR>
                <TD>
                <TABLE BORDER="0" CELLPADDING="2">
                <TR>
                    <TD ALIGN="center">
```

Listing 8.2: HTML for the JavaScript solution (Continued)

```
                    <INPUT TYPE="button" ONCLICK="zoom(1)"
                        VALUE="ZOOM IN">
            </TD>
        </TR>
        <TR>
            <TD ALIGN="center">
                <INPUT TYPE="text" NAME="mag" SIZE=4>
            </TD>
        </TR>
        <TR>
            <TD ALIGN="center">
                <INPUT TYPE="button" ONCLICK="zoom(-1)"
                VALUE="ZOOM OUT">
            </TD>
        </TR>
        </TABLE>
        </TD>
        <TD>
        <TABLE BORDER="0" CELLPADDING="2">
        <TR>
            <TD>
                East/West <INPUT TYPE="text" NAME="londeg"
                    SIZE=4><INPUT TYPE="text" NAME="lonmin"
                    SIZE=2><INPUT TYPE="text" NAME="lonsec"
                    SIZE=10>
            </TD>
            <TD ROWSPAN="2">
            <TABLE BORDER="0" CELLPADDING="0">
            <TR>
                <TD></TD>
                <TD>
                    <PRE><INPUT TYPE="button" VALUE="N"
                    ONCLICK="changeLatitude(1)"></PRE>
                </TD>
                <TD></TD>
            </TR>
            <TR>
                <TD>
                    <PRE><INPUT TYPE="button" VALUE="W"
                    ONCLICK="changeLongitude(-1)"></PRE>
                </TD>
                <TD></TD>
                <TD>
                    <PRE><INPUT TYPE="button" VALUE="E"
                    ONCLICK="changeLongitude(1)"></PRE>
                </TD>
            </TR>
            <TR>
                <TD></TD>
```

Listing 8.2: HTML for the JavaScript solution (Continued)

```
                    <TD>
                        <PRE><INPUT TYPE="button" VALUE="S"
                        ONCLICK="changeLatitude(-1)"></PRE>
                    </TD>
                    <TD></TD>
                </TR>
                </TABLE>
                </TD>
            </TR>
            <TR>
                <TD>
                North/South <INPUT TYPE="text" NAME="latdeg"
                    SIZE=2><INPUT TYPE="text" NAME="latmin"
                    SIZE=2><INPUT TYPE="text" NAME="latsec" SIZE=10>
                </TD>
            </TR>
            </TABLE>
            </TD>
            <TD>
            <TABLE BORDER="0" CELLPADDING="2">
            <TR>
                <TD ALIGN="center">
                <INPUT TYPE="button"
                    ONCLICK="display(getMagnification())"
                VALUE="GO!">
                </TD>
            </TR>
            <TR>
                <TD ALIGN="center"><INPUT TYPE="RESET"></TD>
            </TR>
            </TABLE>
            </TD>
        </TR>
        </TABLE>
    </FORM>
    </CENTER>
  </BODY>
</HTML>
```

IMPROVING THE SOLUTION

There are many ways of enhancing the JavaScript solution. For starters, you can change the image size and you can give the user control over the image size. If you do that, it might be a good idea to define a new window for the image, because the current 320x200 image size already crowds the screen.

Also, as mentioned, the Tiger Mapping Service defines a lot of additional parameters. (For additional details, see the online documentation, which is listed in the Quick Reference). You can add support for such parameters as markers for locations on the map, information layers (grids, place names, and so on), and statistical information.

MODIFYING THE EXAMPLE FOR YOUR OWN USE

In your work, you may need to write Web pages that talk to servers whose interfaces you have no control over. Two common kinds of servers are relational databases, which may require their input in SQL, and search engines like Alta Vista or Yahoo!. These interfaces may not meet the needs of your users, or they may be too complicated for your target audience. Using JavaScript and the principle of form modification, you can create simple, easy-to-use interfaces that meet your user's needs while satisfying the requirements of the server.

Games

THE SCENARIO

THE REQUIREMENTS

THE SOLUTION (WITHOUT JAVASCRIPT)

THE SOLUTION (WITH JAVASCRIPT)

IMPROVING THE SOLUTION

MODIFYING THE EXAMPLE FOR YOUR
   OWN USE

W eb-based games are a realm in which JavaScript shines. Although
you don't need JavaScript to write Web-based games in which the
user interacts with the computer, as a rule games written without
JavaScript are much slower and thus less fun.

THE SCENARIO

Most people know the game of hangman from grade school. The first player
chooses a word and states how many letters it contains; the second player tries
to guess the word. The second player picks a letter, and if that letter is present
in the word, the first player identifies where the letter appears in the word. If
the letter isn't present in the word, the first player draws a stick figure of a person being hanged, one body part at a time. As I recall, you draw the head, followed by the body, the two arms, and the two legs. If the second player makes
six wrong guesses, the stick figure is complete, and the first player has stumped
the second player.

THE REQUIREMENTS

You will create a Web page that allows the user to play hangman against the
computer. The computer, through the Web page, will choose the word, and
the user will attempt to guess the word.

When the word is chosen, a string of underlines separated by spaces is displayed, one underline per letter. For example, if the word "syzygy" is chosen, this is displayed:

The hangman's gallows is also displayed:

```
+ - - +
| /   |
|     Ø
|
|
|
+======
```

When the user guesses a letter, the letter is displayed if it is in the word. For example, if the word is "syzygy" and the user guesses "y," the display is updated like this:

If, on the other hand, the letter is not in the word, another character of the hanged man is added to the gallows. For example, if the word is "syzygy" and the user guesses "e," the gallows display is updated like this:

```
+ - - +
| /   |
|     @
|
|
|
+======
```

On incorrect guesses, the gallows display acquires, in turn, the head, the body, the left arm, the right arm, the left leg, and the right leg. The final gallows display, if the user is stumped, looks like this:

```
+ - - +
| /   |
|     @
|    -|-
|    / \
|
+======
```

The user should not be penalized for guessing the same letter twice, and if possible, should not be permitted to guess the same letter twice. The user is given a score, based on how many letters he or she guessed wrong. A running average (the total scores divided by the total games played) should be displayed.

The solution (without JavaScript)

The conventional solution (non-JavaScript) to writing a game page is to first display a page with the rules and a button to indicate that the user is ready to start playing the game. When the user presses the button, a CGI program generates the first HTML page that the user will play on. The first word is chosen and is contained in an INPUT HIDDEN element. The CGI program writes the HTML to display the underlines and the gallows, and the page includes an INPUT element that the user can use to choose the letter. The user selects a letter, and the form data is sent back to the CGI program. The CGI program then evaluates the new letter, creates a new page with the letter showing or another character in the hanged man. The flow looks like this:

```
User sees welcome page
User presses button to start
-----------------------------------> CGI program activated
New page is displayed <----------------
User selects letter -----------------> CGI program evaluates letter
New page is displayed <----------------
```

And on and on it goes, until the user guesses the word or is stumped.

The heart of this solution is the CGI program that creates each new page. The HTML that you write is almost an afterthought. It simply presents the rules and provides a FORM element with a SUBMIT button, like the code in Listing 9.1, which produces the form shown in Figure 9.1.

Listing 9.1: Welcome page

```
<HTML>
    <HEAD>
        <TITLE>Hangman</TITLE>
    </HEAD>
    <BODY>
        <P>
            Welcome to Hangman! The object of this game is to guess a
            word without getting hanged! You can get five letters wrong
            - and then you're hanged!
        </P>
        <FORM ACTION="http://someserver.somewhere/cgi-bin/hangman"
            METHOD="get">
```

Listing 9.1: Welcome page (Continued)

```
                <INPUT TYPE="submit" VALUE="Play Hangman">
        </FORM>
    </BODY>
</HTML>
```

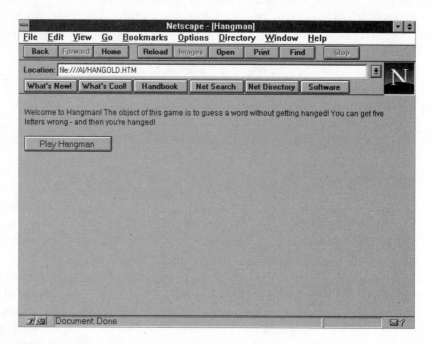

Figure 9.1: Welcome page

THE SOLUTION (WITH JAVASCRIPT)

The big problem with the non-JavaScript solution is the enormous expense in bandwidth. With every guess, a new HTML page is downloaded from the server. That's a lot of traffic!

From the user's perspective, this translates to a slow game. It's okay for the user to deliberate about his or her next move, but the computer is expected to respond instantly! Instead, the user gets to watch the status bar display the number of seconds until the next page is downloaded.

A game of any length—where lots of screens are being loaded—will also eat your user's history. If the user had visited a page before playing the game and wanted to go back to it, the user would be out of luck unless he or she had bookmarked that page.

With JavaScript, the user can get the desired instant feedback.

First, let's lay out the screen. You need a frame that holds the current results—the gallows and the underlines. Another frame holding the running average would be nice. And you need a frame to get the letters from the user. A simple frame document like this will suffice:

```
<HTML>
    <HEAD>
        <TITLE>Hangman II</TITLE>
    </HEAD>
    <FRAMESET ROWS="*,*">
        <FRAMESET COLS="*,*">
            <FRAME SRC="empty.htm" NAME="scoreboard">
            <FRAME SRC="empty.htm" NAME="playingfield">
        </FRAMESET>
        <FRAME SRC="hangctrl.htm" NAME="controls">
    </FRAMESET>
</HTML>
```

The empty.htm file used in the scoreboard and playingfield frames is a simple placeholder file that is repeatedly overwritten as the game progresses. The hangctrl.htm file provides the user controls and the JavaScript code to update the scoreboard and playingfield frames.

Let's start with the score frame. This frame simply displays the running average. To do that, you need data—the current sum of scores and the number of games played. Because the user may play hangman, go visit some other pages, and then come back and play another game of hangman, let's store the data in a cookie. This is a data structure that your JavaScript pages can use to store data on the user's disk and retrieve it later. While you can store much more, you only need to store a variable name and a value. The function that initializes the scoreboard frame will try to load the total points and total words from cookies. If they aren't available, such as when a user plays the games for the first time, the function will create cookies with values of 0 for the total points and total words. Normally, the value displayed will be the total points divided by the total words played, but with initial values of 0, that doesn't work. Division by zero is an illegal operation, so the function to initialize the scoreboard has to take that into account. Finally, the function will display the score on the scoreboard frame:

```
var totalPoints;
var totalWords;
```

```
var runningAverage;
function initializeScoreBoard()
    {
    var tP = getCookie("HMPoints");
    if (tP == null)
        {
        neverPlayed();
        }
    else
        {
        var tW = getCookie("HMCount");
        if (tW == null)
            {
            neverPlayed();
            }
        else
            {
            totalPoints = eval(tP);
            totalWords = eval(tW);
            }
        }
    if (totalWords == 0)
        {
        runningAverage = 0;
        }
    else
        {
        runningAverage = Math.round(100 * (totalPoints / totalWords));
        }
    displayScoreBoard();
    }
```

The function getCookie() tries to find a cookie with the specified name; it returns the special value null if no such cookie exists. Otherwise, it returns the specified cookie's value as a string:

```
function getCookie(s)
    {
    var target = s + "=";
    var targetLength = target.length;
    var index = 0;
    while (1) // search while 1 is nonzero, i.e., forever
        {
        var offset = index + targetLength;
        if (document.cookie.substring(index, offset) == target)
            {
            var tail = document.cookie.indexOf(";", offset);
```

```
        if (tail == -1)
            {
            tail = document.cookie.length;
            }
        return unescape(document.cookie.substring(offset, tail));
        }
    index = 1 + document.cookie.indexOf(" ", index);
    if (index == 0 || index >= document.cookie.length)
        {
        return null;
        }
    }
  return null;
  }
```

The getCookie() function searches the document's cookie property for the specified name followed by an equal sign. If that string is found, the value is the substring that follows the equal sign and ends with a semicolon. If there is no semicolon, the rest of the cookie property string is returned. In either case, the value is passed to the unescape() function to translate escaped characters back into normal text. If the name= string is not found, getCookie() scans ahead to the next space and searches again. If the end of the document's cookie property is reached, the cookie is not there and a null is returned.

The neverPlayed() function creates new total points and total words cookies and sets them to zero; it also sets the variables totalPoints and totalWords to zero:

```
function neverPlayed()
    {
    totalPoints = 0;
    totalWords = 0;
    createCookie("HMPoints", 0);
    createCookie("HMCount", 0);
    }
```

The createCookie() function is very simple; it runs the value parameter through the escape() function to translate special characters like spaces and semicolons into their hexadecimal values. It then creates the cookie:

```
function createCookie(name, value)
    {
    document.cookie = name + "=" + escape(value);
    }
```

Finally, initializeScoreBoard() calls displayScoreBoard() to fill in the scoreboard frame. This creates a new HTML page that uses buttons to contain the score. Notice that the initializeScoreBoard() function multiplied the runningAverage value by 100 and rounded it off—that was to make displayScoreBoard() easier to write and understand:

```
function displayScoreBoard()
    {
    parent.scoreboard.document.close();
    parent.scoreboard.document.open();
    parent.scoreboard.document.open();
    openScoreBoardTag("HTML");
        openScoreBoardTag("BODY");
            openScoreBoardTag("CENTER");
                openScoreBoardTag("FORM");
                    openScoreBoardTag("CODE");
                    writeScoreBoard("Average misses: ");
                    openScoreBoardTag("INPUT TYPE=\"button\" VALUE=\""
                        + Math.floor(runningAverage / 100) + "\"");
                    openScoreBoardTag("INPUT TYPE=\"button\"" +
                        " VALUE=\".\"");
                    openScoreBoardTag("INPUT TYPE=\"button\" VALUE=\""
                        + (Math.floor(runningAverage / 10) % 10) +
                        "\"");
                    openScoreBoardTag("INPUT TYPE=\"button\" VALUE=\"" +
                        (Math.floor(runningAverage) % 10) + "\"");
                    closeScoreBoardTag("CODE");
                closeScoreBoardTag("FORM");
            closeScoreBoardTag("CENTER");
        closeScoreBoardTag("BODY");
    closeScoreBoardTag("HTML");
    }
```

The displayScoreBoard() function closes the scoreboard frame and then opens it again; the open() call is made twice to get around some platform-specific browser problems. The functions openScoreBoardTag(), closeScoreBoardTag(), and writeScoreBoard() write the strings to the scoreboard frame; these functions make it easier to keep track of the logical structure of the document being written:

```
function writeScoreBoard(text)
    {
    parent.scoreboard.document.write(text);
    }

function openScoreBoardTag(tag)
    {
    writeScoreBoard("<" + tag + unescape("%3E"));
    }
```

```
function closeScoreBoardTag(tag)
    {
    openScoreBoardTag("/" + tag);
    }
```

Having set up the scoreboard, you'll need some words to display on the playingfield frame. Using the MakeArray() function from Netscape's online documentation (see Appendix F), you'll create your word list:

```
function MakeArray(n)
    {
    this.length = n;
    for (var i = 1; i <= n; i++)
        {
        this[ i ] = 0;
        }
    return this;
    }


var wordList;


function initializeWordList()
    {
    wordList = new MakeArray(10);
    wordList[ 0 ] = new Word("syzygy");
    wordList[ 1 ] = new Word("pendulum");
    wordList[ 2 ] = new Word("diphtheria");
    wordList[ 3 ] = new Word("phantasm");
    wordList[ 4 ] = new Word("escutcheon");
    wordList[ 5 ] = new Word("marzipan");
    wordList[ 6 ] = new Word("quincunx");
    wordList[ 7 ] = new Word("troglodyte");
    wordList[ 8 ] = new Word("jitterbug");
    wordList[ 9 ] = new Word("vivacious");
    }
```

Here I've created ten words; you'd probably want to use more than that. The Word object contains a BOOLEAN flag that indicates whether the word has been played before, the word itself, and the word's length. The length of the word is accessed so frequently that it's not a bad idea to make it a property of the Word object. As with the total points and total words, let's store the played flag in a cookie; that way, the user isn't given the same word twice:

```
function Word(word)
    {
    var playValue = getCookie("HMW" + word);
    if (playValue == null)
```

```
        {
    this.played = false;
    createCookie("HMW"+word, "0");
        }
    else
        {
    if (eval(playValue) == 0)
        {
        this.played = false;
        }
    else
        {
        this.played = true;
        }
        }
    this.word = word;
    this.wordLength = word.length;
    }
```

Note that the word is prefaced with "HMW"; this is to avoid accidental collisions with other cookies. If the cookie's value is "0", the word has not been played before. If the cookie isn't found, a new cookie with a value of "0" is created.

Keeping track of which words a user has guessed does place a burden on you to provide new words every so often. (Otherwise, what happens when the user has played all of the words?) But this is not necessarily a harsh task. The same kind of CGI programs that provide page hit counts can be adapted to insert a random set of words into the page.

Having defined some words, it's time to put up the gallows! The function newWord() sets up a new word. In so doing, it has to take into account that it might be called in the middle of play of another word, unless you want to lock out the user from giving up in the middle. A variable, buttonsActive, is false if there is no active game in progress and true in the middle of a game.

The newWord() function then has to select a word. Because the Math object's random() method does not work on all platforms, I used the least significant digit of the current time's seconds field to select which word to use. The word list is scanned for the *n*th unplayed word, where *n* is the digit used. If there are fewer than *n* unplayed words left, the set of unplayed words is reused in an "eeny meeny miny mo" fashion. If there are no unplayed words left, the user is informed of this fact.

After a word has been selected, its index is noted in a global variable, currentWord. An array of 26 BOOLEAN values is created and initialized to all false; this keeps track of which letters have been guessed. The score is set to zero, and the playing field is drawn. Finally, the buttonsActive flag is set to true—the game is afoot:

```
var guessedLetters;

function newWord()
    {
    if (buttonsActive == true)
        {
        if (confirm("Are you sure you want to give up?") == true)
            {
            score = 6;
            alert("The word was " + wordList[ currentWord ].word);
            gameOver();
            }
        return;
        }
    var now = new Date();
    var j = now.getSeconds() % 10;
    var index = -1;
    for (var i = 0; i <= j; i++)
        {
        for (k = 0; k < 10; k++) // loop keeps us from circling forever
            {
            index++;
            if (index >= 10)
                {
                index = 0;
                }
            if (wordList[ index ].played == 0)
                {
                break;
                }
            if (index >= 10)
                {
                index = 0;
                }
            }
        if (wordList[ index ].played != 0)
            {
            alert("All current words have been played!");
            return;
            }
        }
    currentWord = index;
    guessedLetters = new MakeArray(26);
```

```
for (var k = 0; k < 26; k++)
    {
    guessedLetters[ k ] = false;
    }
score = 0;
drawPlayingField();
buttonsActive = true;
}
```

The drawPlayingField() function is responsible for redrawing the playing-field frame after each guess, as well as for drawing the initial frame. Like the displayScoreBoard() function you saw earlier, it creates a new HTML page and writes it to the playingfield frame. However, it's more dynamic than display-ScoreBoard(): It uses the global variable score to determine how to draw the gallows and the hanged man, and it uses the guessedLetters array to determine which letters to fill in, and to display which letters the user has already guessed. While determining which letters to fill in, it also notes whether the user has guessed the word:

```
function drawPlayingField()
    {
    parent.playingfield.document.close();
    parent.playingfield.document.open();
    parent.playingfield.document.open();
    openPlayingFieldTag("HTML");
        openPlayingFieldTag("BODY");
            openPlayingFieldTag("PRE");
                writePlayingFieldLine("+---+");
                writePlayingFieldLine("|/  |");
                if (score == 0)
                    {
                    writePlayingFieldLine("|   0"); // the noose
                    }
                else
                    {
                    writePlayingFieldLine("|   @"); // the head
                    }
                if (score < 2)
                    {
                    writePlayingFieldLine("|");
                    }
                else if (score == 2)
                    {
                    writePlayingFieldLine("|   |"); // body
                    }
                else if (score == 3)
```

```
    {
    writePlayingFieldLine("|  -|"); // body and arm
    }
else
    {
    writePlayingFieldLine("|  -|-"); // body and arms
    }
if (score < 5)
    {
    writePlayingFieldLine("|");
    }
else if (score == 5)
    {
    writePlayingFieldLine("|  /"); // left leg
    }
else
    {
    writePlayingFieldLine("|  / \\"); // both legs
    }
writePlayingFieldLine("|");
writePlayingFieldLine("+======");
openPlayingFieldTag("BR");
var missed = 0;
for (var k = 0; k < wordList[ currentWord ].wordLength;
    k++)
    {
    var letter =
        wordList[ currentWord ].word.substring(k,
        k + 1);
    var value = codeOf(letter);
    if (guessedLetters[ value ] == true)
        {
        writePlayingField(letter);
        }
    else
        {
        writePlayingField("_");
        missed++;
        }
    writePlayingField(" ");
    }
openPlayingFieldTag("BR");
if (missed)
    {
    writePlayingFieldLine("Letters guessed so far:");
    for (var x = 0; x < 26; x++)
        {
```

```
                            if (guessedLetters[ x ] == true)
                                {
                                writePlayingField(uc.substring(x, x + 1) +
                                    " ");
                                }
                            }
                        }
                    else
                        {
                        writePlayingFieldLine("You guessed it!");
                        gameOver();
                        }
                closePlayingFieldTag("PRE");
            closePlayingFieldTag("BODY");
        closePlayingFieldTag("HTML");
        }
```

The functions writePlayingField(), writePlayingFieldLine(), openPlaying-FieldTag(), and closePlayingFieldTag() are very simple and similar to their counterparts used to draw the scoreboard frame:

```
function writePlayingFieldLine(text)
    {
    parent.playingfield.document.writeln(text);
    }

function writePlayingField(text)
    {
    parent.playingfield.document.write(text);
    }

function openPlayingFieldTag(tag)
    {
    writePlayingField("<" + tag + unescape("%3E"));
    }

function closePlayingFieldTag(tag)
    {
    openPlayingFieldTag("/" + tag);
    }
```

The drawPlayingField() function also uses a function, codeOf(), to translate the letters used in the word into indices to use with the guessedLetters array:

```
function codeOf(letter)
    {
    if (letter == "a" || letter == "A") return 0;
    if (letter == "b" || letter == "B") return 1;
```

```
if (letter == "c" || letter == "C") return 2;
if (letter == "d" || letter == "D") return 3;
if (letter == "e" || letter == "E") return 4;
if (letter == "f" || letter == "F") return 5;
if (letter == "g" || letter == "G") return 6;
if (letter == "h" || letter == "H") return 7;
if (letter == "i" || letter == "I") return 8;
if (letter == "j" || letter == "J") return 9;
if (letter == "k" || letter == "K") return 10;
if (letter == "l" || letter == "L") return 11;
if (letter == "m" || letter == "M") return 12;
if (letter == "n" || letter == "N") return 13;
if (letter == "o" || letter == "O") return 14;
if (letter == "p" || letter == "P") return 15;
if (letter == "q" || letter == "Q") return 16;
if (letter == "r" || letter == "R") return 17;
if (letter == "s" || letter == "S") return 18;
if (letter == "t" || letter == "T") return 19;
if (letter == "u" || letter == "U") return 20;
if (letter == "v" || letter == "V") return 21;
if (letter == "w" || letter == "W") return 22;
if (letter == "x" || letter == "X") return 23;
if (letter == "y" || letter == "Y") return 24;
if (letter == "z" || letter == "Z") return 25;
return 26;
}
```

Now the game is almost ready to play. The user will need some input elements to pick a letter; you'll use buttons that have a name and value of each letter in the alphabet, like this:

```
<INPUT TYPE="button" ONCLICK="guess(this)" NAME="A" VALUE="A">
```

The guess() function handles the event of a user clicking on the letter. It checks whether the game is active and does nothing otherwise. The codeOf() function translates the button's value property to an index, and the guessedLetters array is checked—if the letter has been guessed, no action is taken. Otherwise, the letter, both uppercase and lowercase, is scanned for in the currently selected word. If the letter is not found, the score variable is incremented. Then the drawPlayingField() function is called to update the playingfield frame. If the score is 6, the user is informed that the game is over, and is told the word:

```
var lc = "abcdefghijklmnopqrstuvwxyz";
var uc = "ABCDEFGHIJKLMNOPQRSTUVWXYZ";
```

```
function guess(button)
    {
    if (buttonsActive == false)
        {
        return;
        }
    var index = codeOf(button.value);
    if (guessedLetters[ index ] == true)
        {
        return;
        }
    guessedLetters[ index ] = true;
    var match = false;
    for (var j = 0; j < wordList[ currentWord ].wordLength; j++)
        {
        if (wordList[ currentWord ].word.substring(j, j + 1) ==
            lc.substring(index, index + 1))
            {
            match = true;
            break;
            }
        if (wordList[ currentWord ].word.substring(j, j + 1) ==
            uc.substring(index, index + 1))
            {
            match = true;
            break;
            }
        }
    if (match == false)
        {
        score++;
        }
    drawPlayingField();
    if (score >= 6)
        {
        alert("I'm sorry, you lose; the word was " +
            wordList[ currentWord ].word);
        gameOver();
        }
    }
```

The gameOver() function is called when the user has guessed the word, given up, or couldn't guess the word. It turns the buttons off, adds the score to the totalPoints variable, and increments the totalWords variable. The total points and total words cookies are replaced with new values, and the word cookie is replaced with a value of "1", indicating that the word has been played. The Word object's played property is also updated. The scoreboard is then updated via the initializeScoreBoard() function:

```
function gameOver()
    {
    buttonsActive = false;
    totalPoints += score;
    totalWords++;
    createCookie("HMPoints", totalPoints);
    createCookie("HMCount", totalWords);
    createCookie("HMW" + wordList[ currentWord ].word, "1");
    wordList[ currentWord ].played = true;
    initializeScoreBoard();
    }
```

There's one last function needed: an initialization function to start the ball rolling. This is the ONLOAD event handler:

```
function initialize()
    {
    buttonsActive = false;
    initializeWordList();
    initializeScoreBoard();
    newWord();
    }
```

The complete code of the JavaScript solution is shown in Listing 9.2. A sample screen is shown in Figure 9.2.

Listing 9.2: The JavaScript hangman game

```
<HTML>
    <HEAD>
        <SCRIPT LANGUAGE="JavaScript">
<!--

var totalPoints;
var totalWords;
var runningAverage;

function initializeScoreBoard()
    {
    var tP = getCookie("HMPoints");
    if (tP == null)
        {
        neverPlayed();
        }
    else
        {
```

Listing 9.2: The JavaScript hangman game (Continued)

```
                var tW = getCookie("HMCount");
                if (tW == null)
                    {
                    neverPlayed();
                    }
                else
                    {
                    totalPoints = eval(tP);
                    totalWords = eval(tW);
                    }
                }
        if (totalWords == 0)
            {
            runningAverage = 0;
            }
        else
            {
            runningAverage = Math.round(100 * (totalPoints / totalWords));
            }
        displayScoreBoard();
        }

function getCookie(s)
    {
    var target = s + "=";
    var targetLength = target.length;
    var index = 0;
    while (1)
        {
        var offset = index + targetLength;
        if (document.cookie.substring(index, offset) == target)
            {
            var tail = document.cookie.indexOf(";", offset);
            if (tail == -1)
                {
                tail = document.cookie.length;
                }
            return unescape(document.cookie.substring(offset, tail));
            }
        index = 1 + document.cookie.indexOf(" ", index);
        if (index == 0 || index >= document.cookie.length)
            {
            return null;
            }
        }
    return null;
    }

function neverPlayed()
    {
```

Listing 9.2: The JavaScript hangman game (Continued)

```javascript
    totalPoints = 0;
    totalWords = 0;
    createCookie("HMPoints", 0);
    createCookie("HMCount", 0);
    }

function createCookie(name, value)
    {
    document.cookie = name + "=" + escape(value);
    }

function displayScoreBoard()
    {
    parent.scoreboard.document.close();
    parent.scoreboard.document.open();
    parent.scoreboard.document.open();
    openScoreBoardTag("HTML");
        openScoreBoardTag("BODY");
            openScoreBoardTag("CENTER");
                openScoreBoardTag("FORM");
                    openScoreBoardTag("CODE");
                    writeScoreBoard("Average misses: ");
                    openScoreBoardTag("INPUT TYPE=\"button\" VALUE=\"" +
                        Math.floor(runningAverage / 100) + "\"");
                    openScoreBoardTag("INPUT TYPE=\"button\"" +
                        " VALUE=\".\"");
                    openScoreBoardTag("INPUT TYPE=\"button\" VALUE=\"" +
                        (Math.floor(runningAverage / 10) % 10) + "\"");
                    openScoreBoardTag("INPUT TYPE=\"button\" VALUE=\"" +
                        (Math.floor(runningAverage) % 10) + "\"");
                    closeScoreBoardTag("CODE");
                closeScoreBoardTag("FORM");
            closeScoreBoardTag("CENTER");
        closeScoreBoardTag("BODY");
    closeScoreBoardTag("HTML");
    }

function writeScoreBoard(text)
    {
    parent.scoreboard.document.write(text);
    }

function openScoreBoardTag(tag)
    {
    writeScoreBoard("<" + tag + unescape("%3E"));
    }

function closeScoreBoardTag(tag)
    {
    openScoreBoardTag("/" + tag);
```

Listing 9.2: The JavaScript hangman game (Continued)

```javascript
        }

function MakeArray(n)
    {
    this.length = n;
    for (var i = 1; i <= n; i++)
        {
        this[ i ] = 0;
        }
    return this;
    }

var wordList;

function initializeWordList()
    {
    buttonsActive = false;
    wordList = new MakeArray(10);
    wordList[ 0 ] = new Word("syzygy");
    wordList[ 1 ] = new Word("pendulum");
    wordList[ 2 ] = new Word("diphtheria");
    wordList[ 3 ] = new Word("phantasm");
    wordList[ 4 ] = new Word("escutcheon");
    wordList[ 5 ] = new Word("marzipan");
    wordList[ 6 ] = new Word("quincunx");
    wordList[ 7 ] = new Word("troglodyte");
    wordList[ 8 ] = new Word("jitterbug");
    wordList[ 9 ] = new Word("vivacious");
    }

function Word(word)
    {
    var playValue = getCookie("HMW" + word);
    if (playValue == null)
        {
        this.played = false;
        createCookie("HMW"+word, "0");
        }
    else
        {
        if (eval(playValue) == 0)
            {
            this.played = false;
            }
        else
            {
            this.played = true;
            }
        }
    this.word = word;
```

Listing 9.2: The JavaScript hangman game (Continued)

```javascript
        this.wordLength = word.length;
        }

var buttonsActive = false;
var currentWord;
var guessedLetters;

function newWord()
    {
    if (buttonsActive == true)
        {
        if (confirm("Are you sure you want to give up?") == true)
            {
            score = 6;
            alert("The word was " + wordList[ currentWord ].word);
            gameOver();
            }
        return;
        }
    var now = new Date();
    var j = now.getSeconds() % 10;
    var index = -1;
    for (var i = 0; i <= j; i++)
        {
        for (k = 0; k < 10; k++)
            {
            index++;
            if (index >= 10)
                {
                index = 0;
                }
            if (wordList[ index ].played == 0)
                {
                break;
                }
            if (index >= 10)
                {
                index = 0;
                }
            }
        if (wordList[ index ].played != 0)
            {
            alert("All current words have been played!");
            return;
            }
        }
    currentWord = index;
    guessedLetters = new MakeArray(26);
    for (var k = 0; k < 26; k++)
```

Listing 9.2: The JavaScript hangman game (Continued)

```
            {
            guessedLetters[ k ] = false;
            }
     score = 0;
     drawPlayingField();
     buttonsActive = true;
     }

function drawPlayingField()
     {
     parent.playingfield.document.close();
     parent.playingfield.document.open();
     parent.playingfield.document.open();
     openPlayingFieldTag("HTML");
         openPlayingFieldTag("BODY");
             openPlayingFieldTag("PRE");
                 writePlayingFieldLine("+---+");
                 writePlayingFieldLine("|/  |");
                 if (score == 0)
                     {
                     writePlayingFieldLine("|   0");
                     }
                 else
                     {
                     writePlayingFieldLine("|   @");
                     }
                 if (score < 2)
                     {
                     writePlayingFieldLine("|");
                     }
                 else if (score == 2)
                     {
                     writePlayingFieldLine("|   |");
                     }
                 else if (score == 3)
                     {
                     writePlayingFieldLine("|  -|");
                     }
                 else
                     {
                     writePlayingFieldLine("|  -|-");
                     }
                 if (score < 5)
                     {
                     writePlayingFieldLine("|");
                     }
                 else if (score == 5)
                     {
                     writePlayingFieldLine("|  /");
                     }
```

Listing 9.2: The JavaScript hangman game (Continued)

```
                else
                    {
                    writePlayingFieldLine("|  / \\");
                    }
            writePlayingFieldLine("|");
            writePlayingFieldLine("+======");
            openPlayingFieldTag("BR");
            var missed = 0;
            for (var k = 0; k < wordList[ currentWord ].wordLength;
                k++)
                {
                var letter =
                    wordList[ currentWord ].word.substring(k,
                    k + 1);
                var value = codeOf(letter);
                if (guessedLetters[ value ] == true)
                    {
                    writePlayingField(letter);
                    }
                else
                    {
                    writePlayingField("_");
                    missed++;
                    }
                writePlayingField(" ");
                }
            openPlayingFieldTag("BR");
            if (missed)
                {
                writePlayingFieldLine("Letters guessed so far:");
                for (var x = 0; x < 26; x++)
                    {
                    if (guessedLetters[ x ] == true)
                        {
                        writePlayingField(uc.substring(x, x + 1) +
                            " ");
                        }
                    }
                }
            else
                {
                writePlayingFieldLine("You guessed it!");
                gameOver();
                }
        closePlayingFieldTag("PRE");
    closePlayingFieldTag("BODY");
closePlayingFieldTag("HTML");
}

function writePlayingFieldLine(text)
```

Listing 9.2: The JavaScript hangman game (Continued)

```
        {
        parent.playingfield.document.writeln(text);
        }

function writePlayingField(text)
        {
        parent.playingfield.document.write(text);
        }

function openPlayingFieldTag(tag)
        {
        writePlayingField("<" + tag + unescape("%3E"));
        }

function closePlayingFieldTag(tag)
        {
        openPlayingFieldTag("/" + tag);
        }

function codeOf(letter)
        {
        if (letter == "a" || letter == "A") return 0;
        if (letter == "b" || letter == "B") return 1;
        if (letter == "c" || letter == "C") return 2;
        if (letter == "d" || letter == "D") return 3;
        if (letter == "e" || letter == "E") return 4;
        if (letter == "f" || letter == "F") return 5;
        if (letter == "g" || letter == "G") return 6;
        if (letter == "h" || letter == "H") return 7;
        if (letter == "i" || letter == "I") return 8;
        if (letter == "j" || letter == "J") return 9;
        if (letter == "k" || letter == "K") return 10;
        if (letter == "l" || letter == "L") return 11;
        if (letter == "m" || letter == "M") return 12;
        if (letter == "n" || letter == "N") return 13;
        if (letter == "o" || letter == "O") return 14;
        if (letter == "p" || letter == "P") return 15;
        if (letter == "q" || letter == "Q") return 16;
        if (letter == "r" || letter == "R") return 17;
        if (letter == "s" || letter == "S") return 18;
        if (letter == "t" || letter == "T") return 19;
        if (letter == "u" || letter == "U") return 20;
        if (letter == "v" || letter == "V") return 21;
        if (letter == "w" || letter == "W") return 22;
        if (letter == "x" || letter == "X") return 23;
        if (letter == "y" || letter == "Y") return 24;
        if (letter == "z" || letter == "Z") return 25;
        return 26;
        }
```

Listing 9.2: The JavaScript hangman game (Continued)

```javascript
var lc = "abcdefghijklmnopqrstuvwxyz";
var uc = "ABCDEFGHIJKLMNOPQRSTUVWXYZ";
var score;

function guess(button)
    {
    if (buttonsActive == false)
    {
    return;
    }
    var index = codeOf(button.value);
    if (guessedLetters[ index ] == true)
        {
        return;
        }
    guessedLetters[ index ] = true;
    var match = false;
    for (var j = 0; j < wordList[ currentWord ].wordLength; j++)
        {
        if (wordList[ currentWord ].word.substring(j, j + 1) ==
            lc.substring(index, index + 1))
            {
            match = true;
            break;
            }
        if (wordList[ currentWord ].word.substring(j, j + 1) ==
            uc.substring(index, index + 1))
            {
            match = true;
            break;
            }
        }
    if (match == false)
        {
        score++;
        }
    drawPlayingField();
    if (score >= 6)
{
alert("I'm sorry, you lose; the word was " +
        wordList[ currentWord ].word);
gameOver();
}
    }

function gameOver()
    {
    buttonsActive = false;
    totalPoints += score;
```

Listing 9.2: The JavaScript hangman game (Continued)

```
        totalWords++;
        createCookie("HMPoints", totalPoints);
        createCookie("HMCount", totalWords);
        createCookie("HMW" + wordList[ currentWord ].word, "1");
        wordList[ currentWord ].played = true;
        initializeScoreBoard();
        }

function initialize()
    {
    initializeWordList();
    initializeScoreBoard();
    newWord();
    }

//-->
      </SCRIPT>
   </HEAD>
   <BODY ONLOAD="initialize()">
      <CENTER>
         <FORM NAME="controller">
            <TABLE>
               <TR>
                  <TD>
                     <INPUT TYPE="button" NAME="start"
                        VALUE="New Word" ONCLICK="newWord()">
                  </TD>
                  <TD>
                     <CODE>
                        <INPUT TYPE="button"
                           ONCLICK="guess(this)" NAME="A"
                           VALUE="A">
                        <INPUT TYPE="button"
                           ONCLICK="guess(this)" NAME="B"
                           VALUE="B">
                        <INPUT TYPE="button"
                           ONCLICK="guess(this)" NAME="C"
                           VALUE="C">
                        <INPUT TYPE="button"
                           ONCLICK="guess(this)" NAME="D"
                           VALUE="D">
                        <INPUT TYPE="button"
                           ONCLICK="guess(this)" NAME="E"
                           VALUE="E">
                        <INPUT TYPE="button"
                           ONCLICK="guess(this)" NAME="F"
                           VALUE="F">
                        <INPUT TYPE="button"
                           ONCLICK="guess(this)" NAME="G"
                           VALUE="G">
```

Listing 9.2: The JavaScript hangman game (Continued)

```
<INPUT TYPE="button"
    ONCLICK="guess(this)" NAME="H"
    VALUE="H">
<INPUT TYPE="button"
    ONCLICK="guess(this)" NAME="I"
    VALUE="I">
<INPUT TYPE="button"
    ONCLICK="guess(this)" NAME="J"
    VALUE="J">
<INPUT TYPE="button"
    ONCLICK="guess(this)" NAME="K"
    VALUE="K">
<INPUT TYPE="button"
    ONCLICK="guess(this)" NAME="L"
    VALUE="L">
<INPUT TYPE="button"
    ONCLICK="guess(this)" NAME="M"
    VALUE="M">
<BR>
<INPUT TYPE="button"
    ONCLICK="guess(this)" NAME="N"
    VALUE="N">
<INPUT TYPE="button"
    ONCLICK="guess(this)" NAME="O"
    VALUE="O">
<INPUT TYPE="button"
    ONCLICK="guess(this)" NAME="P"
    VALUE="P">
<INPUT TYPE="button"
    ONCLICK="guess(this)" NAME="Q"
    VALUE="Q">
<INPUT TYPE="button"
    ONCLICK="guess(this)" NAME="R"
    VALUE="R">
<INPUT TYPE="button"
    ONCLICK="guess(this)" NAME="S"
    VALUE="S">
<INPUT TYPE="button"
    ONCLICK="guess(this)" NAME="T"
    VALUE="T">
<INPUT TYPE="button"
    ONCLICK="guess(this)" NAME="U"
    VALUE="U">
<INPUT TYPE="button"
    ONCLICK="guess(this)" NAME="V"
    VALUE="V">
<INPUT TYPE="button"
    ONCLICK="guess(this)" NAME="W"
    VALUE="W">
<INPUT TYPE="button"
```

Listing 9.2: The JavaScript hangman game (Continued)

```
                                        ONCLICK="guess(this)" NAME="X"
                                        VALUE="X">
                                <INPUT TYPE="button"
                                        ONCLICK="guess(this)" NAME="Y"
                                        VALUE="Y">
                                <INPUT TYPE="button"
                                        ONCLICK="guess(this)" NAME="Z"
                                        VALUE="Z">
                            </CODE>
                        </TD>
                    </TR>
                </TABLE>
            </FORM>
        </CENTER>
    </BODY>
</HTML>
```

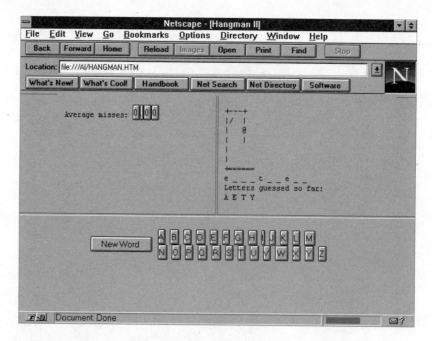

Figure 9.2: The JavaScript hangman game in progress

IMPROVING THE SOLUTION

Besides including more words and using a server-include CGI process to change the words on the fly, you can improve the game itself by adding a timer to increase pressure on the player. You could do this by adding a TEXT INPUT element to the form and displaying an incrementing timer in it. To start the timer you would need a function that should be executed from newWord(), a function to keep the timer running, and a function to stop the timer from gameOver(). You would need to modify the scoring to take the time into account—maybe double the points after some arbitrary number of seconds.

MODIFYING THE EXAMPLE FOR YOUR OWN USE

Besides improving this example, you can devise other interactive games using this medium. Basically, any game that can be played one-on-one against the computer should work well in JavaScript—checkers, chess, Othello, Go, Parcheesi. With GIF or JPEG images, you could even play card games or board games such as Monopoly. The only limitation is your ability to translate the rules of the game into JavaScript code!

Part 3

Quick Reference

ISO Latin-1 Character Set

JavaScript Reserved Words

A Review of HTML

JavaScript Operators

Built-in Objects and Functions

Online Resources

Appendix A:
ISO Latin-1 Character Set

HTML—and, by extension, JavaScript—uses the ISO Latin-1 character set. Because many of these characters are difficult or impossible to use with text editors, you can enter them by means of an entity code. Entity codes consist of an ampersand, a pound sign, the decimal representation of the character, and a semicolon. An example of an entity code is 0, which is the entity code for the digit 0.

Entity codes are difficult to use without memorizing a list of characters and their decimal representations. Fortunately, you can also enter many characters by using their entity names. An entity name consists of an ampersand, the character's name, and a semicolon. An example of an entity name is <, which is the entity name for the less-than (<) sign. Not all characters in the ISO Latin-1 character set have entity names. The following table lists all the ISO Latin-1 characters and their entity codes, also listing entity names where applicable.

Character	Description	Entity Code	Entity Name
	(unused)	&#0; through &#8;	
	horizontal tab	&#9;	
	line feed	&#10;	
	(unused)	&#11; through &#31;	
	space	&#32;	

Character	Description	Entity Code	Entity Name
!	exclamation mark	&#33;	
"	quotation mark	&#34;	&quot;
#	number sign	&#35;	
$	dollar sign	&#36;	
%	percent sign	&#37;	
&	ampersand	&#38;	&amp;
'	apostrophe	&#39;	
(	left parenthesis	&#40;	
)	right parenthesis	&#41;	
*	asterisk	&#42;	
+	plus sign	&#43;	
,	comma	&#44;	
-	hyphen	&#45;	
.	period (fullstop)	&#46;	
/	solidus (slash)	&#47;	
0 through 9	digits 0 through 9	0 through 9	
:	colon	&#58;	
;	semicolon	&#59;	
<	less-than sign	&#60;	&lt;
=	equal sign	&#61;	
>	greater-than sign	&#62;	&gt;
?	question mark	&#63;	
@	commercial at sign	&#64;	
A through Z	letters A through Z	A through Z	
[	left square bracket	&#91;	

Character	Description	Entity Code	Entity Name
\	reverse solidus (backslash)	&#92;	
]	right square bracket	&#93;	
^	caret	&#94;	
_	horizontal bar	&#95;	
`	grave accent	&#96;	
a through z	letters a through z	a through z	
{	left curly brace	&#123;	
|	vertical bar	|	
}	right curly brace	&#125;	
~	tilde	&#126;	
	(unused)	&#127; through Ÿ	
	nonbreaking space		
¡	inverted exclamation	&#161;	&iexcl;
¢	cent sign	&#162;	&cent;
£	pound sterling	&#163;	&pound;
¤	general currency sign	&#164;	&curren;
¥	yen sign	&#165;	&yen;
¦	broken vertical bar	&#166;	¦ &brkbar;
§	section sign	&#167;	&sect;
¨	umlaut dieresis	&#168;	¨ ¨
©	copyright	&#169;	&copy;
ª	feminine ordinal	&#170;	&ordf;

Character	Description	Entity Code	Entity Name
«	left angle quote guillemotleft	&#171;	&laquo;
¬	not sign	&#172;	&not;
—	soft hyphen	&#173;	&shy;
®	registered trademark	&#174;	&reg;
¯	macron accent	&#175;	¯ &hibar;
°	degree sign	&#176;	&deg;
±	plus or minus	&#177;	&plusmn;
2	superscript 2	&#178;	&sup2;
3	superscript 3	&#179;	&sup3;
´	acute accent	&#180;	&acute;
µ	micro sign	&#181;	&micro;
¶	paragraph sign	&#182;	&para;
·	middle dot	&#183;	&middot;
¸	cedilla	&#184;	&cedil;
1	superscript one	&#185;	&sup1;
º	masculine ordinal	&#186;	&ordm;
»	right angle quote guillemotright	&#187;	&raquo;
¼	fraction one-fourth	&#188;	&frac14;
½	fraction one-half	&#189;	&frac12;
¾	fraction three-fourths	&#190;	&frac34;
¿	inverted question mark	&#191;	&iquest;
À	capital A, grave accent	&#192;	&Agrave;
Á	capital A, acute accent	&#193;	&Aacute;
Â	capital A, circumflex accent	&#194;	&Acirc;

Character	Description	Entity Code	Entity Name
Ã	capital A, tilde	&#195;	&Atilde;
Ä	capital A, dieresis capital A, umlaut mark	&#196;	&Auml;
Å	capital A, ring	&#197;	&Aring;
Æ	capital AE diphthong (ligature)	&#198;	&Aelig;
Ç	capital C, cedilla	&#199;	&Ccedil;
È	capital E, grave accent	&#200;	&Egrave;
É	capital E, acute accent	&#201;	&Eacute;
Ê	capital E, circumflex accent	&#202;	&Ecirc;
Ë	capital E, dieresis capital E, umlaut mark	&#203;	&Euml;
Ì	capital I, grave accent	&#204;	&Igrave;
Í	capital I, acute accent	&#205;	&Iacute;
Î	capital I, circumflex accent	&#206;	&Icirc;
Ï	capital I, dieresis capital I, umlaut mark	&#207;	&Iuml;
	capital Eth, Icelandic	&#208;	Ð Đ
Ñ	capital N, tilde	&#209;	&Ntilde;
Ò	capital O, grave accent	&#210;	&Ograve;
Ó	capital O, acute accent	&#211;	&Oacute;
Ô	capital O, circumflex accent	&#212;	&Ocirc;
Õ	capital O, tilde	&#213;	&Otilde;
Ö	capital O, dieresis capital O, umlaut mark	&#214;	&Ouml;
x	multiply sign	&#215;	&times;

Character	Description	Entity Code	Entity Name
Ø	capital O, slash	Ø	Ø
Ù	capital U, grave accent	Ù	Ù
Ú	capital U, acute accent	Ú	Ú
Û	capital U, circumflex accent	Û	Û
Ü	capital U, dieresis capital U, umlaut mark	Ü	Ü
Ý	capital Y, acute accent	Ý	Ý
	capital THORN, Icelandic	Þ	Þ
ß	small sharp s, German (sz ligature)	ß	ß
à	small a, grave accent	à	à
á	small a, acute accent	á	á
â	small a, circumflex accent	â	â
ã	small a, tilde	ã	ã
ä	small a, dieresis small a, umlaut mark	ä	ä
å	small a, ring	å	å
æ	small ae dipthong (ligature)	æ	æ
ç	small c, cedilla	ç	ç
è	small e, grave accent	è	è
é	small e, acute accent	é	é
ê	small e, circumflex accent	ê	ê
ë	small e, dieresis small e, umlaut mark	ë	ë
ì	small I, grave accent	ì	ì
í	small I, acute accent	í	í
î	small i, circumflex accent	î	î

Character	Description	Entity Code	Entity Name
ï	small i, dieresis small i, umlaut mark	&#239;	&iuml;
∂	small eth, Icelandic	&#240;	&eth;
ñ	small n, tilde	&#241;	&ntilde;
ò	small o, grave accent	&#242;	&ograve;
ó	small o, acute accent	&#243;	&oacute;
ô	small o, circumflex accent	&#244;	&ocirc;
õ	small o, tilde	&#245;	&otilde;
ö	small o, dieresis small o, umlaut mark	&#246;	&ouml;
÷	division sign	&#247;	&divide;
ø	small o, slash	&#248;	&oslash;
ù	small u, grave accent	&#249;	&ugrave;
ú	small u, acute accent	&#250;	&uacute;
û	small u, circumflex accent	&#251;	&ucirc;
ü	small u, dieresis small u, umlaut mark	&#252;	&uuml;
y	small y, acute accent	&#253;	&yacute;
	small thorn, Icelandic	&#254;	&thorn;
ÿ	small y, dieresis small y, umlaut mark	&#255;	&yuml;

Appendix B:
JavaScript Reserved Words

The JavaScript language sets aside certain words that you cannot use as the names of variables, functions, methods, or objects. Some of these words are currently used by JavaScript; others are reserved for future use.

The reserved words are

abstract	float	public
Boolean	for	return
break	function	short
byte	goto	static
case	if	super
catch	implements	switch
char	import	synchronized
class	in	this
const	instanceof	throw
continue	int	throws
default	interface	transient
do	long	true
double	native	try
else	new	var
extends	null	void
false	package	while
final	private	with
finally	protected	

Appendix C:
A Review of HTML

Before you can use JavaScript in a Web page, you need to know how to write a Web page. This appendix reviews the basic HTML you need to know to put together Web pages. It also reviews the structure of a good Web page.

The basic structure of a Web page

Web pages are composed of HTML tags, content, and comments. The content—the plain text of the page—should be contained within HTML tags. Most browsers will display content that is not contained within HTML tags, but HTML standards don't require them to display uncontained content.

The content, not the tags, should contain comments, if for no better reason than that it makes the page more readable and easier to maintain. Comments begin with <!-- and end with -->. It's a good practice never to place a double dash (--) or a right angle bracket (>) within a comment. Some browsers may prematurely terminate the comment when they read these character sequences. It's important to remember this when writing JavaScript code, which you usually place inside comments to keep JavaScript-ignorant browsers from displaying the code on the screen.

HTML tags are special keywords enclosed within angle brackets (< and >). They may have attributes that refine the behavior of the tag; attributes are typically of the form *name=value*. When a tag has attributes, some of them are mandatory and the others are optional. Certain browsers may let you get away with omitting mandatory attributes, but you shouldn't expect all browsers to do so. The attribute values may be numeric or text, and may be enclosed within quotes. Some tools you can use to verify the syntax of your pages have trouble with attribute values; enclosing the values within quotes usually helps.

Tag and attribute names are case-insensitive. Attribute values are almost always case-sensitive. Because most content is lowercase (uppercase text is perceived as shouting), I prefer to write tag and attribute names in uppercase. It makes them stand out from the content.

Most tags have corresponding end tags. The end tag contains the same keyword as the first tag, or start tag, but with a leading slash (/) character. Like the start tag, it is enclosed within angle brackets. Unlike start tags, end tags do not have attributes.

Some tags contain text, and these tags have end tags. In certain specialized circumstances, the end tag is implied; for example, within a table row, a table cell that starts with a <TD> tag is implicitly ended by another <TD> tag. It is a good practice, however, always to use end tags. It makes your code easier to read and maintain.

An HTML element consists of either a tag that contains no text, such as an <IMG> tag, or a tag and its end tag and the text between them, such as

```
<B>Some bold text</B>
```

In the first case, the element is called an empty element. In the second case, the element is called a container element.

Certain rules dictate which HTML elements can exist within which other HTML elements. You can nest HTML elements, but their start and end tags cannot overlap. For example, you may wish to render text in a bold italic font. You can do so by enclosing the text within <B> and </B>, and within <I> and </I>. <B><I>text</I></B> will work. <I><B>text</B></I> will work. <B><I>text</B></I> will not work.

Some tags have attributes in common with each other. These common attributes take common values, and these values may not be very obvious as to what they do. Uniform Resource Locators, colors, the ALIGN attribute, and the CLEAR attribute are not well understood.

UNIFORM RESOURCE LOCATORS

Uniform Resource Locators, or URLs, specify the location of documents on the Internet, and the protocol that is used to retrieve them. The general format of a URL is

```
protocol hostname port pathname search hash
```

These are defined as follows:

protocol   The beginning of a URL, up to the first colon. Common protocols include javascript: (JavaScript code), about: (navigator information), http: (World Wide Web), file: (local file), ftp: (FTP), mailto: (mail), news: (Usenet news), and gopher: (Gopher). The protocol may be separated from the rest of the URL by two slashes (http:, ftp:, news:), three slashes (file:), or no slashes (javascript:, about:, mailto:, gopher:).

hostname   The host and domain name, or IP address, of a network host.

port   The number of the communications port used by the network host for communication. Many protocols define a "well-known" port number (21 for FTP, 70 for Gopher, 80 for the World Wide Web, 119 for Usenet news, to name a few) for the protocol, and because most hosts use the well-known port numbers, the port component is rarely used.

pathname   The path of the file, including the file name, on the network host.

search   Query information, beginning with a question mark.

hash   An anchor name, beginning with a hash mark (#)

An absolute URL has a protocol, host name, and path name, and may include a port, search, and hash field.

A relative URL has no protocol or host name, and the path name is not usually a full path name.

COLORS

Tags that take color attributes may specify the color values in two different ways: by name or by hex triplet.

There are 140 defined color names, such as red, black, and turquoise. For a complete list of these defined colors, check the code listings for Chapter 6.

Hex triplets consist of a pound sign followed by the hexadecimal values of the red component, the green component, and the blue component. Each component may have a value from 00 to FF, and must have two digits.

ALIGNMENT

Some elements can float freely within a stream of text, and have ALIGN attributes that permit you to dictate where the element will appear on the screen. The most common values for the ALIGN attribute are left, right, top, texttop, middle, absmiddle, baseline, bottom, and absbottom.

Left and right alignment (ALIGN="left" and ALIGN="right") place a free-floating element below the current line of text, on either the left margin or the right margin. Text flows around the element.

Top and texttop alignment (ALIGN="top" and ALIGN="texttop") place a free-floating element on the screen so that the top of the element is lined up with the top of the line up to that point. In other words, alignment is with respect to text and elements to the left of the current element. The difference between top and texttop alignment is that top alignment takes text and elements into account, and texttop alignment only considers text.

Middle and absmiddle alignment (ALIGN="middle" and ALIGN="absmiddle") place a free-floating element on the screen so that the middle of the element is lined up with either the baseline of the text (ALIGN="middle") or with the middle of the text and elements to the left (ALIGN="absmiddle"). When there is nothing but text to the left, there is almost no difference between the two.

Baseline, bottom, and absbottom alignment (ALIGN="baseline", ALIGN="bottom", and ALIGN="absbottom") place a free-floating element on the screen so that the bottom of the element is lined up either with the baseline of the text (ALIGN="baseline" and ALIGN="bottom"—they are synonymous) or with the bottom of the lowest text or element to the left of the free-floating element (ALIGN="absbottom").

CLEAR

CLEAR is a common attribute used by elements. This attribute specifies that the browser should go farther down the screen until the specified margin is clear before displaying the element's text. Typical values are left, right, and all (both left and right margins must be clear).

In Figures C.1 through C.4, a BR (line break) element, which can take a CLEAR attribute, is inserted into the text following the word "break." In Figure C.1, with CLEAR="left", the text stops until the image on the left is cleared, and then resumes. In Figure C.2, with CLEAR="right", the text stops until the image on the right is cleared, and then resumes. In Figure C.3, with CLEAR="all", the text stops until both images are cleared, and then resumes. Finally, in Figure C.4, there is no CLEAR attribute and text resumes on the next line, between the two images.

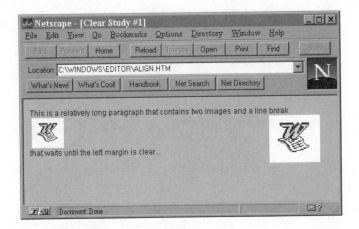

Figure C.1: <BR CLEAR="left">

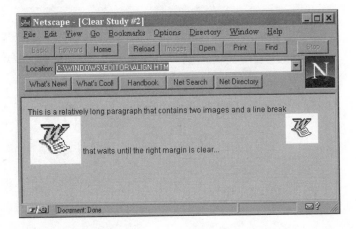

Figure C.2: <BR CLEAR="right">

NETSCAPE-SUPPORTED HTML ELEMENTS

This section includes short descriptions of the HTML elements currently supported by Netscape. These elements do not pertain solely to JavaScript. Each element description mentions commonly used attributes of the element, explains the function of the element, includes special notes about the element, and tells what elements may be contained within that element.

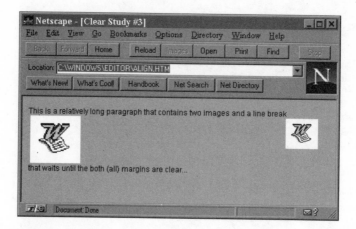

Figure C.3: <BR CLEAR="all">

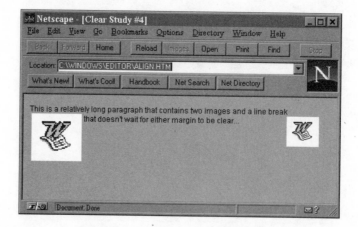

Figure C.4: <BR> with no CLEAR attribute

A (ANCHOR)

The A element marks the beginning of a hypertext link if it uses the HREF attribute or the destination of a hypertext link if it uses the NAME attribute. In JavaScript, it's a link object if it uses the HREF attribute and an anchor object if it contains the NAME attribute. There are five attributes, but an A element must have an HREF or NAME attribute. Both can be used in the same element—an A element may be both a link object and an anchor object.

HREF=*string*	The value specifies the target of a hypertext link.
NAME=*string*	The value creates a destination for a hypertext link.
ONCLICK=*string*	The value specifies a JavaScript expression to be executed when the user clicks on the element. This only applies to A elements that have an HREF attribute defined.
ONMOUSEOVER= *string*	The value specifies a JavaScript expression to be executed when the user moves the mouse pointer over the element. This only applies to A elements that have an HREF attribute defined.
TARGET=*string*	The value specifies a window or frame into which the link will be loaded. This only applies to A elements that have an HREF attribute defined.

The A element is a container element that can contain content text and B, BASEFONT, BIG, BLINK, BR, CITE, CODE, EM, FONT, H1, H2, H3, H4, H5, H6, I, IMG, KBD, NOBR, SAMP, SMALL, STRIKE, SUB, SUP, TT, VAR, and WBR elements. It may not contain another A element. Its contents are usually highlighted by the browser when the HREF attribute is used.

ADDRESS

The ADDRESS element indicates that its contents constitute an address. Typical usage would include electronic signatures and lists of authors. This element has no attributes, and it is a container element that may contain content text and A, B, BASEFONT, BIG, BLINK, BR, CITE, CODE, EM, FONT, I, IMG, KBD, NOBR, P, SAMP, SMALL, STRIKE, STRONG, SUB, SUP, TT, VAR, and WBR elements.

APPLET

The APPLET element loads a Java applet and executes it. It has eight attributes:

ALIGN=*string*   The value specifies the applet's alignment on the page. Permitted values include left, right, top, texttop, middle, absmiddle, baseline, bottom, and absbottom.

CODE=*string*   The value specifies the relative URL of the applet. This attribute is mandatory.

CODEBASE=*string*   The value specifies a base URL for the CODE attribute's relative URL. In the absence of this attribute, the document URL becomes the base URL.

HEIGHT=*number*   The value specifies the height, in pixels, of the applet. This attribute is mandatory.

HSPACE=*number*   The value specifies the horizontal distance, in pixels, between the applet and surrounding text.

NAME=*string*   The value creates a destination for a hypertext link.

VSPACE=*number*   The value specifies the vertical distance, in pixels, between the applet and surrounding text.

WIDTH=*number*   The value specifies the width, in pixels, of the applet. This attribute is mandatory.

The APPLET element is a container element that may contain content text and A, B, BASEFONT, BIG, BLINK, BR, CITE, CODE, EM, FONT, I, IMG, KBD, NOBR, PARAM, SAMP, SMALL, STRIKE, STRONG, SUB, SUP, VAR, and WBR elements.

AREA

The AREA element defines a region within a MAP element that the user may select. If the HREF attribute is used, the area acts like the beginning of a hypertext link. If the NOHREF attribute is used, the area acts like a "dead zone"; if the user clicks in such an area, nothing happens. There can be multiple AREA elements within a MAP element. In case of overlap, the first AREA element that contains the coordinates the user selected will be the active element. The coordinates start in the image's upper-left corner.

There are four attributes:

COORDS=*string*   The value specifies the coordinates that define the area. If the area is a rectangle, there are four coordinates: left, top, right, and bottom. If the area is a circle, there are three coordinates: the center of the circle (horizontal coordinate and then vertical coordinate) followed by the radius. If the area is a polygon, there are an arbitrary number of coordinate pairs. In this case, each pair describes a vertex of the polygon. The vertex's horizontal coordinate is first, followed by the vertical coordinate. The last pair does not need to match the first pair; in that case, the browser will assume a line segment between the first vertex and the last vertex.

HREF=*string*   The value identifies a hypertext link that will be the target if a point within this area's coordinates is selected.

NOHREF   This attribute means that this area describes a dead zone; nothing will happen if you select a point within this area's coordinates.

SHAPE=*string*   The value specifies the shape of the area. Valid values include circle, rect (rectangle), and poly (polygon). The default shape is a rectangle.

The AREA element is an empty element.

B (BOLDFACE)

The B element specifies that the browser should render the contents in a bold font.

There are no attributes. The B element is a container element that may contain content text and A, B, BASEFONT, BIG, BLINK, BR, CITE, CODE, EM, FONT, I, IMG, KBD, NOBR, SAMP, SMALL, STRIKE, STRONG, SUB, SUP, TT, VAR, and WBR elements.

BASE

The BASE element overrides the Web page's URL as the base for relative URLs. It has one mandatory attribute, HREF=string, where the value specifies the base for relative URLs.

The BASE element is empty.

BASEFONT

The BASEFONT element overrides the value of the base font size (which by default is 3). The browser adds relative FONT element values to the base font size. The BASEFONT element has one mandatory attribute, SIZE=*number*, where the number value is the base font size.

The BASEFONT element is a container element that may contain content text and A, ADDRESS, APPLET, B, BASEFONT, BIG, BLINK, BLOCK-QUOTE, BR, CENTER, CITE, CODE, DIR, DIV, DL, EM, FONT, FORM, H1, H2, H3, H4, H5, H6, HR, I, IMG, KBD, MAP, MENU, NOBR, OL, P, PRE, SAMP, SMALL, STRIKE, STRONG, SUB, SUP, TABLE, TT, UL, VAR, and WBR elements.

BIG

The BIG element specifies that the browser should render the contents in a larger than normal font.

There are no attributes. The BIG element is a container element that may contain content text and A, B, BASEFONT, BIG, BLINK, BR, CITE, CODE, EM, FONT, I, IMG, KBD, NOBR, SAMP, SMALL, STRIKE, STRONG, SUB, SUP, TT, VAR, and WBR elements.

BLINK

The BLINK element requests that contained elements be rendered in a blinking font. The blinking effect is as alarming as a shout of "Fire!" Just as most of us don't have a reason to pull the fire alarm every day, there is hardly ever a good reason to include blinking text in an ordinary document. Use of BLINK is considered even more vulgar than writing text in all uppercase.

There are no attributes. The BLINK element is a container element that may contain content text and A, B, BASEFONT, BIG, BLINK, BR, CITE, CODE, EM, FONT, I, IMG, KBD, NOBR, SAMP, SMALL, STRIKE, STRONG, SUB, SUP, TT, VAR, and WBR elements.

BLOCKQUOTE

The BLOCKQUOTE element indicates that its contents constitute a quotation.

The BLOCKQUOTE element has no attributes. It is a container element that may contain content text and A, ADDRESS, APPLET, B, BASEFONT, BIG, BLINK, BLOCKQUOTE, BR, CENTER, CITE, CODE, DIR, DIV, DL, EM, FONT, FORM, H1, H2, H3, H4, H5, H6, HR, I, IMG, KBD, MAP, MENU, NOBR, OL, P, PRE, SAMP, SMALL, STRIKE, STRONG, SUB, SUP, TABLE, TT, UL, VAR, and WBR elements.

BODY

The BODY element contains the visible contents of the document.

The BODY element has eight optional attributes:

ALINK=*color*   The value specifies the color for the active link (the link currently selected by the user).

BACKGROUND=*string*   The value specifies the URL of an image file that will be tiled to form the background.

BGCOLOR=*color*   The value specifies the color for the background.

LINK=*color*   The value specifies the color of unvisited links.

ONLOAD=*string*   The value specifies a JavaScript expression to be executed when the Web page finishes loading.

ONUNLOAD=*string*   The value specifies a JavaScript expression to be executed when the user leaves the Web page.

TEXT=*color*   The value specifies the color of ordinary text.

VLINK=*color*   The value specifies the color of visited links.

The BODY element is a container element that may contain content text and A, ADDRESS, APPLET, B, BASEFONT, BIG, BLINK, BLOCKQUOTE, BR, CENTER, CITE, CODE, DIR, DIV, DL, EM, FONT, FORM, H1, H2, H3, H4, H5, H6, HR, I, IMG, KBD, MAP, MENU, NOBR, OL, P, PRE, SAMP, SMALL, STRIKE, STRONG, SUB, SUP, TABLE, TT, UL, VAR, and WBR elements.

BR (LINE BREAK)

The BR element forces a line break. It has one optional attribute, CLEAR=*string*, where the value indicates how far down the browser should space until the indicated margin is clear of text and images. Valid values include left, right, and all.

The BR element is an empty element.

CAPTION

The CAPTION element defines a table caption. It has two attributes:

ALIGN=*string*   The value indicates how the caption should be horizontally aligned with its table. Valid values include top, bottom, left, and right.

ID=*string*   The value defines a hypertext link target.

The CAPTION element is a container element that may contain content text and A, B, BASEFONT, BIG, BLINK, BR, CITE, CODE, EM, FONT, I, IMG, KBD, NOBR, SAMP, SMALL, STRIKE, STRONG, SUB, SUP, TT, VAR, and WBR elements.

CENTER

The CENTER element indicates that the browser should horizontally center the contained text. It has no attributes. The CENTER element is a container element that may contain content text and A, ADDRESS, APPLET, B, BASE-FONT, BIG, BLINK, BLOCKQUOTE, BR, CENTER, CITE, CODE, DIR, DIV, DL, EM, FONT, FORM, H1, H2, H3, H4, H5, H6, HR, I, IMG, KBD, MAP, MENU, NOBR, OL, P, PRE, SAMP, SMALL, STRIKE, STRONG, SUB, SUP, TABLE, TT, UL, VAR, and WBR elements.

CITE

The CITE element indicates that the contained text is a citation.

There are no attributes. The CITE element is a container element that may contain content text and A, B, BASEFONT, BIG, BLINK, BR, CITE, CODE, EM, FONT, I, IMG, KBD, NOBR, SAMP, SMALL, STRIKE, STRONG, SUB, SUP, TT, VAR, and WBR elements.

CODE

The CODE element indicates that the contained text is computer code and should be rendered in a suitable font. This element is recommended for short, single-line text; the PRE element is the element of choice for longer text, especially multiline text.

There are no attributes. The CODE element is a container element that may contain content text and A, B, BASEFONT, BIG, BLINK, BR, CITE, CODE, EM, FONT, I, IMG, KBD, NOBR, SAMP, SMALL, STRIKE, STRONG, SUB, SUP, TT, VAR, and WBR elements.

DD (DEFINITION DESCRIPTION)

The DD element contains the definition portion of a definition list item. It has no attributes, and is a container element that may contain content text and A, APPLET, B, BASEFONT, BIG, BLINK, BLOCKQUOTE, BR, CENTER, CITE, CODE, DIR, DL, EM, FONT, FORM, I, IMG, KBD, MENU, NOBR, OL, P, PRE, SAMP, SMALL, STRIKE, STRONG, SUB, SUP, TABLE, TT, UL, VAR, and WBR elements.

DIR (DIRECTORY)

The DIR element creates a list of short text items, such as file names. It has no attributes, and is a container element that may contain LI elements and their contents. A DIR element cannot contain APPLET, BLOCKQUOTE, CENTER, DIR, DL, FORM, MENU, OL, P, PRE, TABLE, or UL elements.

DIV (DIVISION)

The DIV element breaks a document into major subdivisions. It has five attributes:

ALIGN=*string*   The value specifies the horizontal alignment of the division. Valid values include left, center, and right.

CLEAR=*string*   The value indicates how far down the browser should space until the indicated margin is clear of text and images. Valid values include left, right, and all.

ID=*string*   The value defines a hypertext link target.

NEEDS=*number*   The value specifies the minimal width required for this element.

NOWRAP   This attribute disables line wrap.

The DIV element is a container element that may contain content text and A, ADDRESS, APPLET, B, BASEFONT, BIG, BLINK, BLOCKQUOTE, BR, CENTER, CITE, CODE, DIR, DIV, DL, EM, FONT, FORM, H1, H2, H3, H4, H5, H6, HR, I, IMG, KBD, MAP, MENU, NOBR, OL, P, PRE, SAMP, SMALL, STRIKE, STRONG, SUB, SUP, TABLE, TT, UL, VAR, and WBR elements.

DL (DEFINITION LIST)

The DL element contains a list of definitions. It has one attribute, COMPACT, which suggests that the list be rendered in a more compact form.

The DL element is a container element that may contain DD and DT elements.

DT (DEFINITION TERM)

The DT element contains a term in a list of definitions. It has no attributes, and is a container element that may contain content text and A, B, BASE-FONT, BIG, BLINK, BR, CITE, CODE, EM, FONT, I, IMG, KBD, NOBR, SAMP, SMALL, STRIKE, STRONG, SUB, SUP, TT, VAR, and WBR elements.

EM (EMPHASIS)

The EM element indicates that the browser should emphasize the contents. Browsers typically render the contents in an italic font.

There are no attributes. The EM element is a container element that may contain content text and A, B, BASEFONT, BIG, BLINK, BR, CITE, CODE, EM, FONT, I, IMG, KBD, NOBR, SAMP, SMALL, STRIKE, STRONG, SUB, SUP, TT, VAR, and WBR elements.

FONT

The FONT element defines the font size for contained text. The size may be absolute or relative; the browser adds the base font value to relative font sizes. This element has two attributes:

COLOR=*color*   The value specifies the color for normal text within the FONT element.

SIZE=*string*   The value may be a number (absolute size) or a number preceded by a + or – character (relative size).

The FONT element is a container element that may contain content text and A, B, BASEFONT, BIG, BLINK, BR, CITE, CODE, EM, FONT, I, IMG, KBD, NOBR, SAMP, SMALL, STRIKE, STRONG, SUB, SUP, TT, VAR, and WBR elements.

FORM

The FORM element defines a block of input fields that the user may fill in. The browser usually sends the user's data to a CGI application on the server. If the GET method is used, the CGI application can access an environment variable with the name QUERY_STRING. If the POST method is used, the CGI application can read the data from the standard input stream (stdin); the environment variable CONTENT_LENGTH contains the length of the data. Data is sent as *name=value* pairs separated by ampersands (&). The *name=value* pairs are URL-encoded—spaces are converted to pluses (+) and some characters are converted to a percent (%) character followed by the character's two-digit hexadecimal value.

The FORM element has six attributes:

ACTION=*string*   The value specifies either a CGI URL or a mailto: URL. This attribute is mandatory.

ENCTYPE=*string*   The value specifies the MIME encoding for the data when it is sent to the server. The values can be application/x-www-form-urlencoded (the default value) or multipart/form-data.

METHOD=*string*   The value specifies how the data should be sent. The valid values are GET (the default) and POST.

NAME=*string*   The value specifies the name of the corresponding JavaScript form object

ONSUBMIT=*string*   The value specifies a JavaScript expression to be executed when the user clicks on the SUBMIT button.

TARGET=*string*   The value specifies the name of a window or frame object into which the form responses will be written.

A FORM element is a container element that may contain content text and A, ADDRESS, APPLET, B, BASEFONT, BIG, BLINK, BLOCKQUOTE, BR, CENTER, CITE, CODE, DIR, DIV, DL, EM, FONT, H1, H2, H3, H4, H5, H6, HR, I, IMG, INPUT, KBD, MAP, MENU, NOBR, OL, P, PRE, SAMP, SELECT, SMALL, STRIKE, STRONG, SUB, SUP, TABLE, TEXTAREA, TT, UL, VAR, and WBR elements. A FORM element may not contain another FORM element. A FORM element must contain at least one INPUT, SELECT, or TEXTAREA element.

FRAME

The FRAME element defines a frame, which is a subsection of the browser screen. It has six attributes:

MARGINHEIGHT=*number*   The value specifies the size of the top and bottom margins of the frame. The value cannot be zero; you cannot use this attribute to erase the line between frames, and you cannot make the value so large as to squeeze another frame out of existence. If you do not use this attribute, the browser sets the upper and lower margins as it sees fit.

MARGINWIDTH=*number*   The value specifies the size of the left and right margins of the frame. The value cannot be zero; you cannot use this attribute to erase the line between frames, and you cannot make the value so large as to squeeze another frame out of existence. If you do not use this attribute, the browser sets the left and right margins as it sees fit.

NAME=*string*   The value is assigned to its frame so that the frame can be targeted by other links. This is the corresponding frame object's name attribute. By default, frames are unnamed.

NORESIZE   This attribute prevents the user from being able to resize this frame. Frames that share an edge with this frame cannot be resized if doing so would force this frame to be resized.

SCROLLING=*string*   The value indicates how scroll bars should be used with the frame. Valid values are yes, no, and auto. The browser will always display the scroll bar if the value is yes. The browser will never display the scrollbar if the value is no. The browser will display the scrollbar as it sees fit if the value is auto. The default value is auto.

SRC=*string*   The value specifies the URL for the document to be loaded into the frame. The frame will be empty if you do not use this attribute. The frame will also be empty if the specified URL happens to be the URL of an ancestor to this frame. This helps prevent infinite recursion.

The FRAME element is an empty element.

FRAMESET

The FRAMESET element defines a set of frames and how the containing window or frame will be divided to hold them.

A FRAMESET element has four attributes:

COLS=*string*   The value describes how the columns of frames will be allocated window space.

ONLOAD=*string*   The value specifies a JavaScript expression to be executed when the Web page has been loaded.

ONUNLOAD=*string*   The value specifies a JavaScript expression to be executed when the user leaves the Web page.

ROWS=*string*   The value describes how the rows of frames will be allocated window space.

A FRAMESET element must have either a COLS or a ROWS attribute, but not both. The COLS and ROW attribute values consist of frame widths or heights separated by commas. There should be no spaces in the value, and there should be one frame width or height for each FRAME or FRAMESET contained in the FRAMESET element. Frame widths and heights may be numbers, percentages (number followed by a percent sign), or relative values (an asterisk preceded by an optional number). Values that are numbers specify the height or width of the corresponding FRAME or FRAMESET element in pixels. Percentage values specify the percentage of the available space that should be allocated to the corresponding FRAME or FRAMESET element. Relative valued elements are allocated after all number and percentage valued elements have been allocated. If there are no relative values and the percentage values do not add up to 100 percent, the browser will adjust the percentage values to add up to 100 percent.

A FRAMESET element is a container element that may contain FRAME, NOFRAME, and FRAMESET elements.

H1, H2, H3, H4, H5, AND H6 (HEADINGS)

The H1, H2, H3, H4, H5, and H6 elements create headings. The most prominent is H1 and the least prominent is H6. These elements have three attributes:

ALIGN=*string*   The value specifies the horizontal alignment of the heading. Valid values include left, center, right, and justify.

CLEAR=*string*   The value indicates how far down the browser should space until the indicated margin is clear of text and images. Valid values include left, right, and all.

ID=*string*   The value defines a hypertext link target.

Heading elements are container elements that may contain content text and A, B, BASEFONT, BIG, BLINK, BR, CITE, CODE, EM, FONT, I, IMG, KBD, NOBR, SAMP, SMALL, STRIKE, STRONG, SUB, SUP, TT, VAR, and WBR elements.

HEAD

The HEAD element contains information about the document. It has no attributes and is a container element that may contain BASE, ISINDEX, LINK, META, NEXTID, SCRIPT, and TITLE elements. A TITLE element is considered mandatory by HTML specifications, but if the document is intended solely as a frame within a larger document, the TITLE element will be ignored and is not necessary. The NEXTID element is used only by automated hypertext editors, and its use is not recommended.

HR (HORIZONTAL RULE)

The HR element draws a horizontal line across the page. There are four attributes:

ALIGN=*string*   The value specifies the horizontal alignment of the rule. Valid values include left, center, and right.

NOSHADE   This attribute indicates that the rule should not include shading.

SIZE=*number*   The value specifies the thickness of the line.

WIDTH=*string*   The value specifies the width of the line, possibly as a percentage of the window width.

The HR element is an empty element.

HTML

The HTML element contains the entire document. It has no attributes, and it should contain a HEAD element followed by a BODY or FRAMESET element. In your JavaScript code, either or both elements may be superfluous.

I (ITALIC)

The I element specifies that the browser should render the contents in an italic font.

There are no attributes. The I element is a container element that may contain content text and A, B, BASEFONT, BIG, BLINK, BR, CITE, CODE, EM, FONT, I, IMG, KBD, NOBR, SAMP, SMALL, STRIKE, STRONG, SUB, SUP, TT, VAR, and WBR elements.

IMG (IMAGE)

The IMG element embeds an inline image in the document. The image may be used as an *image map*—an image that contains clickable areas that act as a links to other URLs.

An image has height and width. You can specify these two quantities in the IMG element. Although they are not mandatory, there are two good reasons to treat them as mandatory:

▸ It makes it easier for the browser to map out the document's real estate.

▸ Bizarre errors will occur in JavaScript code if you do not specify the height and width of every image.

The IMG element has 11 attributes:

ALIGN=*string* The value specifies the horizontal alignment of the image. Valid values include left, right, center, top, texttop, middle, absmiddle, baseline, bottom, and absbottom.

ALT=*string* The value provides text that a nongraphics browser may display instead of the image.

BORDER=*number* The value specifies the thickness of the border around the image.

HEIGHT=*number* The value specifies the height, in pixels, of the image. For pages using JavaScript, this attribute is mandatory.

HSPACE=*number* The value specifies how far, in pixels, to separate the image from text on either side.

ISMAP This attribute indicates that the image is a server-side image map. To be useful, an IMG element with an ISMAP attribute has to be enclosed within an A element that has an HREF attribute (a link object). When the user clicks on a point in the image, the coordinates of the point are sent to the URL specified in the enclosing A element's HREF attribute. The URL is typically the location of a CGI application on the server.

LOWSRC=*string* The value specifies the URL of a lower resolution version of the image that can be quickly loaded. The idea is that, as time permits, the browser will replace the image with the real image.

SRC=*string* The value specifies the URL of the image file. This attribute is mandatory.

USEMAP=*string* The value specifies the relative URL of a MAP element; this image is a client-side image map.

VSPACE=*number* The number value specifies how far, in pixels, to separate the image from text above and below it.

WIDTH=*number* The number value specifies the width, in pixels, of the image. For pages using JavaScript, this attribute is mandatory.

The IMG element is an empty element.

INPUT

The INPUT element creates an input field. There are nine types of input fields.

▸ Button fields are specifically for use in JavaScript code; they send no data to the server.

▸ Checkbox fields are either selected or not selected. Only selected checkbox fields are sent to the server.

▸ Hidden fields are not displayed and are always sent to the server. Hidden fields can be used to send hardcoded data to the server.

▸ Image fields are images that the user can click on; the browser keeps track of where the cursor is when the user clicks on the picture and calculates the coordinates on the picture. Data is sent as two *name=value* pairs; the horizontal coordinate is sent first, followed by the vertical coordinate. The names have "x" and "y" appended; for example, if the image field name were imagefield and the user clicked on the point (100,50), the browser would send imagefield.x=100&imagefield.y=50.

▸ Password fields act like text fields except that the user's text is not displayed on the screen.

▸ Radio fields form linked radio fields. Like checkbox fields, radio fields are either selected or not selected. Unlike checkbox fields, radio fields are mutually exclusive. Only one radio field within a linked radio field can be selected at a time. You link radio fields by giving them the same names. Radio fields must have values assigned to them.

▸ A reset field creates a reset button that, when selected, resets all INPUT elements in the containing FORM element to their initial values.

▸ A submit field creates a submit button that, when selected, sends all data from the enclosing FORM element to the server. A submit field's value, if defined, cannot be changed and is used as the label for the button.

▸ Text fields allow the user to enter a single line of text (the TEXTAREA element enables the user to enter multiple lines of text).

The INPUT element has 13 attributes:

ALIGN=*string*	The value specifies the alignment of the field on the page. Valid values include top, middle, and bottom.
CHECKED	This attribute is used for checkbox and radio button input fields and specifies that the field be in the selected state.

MAXLENGTH= *number* The value specifies the maximum length for text in a text or password input field.

NAME=*string* The value specifies the name of the field. This attribute is mandatory. All radio fields that define a set of radio buttons must have the same name value.

ONBLUR=*string* The value specifies a JavaScript expression to be executed when the user transfers focus from this input field to another. This applies to password and text fields.

ONCHANGE= *string* The value specifies a JavaScript expression to be executed when the user changes the data in the field and presses Enter or transfers focus from this input field to another. This applies to text fields.

ONCLICK= *string* The value specifies a JavaScript expression to be executed when the user clicks on the INPUT element. This applies to button, checkbox, radio, reset, and submit fields.

ONFOCUS= *string* The value specifies a JavaScript expression to be executed when the user clicks on the INPUT element. This applies to password and text fields.

ONSELECT= *string* The value specifies a JavaScript expression to be executed when the user highlights some or all of the INPUT field's contents. This applies to password and text fields.

SIZE=*number* The value specifies the size of the field. For text and password fields, this is the number of characters that can be entered in the box without scrolling.

SRC=*string* The value specifies the URL of the image for an image field.

TYPE=*string* The value specifies the kind of field. Valid values are button, checkbox, hidden, image, password, radio, reset, submit, and text. This attribute is mandatory.

VALUE=*string*   The value used depends on the field type. It speci-
                      fies the initial value displayed in a text field. It speci-
                      fies the button label for a button, reset, or submit
                      field. It specifies the value returned to the server for
                      a checkbox or radio field. It specifies a default (un-
                      displayable) value for a password field. It specifies
                      the initial (unseen) value for a hidden field.

The INPUT element is an empty element.

ISINDEX (IS INDEXED)

The ISINDEX element indicates that the document is a searchable index. It
has one attribute:

PROMPT=*string*   The string value specifies a string to be used before
                      the text input field of the index. The default value is
                      "This is a searchable index. Enter search keywords:".

The ISINDEX element is an empty element.

KBD (KEYBOARD)

The KBD element specifies that the browser should render contained text as
keyboard input.

There are no attributes. The KBD element is a container element that may
contain content text and A, B, BASEFONT, BIG, BLINK, BR, CITE, CODE,
EM, FONT, I, IMG, KBD, NOBR, SAMP, SMALL, STRIKE, STRONG, SUB,
SUP, TT, VAR, and WBR elements.

LI (LIST ITEM)

The LI element creates an item in a list. It has two attributes:

TYPE=*string*   The value specifies the type of bullet or numbering to
                      be used in front of the contained text. Valid values in-
                      clude disc, circle, square, a, A, i, I, and 1. A and a refer
                      to lowercase and uppercase letters; I and i refer to low-
                      ercase and uppercase roman numerals; 1 refers to or-
                      dinary numerals.

VALUE=*number*   The value indicates where to start numbering for letters, Roman numerals, and numerals. The number is incremented with each LI element that follows. A value of 6, as an example, would be represented as F or f (letters), VI or vi (roman numerals), or 6 (numerals).

The LI element is a container element that may contain content text and A, APPLET, B, BASEFONT, BIG, BLINK, BLOCKQUOTE, BR, CENTER, CITE, CODE, DIR, DL, EM, FONT, FORM, I, IMG, KBD, MENU, NOBR, OL, P, PRE, SAMP, SMALL, STRIKE, STRONG, SUB, SUP, TABLE, TT, UL, VAR, and WBR elements. It may not contain another LI element.

LINK

The LINK element describes an association with another document. The LINK element is rarely used; its chief value lies in statically documenting an association with another document. It has two attributes:

HREF=*string*   The value specifies the URL of the other document. This attribute is mandatory.

TITLE=*string*   The value specifies the title of the other document.

The LINK element is an empty element.

MAP

The MAP element describes a set of selectable areas within a client-side image map. It has one mandatory attribute, NAME=*string*, where the value gives a name that can be used by the IMG element in its USEMAP attribute.

The MAP element is a container element that contains only AREA elements.

MENU

The MENU element contains a list of items. It has no attributes, and is a container element that may contain APPLET, BLOCKQUOTE, CENTER, DIR, DL, FORM, LI, OL, P, PRE, TABLE, and UL elements.

META (DOCUMENT META-INFORMATION)

The META element adds information to the document's HEAD element that does not fit anywhere else. It has three attributes:

CONTENT=*string*   The value specifies the content associated with this element. This attribute is mandatory.

HTTP-EQUIV= *string*   The value specifies a field to be sent by the server in an HTTP response header.

NAME=*string*   The value specifies a string that the client browser may be expected to understand.

You should use either the HTTP-EQUIV or the NAME attribute, but not both. The META element is an empty element.

NOBR (NO BREAK)

The NOBR element prevents the browser from inserting line breaks. It has no attributes. The NOBR element is a container element that may contain content text and A, B, BASEFONT, BIG, BLINK, BR, CITE, CODE, EM, FONT, I, IMG, KBD, NOBR, SAMP, SMALL, STRIKE, STRONG, SUB, SUP, TT, VAR, and WBR elements.

NOFRAME

The NOFRAME element allows you to provide content for browsers that do not understand FRAMESET and FRAME elements. It has no attributes, and is a container element that may contain content text and A, ADDRESS, APPLET, B, BASEFONT, BIG, BLINK, BODY, BLOCKQUOTE, BR, CENTER, CITE, CODE, DIR, DIV, DL, EM, FONT, FORM, H1, H2, H3, H4, H5, H6, HR, I, IMG, KBD, MAP, MENU, NOBR, OL, P, PRE, SAMP, SMALL, STRIKE, STRONG, SUB, SUP, TABLE, TT, UL, VAR, and WBR elements.

OL (ORDERED LIST)

The OL element contains a list that is strongly ordered in some fashion, such as an alphabetized list. It has three attributes:

COMPACT   This attribute advises the browser to display the list in a more compact fashion than it normally would.

START=*number*   The value indicates where the first LI element should start numbering. The number is incremented with each subsequent LI element. A value of 6, as an example, would be represented as F or f (letters), VI or vi (Roman numerals), or 6 (numerals).

TYPE=*string*   The value specifies how the list items should be numbered. Valid values include a (lowercase letters), A (uppercase letters), i (lowercase Roman numerals), I (uppercase Roman numerals), and 1 (numerals).

The OL element is a container element that may only contain LI elements.

OPTION

The OPTION element specifies an option within a SELECT element. It has two attributes:

SELECTED   This attribute marks the option as selected.

VALUE=*string*   The value is the value of the element when the form is submitted. If this attribute is not used, the value will be the text contained in the element.

The OPTION element is a container element that may only contain content text.

P (PARAGRAPH)

The P element contains a paragraph. It forces a break before and after the contained text. In response to strings of empty P elements, some browsers will increase the thickness of the break; others will not. The P element has five attributes:

ALIGN=*string*   The value specifies how the paragraph should be aligned. Valid values include left, center, and right.

CLEAR=*string*   The value indicates how far down the browser should space until the indicated margin is clear of text and images. Valid values include left, right, and all.

ID=*string*   The value defines a hypertext link target.

NEEDS=*number*   The value specifies the minimal width needed for the paragraph.

NOWRAP   This attribute specifies that line wrap is disabled.

The P element is a container element and may contain content text and A, B, BASEFONT, BIG, BLINK, BR, CITE, CODE, EM, FONT, I, IMG, KBD, NOBR, SAMP, SMALL, STRIKE, STRONG, SUB, SUP, TT, VAR, and WBR elements.

PARAM (APPLET PARAMETER)

The PARAM element specifies a parameter for the containing APPLET element. It has two attributes:

NAME=*string*   The value specifies the name of a parameter. This attribute is mandatory.

VALUE=*string*   The string value specifies the value of the parameter.

The PARAM element is an empty container.

PRE (PREFORMATTED TEXT)

The PRE element specifies that the browser is to render text as is, with its embedded line breaks and spaces intact. It has one attribute, WIDTH=*number*, where the value specifies the width of the text in characters. The browser should break the line after reaching the specified number of characters.

The PRE element is a container element and may contain content text and the elements A, BR, and HR.

SAMP (LITERAL CHARACTERS)

The SAMP element indicates that the browser should render contained text as a sequence of literal characters.

There are no attributes. The SAMP element is a container element that may contain content text and A, B, BASEFONT, BIG, BLINK, BR, CITE, CODE, EM, FONT, I, IMG, KBD, NOBR, SAMP, SMALL, STRIKE, STRONG, SUB, SUP, TT, VAR, and WBR elements.

SCRIPT

The SCRIPT element contains JavaScript code. It has one attribute, LANGUAGE=*string*, which is used to specify the language. It has two values, LiveScript and JavaScript. There is very little difference between the two. You should always use the JavaScript value.

The SCRIPT element is a container element that contains content text as JavaScript code.

SELECT

The SELECT element specifies a set of options from which the user may choose. It has six attributes:

MULTIPLE	This attribute indicates that more than one enclosed OPTION element may be selected at the same time.
NAME=*string*	The value specifies the name of the variable. This attribute is mandatory.
ONBLUR=*string*	The value specifies a JavaScript expression to be executed when focus is moved from this element to another.
ONCHANGE=*string*	The value specifies a JavaScript expression to be executed when the user changes the selected value and focus is moved from this element to another.

| ONFOCUS= *string* | The value specifies a JavaScript expression to be executed when the user gives this element focus. |
| SIZE=*number* | The value specifies the number of displayed options. |

The SELECT element is a container that may only contain OPTION elements.

SMALL

The SMALL element specifies that the browser should render the contents in a smaller than normal font.

There are no attributes. The SMALL element is a container element that may contain content text and A, B, BASEFONT, BIG, BLINK, BR, CITE, CODE, EM, FONT, I, IMG, KBD, NOBR, SAMP, SMALL, STRIKE, STRONG, SUB, SUP, TT, VAR, and WBR elements.

STRIKE

The STRIKE element specifies that the browser should render the contents in a strikethrough font.

There are no attributes. The STRIKE element is a container element that may contain content text and A, B, BASEFONT, BIG, BLINK, BR, CITE, CODE, EM, FONT, I, IMG, KBD, NOBR, SAMP, SMALL, STRIKE, STRONG, SUB, SUP, TT, VAR, and WBR elements.

STRONG (STRONG EMPHASIS)

The STRONG element indicates that the browser should strongly emphasize the contained text.

There are no attributes. The STRONG element is a container element that may contain content text and A, B, BASEFONT, BIG, BLINK, BR, CITE, CODE, EM, FONT, I, IMG, KBD, NOBR, SAMP, SMALL, STRIKE, STRONG, SUB, SUP, TT, VAR, and WBR elements.

SUB (SUBSCRIPT)

The SUB element specifies that the browser should render the contents as subscript.

There are no attributes. The SUB element is a container element that may contain content text and A, B, BASEFONT, BIG, BLINK, BR, CITE, CODE, EM, FONT, I, IMG, KBD, NOBR, SAMP, SMALL, STRIKE, STRONG, SUB, SUP, TT, VAR, and WBR elements.

SUP (SUPERSCRIPT)

The SUP element specifies that the browser should render the contents as superscript.

There are no attributes. The SUP element is a container element that may contain content text and A, B, BASEFONT, BIG, BLINK, BR, CITE, CODE, EM, FONT, I, IMG, KBD, NOBR, SAMP, SMALL, STRIKE, STRONG, SUB, SUP, TT, VAR, and WBR elements.

TABLE

The TABLE element defines a table. It has ten attributes:

ALIGN=*string*	The value specifies the alignment of the table. Valid values include bleedleft, left, center, right, bleedright, and justify. The default value is center.
BORDER=*number*	The value specifies the width of the border around the table. A value of 0 indicates no border.
CELLPADDING=*number*	The value specifies the width of the space, in pixels, between the contents of each cell and its border. The default value is 1.
CELLSPACING=*number*	The value specifies the distance between cells, in pixels. The default value is 2.
CLEAR=*string*	The value specifies that the browser should space down the page until the indicated margin is clear of text and images. The value may be left, right, or all.
ID=*string*	The value specifies a name that can be used in a fragment URL.
NEEDS=*number*	The value specifies the minimal width needed for this element.
NOWRAP	This attribute specifies that line wrap is disabled.
UNITS=*string*	The value specifies the units of measure. Valid values are em, pixels, and relative. The default value is em. An em is a printer's measurement, the width of the letter "M."
WIDTH=*number*	The value specifies the width of the table in pixels or as a percentage of the width that the browser would try to put it in.

The TABLE element is a container element that may contain CAPTION and TR elements.

TD (TABLE DATA) AND TH (TABLE HEADER)

The TD element specifies the contents of a table cell. The TH element creates a header cell for a table. Typically, the browser will render the text of a TH element in a bold font; this is the only real difference between a TH element and a TD element.

The TD and TH elements have seven attributes:

ALIGN=*string*	The value specifies the alignment that should be used for the data. Valid values are left, center, right, and justify.
COLSPAN=*number*	The value specifies the number of columns that this cell spans.
ID=*string*	The value specifies a name that can be used in fragment URLs.
NOWRAP	This attribute specifies that line wrap is disabled.
ROWSPAN=*number*	The value specifies the number of rows that this cell spans.
VALIGN=*string*	The value specifies the vertical alignment that should be used for the data. Valid values are top, middle, bottom, and baseline.
WIDTH=*number*	The value specifies the width in pixels or as a percentage of the calculated width that the cell data should be forced to occupy.

TD and TH elements are container elements that may contain content text and A, ADDRESS, APPLET, B, BASEFONT, BIG, BLINK, BLOCKQUOTE, BR, CENTER, CITE, CODE, DIR, DIV, DL, EM, FONT, FORM, H1, H2, H3, H4, H5, H6, HR, I, IMG, KBD, MAP, MENU, NOBR, OL, P, PRE, SAMP, SMALL, STRIKE, STRONG, SUB, SUP, TABLE, TT, UL, VAR, and WBR elements. An interesting "gotcha" is that a TD or TH element containing an IMG element, and nothing else, must contain no line breaks in the source. In other words,

```
<TD>
<IMG SRC="image.gif" WIDTH=40 HEIGHT=20>
</TD>
```

will result in spaces before and after the image. Usually the goal is to have the image fill the cell completely. Here is the right way to do it:

```
<TD><IMG SRC="image.gif" WIDTH=40 HEIGHT=20></TD>
```

TEXTAREA

The TEXTAREA element defines an input field in which multiple lines may be entered. It has eight attributes:

COLS=*number*	The value specifies the number of columns for the text box. This attribute is mandatory.
NAME=*string*	The value specifies the name of the variable. This attribute is mandatory.
ONBLUR=*string*	The value specifies a JavaScript expression to be executed when the user moves focus from this element to another input field.
ONCHANGE=*string*	The value specifies a JavaScript expression to be executed when the user changes the data in the field and moves focus to another input field.
ONFOCUS=*string*	The value specifies a JavaScript expression to be executed when the user moves focus from another input field to this field.
ONSELECT=*string*	The value specifies a JavaScript expression to be executed when the user highlights some or all of the text in the field.
ROWS=*number*	The value specifies the number of rows for the text box. This attribute is mandatory.
WRAP=*string*	The value specifies how line wrap should be performed. Valid values include off, soft, and hard. The default value is off, meaning that lines are sent as entered. Soft wrap specifies that long lines are displayed with line wrapping, but the lines are sent as entered. Hard wrap specifies that long lines are displayed and sent with line wrapping.

The TEXTAREA element is a container element that may only contain content text.

TITLE

The TITLE element contains the document title, which is usually displayed in the browser window's decoration. It has no attributes, and is a container element that may only contain content text. You should limit the length of this element to 64 or fewer characters.

TR (TABLE ROW)

The TR element defines a table row. It has four attributes:

ALIGN=*string*   The value specifies the alignment that should be used for the data. Valid values are left, center, right, and justify.

ID=*string*   The value specifies a name that can be used in fragment URLs.

NOWRAP   This attribute specifies that line wrap is disabled.

VALIGN=*string*   The value specifies the vertical alignment that should be used for the data. Valid values are top, middle, bottom, and baseline.

The TR element is a container element that may contain TD and TH elements.

TT (TELETYPE)

The TT element specifies that the browser should render the contents in a fixed width teletype font.

There are no attributes. The TT element is a container element that may contain content text and A, B, BASEFONT, BIG, BLINK, BR, CITE, CODE, EM, FONT, I, IMG, KBD, NOBR, SAMP, SMALL, STRIKE, STRONG, SUB, SUP, TT, VAR, and WBR elements.

UL (UNORDERED LIST)

The UL element creates a list that is not ordered. It has two attributes:

COMPACT   This attribute specifies that the browser should try to render the contents in a more compact way.

TYPE=*string*   The value specifies how the list items should be numbered. Valid values include disc (a filled circle), circle (an empty circle), and square.

The UL element is a container element that may contain LI elements.

VAR (VARIABLE)

The VAR element specifies that the browser should render the contained text as a variable name.

There are no attributes. The VAR element is a container element that may contain content text and A, B, BASEFONT, BIG, BLINK, BR, CITE, CODE, EM, FONT, I, IMG, KBD, NOBR, SAMP, SMALL, STRIKE, STRONG, SUB, SUP, TT, VAR, and WBR elements.

WBR (WORD BREAK)

The WBR element informs the browser where it can break a word. Unlike BR, it does not force a line break. You can use WBR elements within a NOBR element to dictate precisely where the browser may break a line and where it may not. The WBR element has no attributes and is an empty element.

APPENDIX D:
JavaScript Operators

JavaScript expressions use special symbols called operators to perform arithmetic and string manipulation. This appendix explains what the various operators do, as well as operator precedence (which operator is used first).

Operators

Operators may be unary, binary, or ternary. A unary operator uses a single value, or operand. A binary operator uses two operands. A ternary operator uses three operands.

ADDITION OPERATOR

The addition operator is a binary operator. The syntax is

```
operand1 + operand2
```

The value of this expression is the arithmetic sum of *operand1* and *operand2*.
   Example:

```
var tmp = 4 + 7.3;
```

In this example, *operand1* is 4 and *operand2* is 7.3. tmp is set to 11.3, the arithmetic sum of *operand1* (4) and *operand2* (7.3).

ASSIGNMENT OPERATOR

The assignment operator is a binary operator. The syntax is

```
operand1 = operand2
```

The value of this expression is that of *operand2*. The value of *operand2* is copied to *operand1*.

Example:

```
var tmp = 2;
```

In this example, *operand1* is tmp and *operand2* is 2. *operand1* (tmp) is set to the value of *operand2* (2).

BITWISE AND OPERATOR

The bitwise AND operator is a binary operator. The syntax is

```
operand1 & operand2
```

You obtain the result of this expression by treating *operand1*, *operand2*, and the result as sets of 32 bits. Each bit of the result is the corresponding bits of *operand1* and *operand2* ANDed together. The result of AND on two bits is 1 if both bits are 1, and 0 otherwise.

Example:

```
var tmp = 79 & 31;
```

In this example, *operand1* is 79 (00000000000000000000000001001111) and *operand2* is 31 (00000000000000000000000000011111). tmp is set to 15 (00000000000000000000000000001111).

BITWISE EXCLUSIVE-OR (XOR) OPERATOR

The bitwise exclusive-or (XOR) operator is a binary operator. The syntax is

```
operand1 ^ operand2
```

You obtain the result of this expression by treating *operand1*, *operand2*, and the result as sets of 32 bits. Each bit of the result is the corresponding bits of *operand1* and *operand2* XORed together. The result of XOR on two bits is 1 if only one of the bits is 1, and 0 if both bits are identical.

Example:

```
var tmp = 79 ^ 96;
```

In this example, *operand1* is 79 (00000000000000000000000001001111) and *operand2* is 96 (00000000000000000000000001100000). tmp is set to 47 (00000000000000000000000000101111).

BITWISE OR OPERATOR

The bitwise OR operator is a binary operator. The syntax is

```
operand1 | operand2
```

You obtain the result of this expression by treating *operand1*, *operand2*, and the result as sets of 32 bits. Each bit of the result is the corresponding bits of *operand1* and *operand2* ORed together. The result of OR on two bits is 1 if either bit is 1, and 0 if both bits are 0.

Example:

```
var tmp = 79 | 96;
```

In this example, *operand1* is 79 (00000000000000000000000001001111) and *operand2* is 96 (00000000000000000000000001100000). tmp is set to 111 (00000000000000000000000001101111).

BITWISE NEGATE OPERATOR

The bitwise negate operator is a unary operator. The syntax is

```
~ operand1
```

You obtain the result of this expression by treating *operand1* and the result as sets of 32 bits. Each bit of the result is the inverse of the corresponding bit of *operand1*.

Example:

```
var tmp = ~79;
```

In this example, *operand1* is 79 (00000000000000000000000001001111). tmp is set to -80 (11111111111111111111111110110000).

CONCATENATION OPERATOR

The concatenation operator is binary. The syntax is

```
operand1 + operand2
```

The result of this expression is a string that concatenates the contents of the string *operand1* and the string *operand2*.

Example:

```
var tmp = "Hello" + " world";
```

In this example, *operand1* is "Hello" and *operand2* is " world". The result is "Hello world".

CONDITIONAL OPERATOR

The conditional operator is the only ternary operator. The syntax is

```
operand1 ? operand2 : operand3
```

The value of this expression depends on *operand1*. If *operand1* evaluates as true, the value is *operand2*. Otherwise, the value is *operand3*.

Example:

```
var tmp = (x == 1) ? 7.2 : foo();
```

In this example, *operand1* is (x == 1), *operand2* is 7.2, and *operand3* is foo(). If *operand1* is true (x is equal to 1), tmp is set to *operand2* (7.2). If *operand1* is false (x is not equal to 1), tmp is set to *operand3* (the return value of foo()).

DIVISION OPERATOR

The division operator is binary. The syntax is

```
operand1 / operand2
```

The value of this expression is the value of *operand1* divided by *operand2*. *operand2* cannot be equal to 0.

Example:

```
var tmp = 24 / 5;
```

In this example, *operand1* is 24 and *operand2* is 5. tmp is set to *operand1* divided by *operand2*, which is 4.8.

EQUALITY OPERATOR

The equality operator is binary. The syntax is

```
operand1 == operand2
```

The value of this expression is true if *operand1* is equal to *operand2*, and false if *operand1* is not equal to *operand2*.

Example:

```
var tmp = (foo == bar);
```

In this example, *operand1* is foo and *operand2* is bar. If foo and bar are equal, tmp is set to true. Otherwise, tmp is set to false.

GREATER THAN OPERATOR

The greater than operator is binary. The syntax is

```
operand1 > operand2
```

The value of this expression is true if *operand1* is greater than *operand2*, and false if *operand1* is less than or equal to *operand2*.

Example:

```
var tmp = (foo > bar);
```

In this example, *operand1* is foo and *operand2* is bar. If foo is greater than bar, tmp is set to true. Otherwise, tmp is set to false.

GREATER THAN OR EQUAL OPERATOR

The greater than or equal operator is binary. The syntax is

```
operand1 >= operand2
```

The value of this expression is true if *operand1* is greater than or equal to *operand2*, and false if *operand1* is less than *operand2*.

Example:

```
var tmp = (foo >= bar);
```

In this example, *operand1* is foo and *operand2* is bar. If foo is greater than or equal to bar, tmp is set to true. Otherwise, tmp is set to false.

INEQUALITY OPERATOR

The inequality operator is binary. The syntax is

```
operand1 != operand2
```

The value of this expression is true if *operand1* is not equal to *operand2*, and false if *operand1* is equal to *operand2*.

Example:

```
var tmp = (foo != bar);
```

In this example, *operand1* is foo and *operand2* is bar. If foo and bar are not equal, tmp is set to true. Otherwise, tmp is set to false.

LESS THAN OPERATOR

The less than operator is binary. The syntax is

```
operand1 < operand2
```

The value of this expression is true if *operand1* is less than *operand2*, and false if *operand1* is greater than or equal to *operand2*.

Example:

```
var tmp = (foo < bar);
```

In this example, *operand1* is foo and *operand2* is bar. If foo is less than bar, tmp is set to true. Otherwise, tmp is set to false.

LESS THAN OR EQUAL OPERATOR

The less than or equal operator is binary. The syntax is

```
operand1 <= operand2
```

The value of this expression is true if *operand1* is less than or equal to *operand2*, and false if *operand1* is greater than *operand2*.

Example:

```
var tmp = (foo <= bar);
```

In this example, *operand1* is foo and *operand2* is bar. If foo is less than or equal to bar, tmp is set to true. Otherwise, tmp is set to false.

LOGICAL AND OPERATOR

The logical AND operator is binary. The syntax is

```
operand1 && operand2
```

This expression is true if both *operand1* and *operand2* are true; otherwise, it's false.

Example:

```
var tmp = foo && bar;
```

In this example, *operand1* is foo and *operand2* is bar. tmp is set to true if both foo and bar are true, and false if either foo or bar is false.

LOGICAL NOT OPERATOR

The logical NOT operator is unary. The syntax is

```
! operand1
```

This expression is true if *operand1* is false; otherwise, it's false.

Example:

```
var tmp = !bar;
```

In this example, *operand1* is bar. tmp is set to true if bar is false, and false if bar is true.

LOGICAL OR OPERATOR

The logical OR operator is binary. The syntax is

```
operand1 || operand2
```

This expression is true if either *operand1* or *operand2* is true; otherwise, it's false.
Example:

```
var tmp = foo || bar;
```

In this example, *operand1* is foo and *operand2* is bar. tmp is set to true if either foo or bar is true, and false if both foo and bar are false.

MODULO OPERATOR

The modulo operator is binary. The syntax is

```
operand1 % operand2
```

The value of this expression is the remainder of performing an integer division of *operand1* by *operand2*. *operand2* cannot be equal to 0. The absolute value of the result will be less than the absolute value of *operand2*, and the sign of the result will be the same as the sign of *operand1*.
Example:

```
var tmp = 12.1 % 3.7
```

In this example, *operand1* is 12.1 and *operand2* is 3.7. tmp is set to the remainder of dividing *operand1* divided by *operand2*. 12.1 divided by 3.7 is 3 with a remainder of 1, so tmp is set to 1.

MULTIPLICATION OPERATOR

The multiplication operator is binary. The syntax is

```
operand1 * operand2
```

The value of this expression is the value of *operand1* multiplied by *operand2*.
Example:

```
var tmp = foo * bar;
```

In this example, *operand1* is foo and *operand2* is bar. tmp is set to the product of *operand1* (foo) multiplied by *operand2* (bar).

NEGATION OPERATOR

The negation operator is unary. The syntax is

```
- operand1
```

The value of this expression is the value of *operand1* subtracted from 0.
Example:

```
var tmp = -foo;
```

In this example, *operand1* is foo. If *operand1* (foo) is equal to 3, tmp is set to −3 (the value of foo subtracted from 0).

It is customary not to include spaces between the operator and the operand.

POST-DECREMENT OPERATOR

The post-decrement operator is unary. The syntax is

```
operand1 --
```

The value of this expression is *operand1*. As a side effect, 1 is subtracted from *operand1*.

Example:

```
var tmp = foo--;
```

In this example, *operand1* is foo. tmp is set to foo, and foo is set to foo - 1.

The result of this expression

```
foo = foo--;
```

is not defined.

It is customary not to include spaces between the operator and the operand.

POST-INCREMENT OPERATOR

The post-increment operator is unary. The syntax is

```
operand1 ++
```

The value of this expression is *operand1*. As a side effect, 1 is added to *operand1*.

Example:

```
var tmp = foo++;
```

In this example, *operand1* is foo. tmp is set to foo, and foo is set to foo + 1.

The result of this expression:

```
foo = foo++;
```

is not defined.

It is customary not to include spaces between the operator and the operand.

PRE-DECREMENT OPERATOR

The pre-decrement operator is unary. The syntax is

```
-- operand1
```

The value of this expression is *operand1* minus 1. As a side effect, 1 is subtracted from *operand1*.

Example:

```
var tmp = --foo;
```

In this example, *operand1* is foo. tmp is set to foo - 1, and foo is set to foo - 1.

The result of this expression:

```
foo = --foo;
```

is not defined.

It is customary not to include spaces between the operator and the operand.

PRE-INCREMENT OPERATOR

The pre-increment operator is unary. The syntax is

```
++ operand1
```

The value of this expression is 1 plus *operand1*. As a side effect, 1 is added to *operand1*.

Example:

```
var tmp = ++foo;
```

In this example, *operand1* is foo. tmp is set to foo + 1, and foo is set to foo + 1.

The result of this expression:

```
foo = ++foo;
```

is not defined.

It is customary not to include spaces between the operator and the operand.

SHIFT LEFT OPERATOR

The shift left operator is binary. The syntax is

```
operand1 << operand2
```

You obtain the result of the expression by treating *operand1* as a set of 32 bits and shifting the bits left by the value in *operand2*. High-order bits are discarded, and the low-order bits are filled with 0's.

Example:

```
var tmp = 31 << 3;
```

In this example, *operand1* is 31 (00000000000000000000000000011111) and *operand2* is 3. tmp is set to 248 (00000000000000000000000011111000).

SIGN-PROPAGATING SHIFT RIGHT OPERATOR

The sign-propagating shift right operator is binary. The syntax is

```
operand1 >> operand2
```

You obtain the result of the expression by treating *operand1* as a set of 32 bits and shifting the bits right by the value in *operand2*. High-order bits are copied from the highest-order bit (which dictates the sign of the value, hence sign-propagating), and low-order bits are discarded.

Example:

```
var tmp = -9 >> 2;
```

In this example, *operand1* is -9 (11111111111111111111111111110111) and *operand2* is 2. tmp is set to -3 (11111111111111111111111111111101).

SHORTHAND ASSIGNMENT OPERATOR

The shorthand assignment operator is a binary operator. The syntax is

```
operand1 op= operand2
```

The value of this expression is the value of *operand1 op operand2*, where *op* can be addition (+), bitwise and (&), bitwise exclusive-or (^), bitwise or (|), division (/), modulo (%), multiplication (*), shift left (<<), sign-propagating shift right (>>), subtraction(-), or zero-fill shift right (>>>). As a side effect, *operand1* is also assigned the result of *operand1 op operand1*. This is equivalent to:

```
operand1 = operand1 op operand2
```

Example:

```
tmp += 2;
```

In this example, *operand1* is tmp, *op* is +, and *operand2* is 2. *operand2* (2) is added to *operand1* (tmp).

SUBTRACTION OPERATOR

The subtraction operator is binary. The syntax is

```
operand1 - operand2
```

The value of this expression is the value of *operand2* subtracted from *operand1*.

Example:

```
var tmp = 14 - foo();
```

In this example, *operand1* is 14 and *operand2* is foo(). tmp is set to the value of *operand2* (the return value of foo()) subtracted from *operand1* (14).

ZERO-FILL SHIFT RIGHT OPERATOR

The zero-fill shift right operator is binary. The syntax is

```
operand1 >>> operand2
```

You obtain the result of the expression by treating *operand1* as a set of 32 bits and shifting the bits right by the value in *operand2*. High-order bits are filled with 0's (hence zero-fill), and low-order bits are discarded.

Example:

```
var tmp = -9 >>> 2;
```

In this example, *operand1* is –9 (11111111111111111111111111110111) and *operand2* is 2. tmp is set to 1,073,741,821 (00111111111111111111111111111101).

ORDER OF PRECEDENCE

The order of precedence determines the order in which the browser applies operators to operands when evaluating an expression. This determines how to evaluate an expression such as:

```
var tmp = 4 + 5 * 6;
```

If you assume that addition has higher priority than multiplication, tmp has the value 54 (4 + 5 * 6 = 9 * 6 = 54). If you assume that multiplication has higher priority than addition, tmp has the value 34 (4 + 5 * 6 = 4 + 30 = 34).

The order of precedence, from highest (perform first) to lowest (perform last) is

▶ Bitwise negate, logical not, negate, post-decrement, post-increment, pre-decrement, pre-increment

▶ Division, modulo, multiplication

▶ Addition, concatenation, subtraction

▶ Shift left, sign-propagating shift right, zero-fill shift right

▶ Greater than, greater than or equal, less than, less than or equal

▶ Equality, inequality

▶ Bitwise and

▶ Bitwise exclusive-or

▶ Bitwise or

▶ Logical and

- ▸ Logical or
- ▸ Conditional
- ▸ Assignment, shorthand assignment

You can override the order of precedence by using parentheses to block off subexpressions that the browser must evaluate first.

Appendix E:
Built-in Objects and Functions

This appendix describes JavaScript's built-in objects and functions. The browser creates some of the objects in response to HTML elements in your Web page, and others are simply part of the language and available all the time.

Built-in objects

JavaScript defines several intrinsic objects. Like the objects that you can define, they have methods and properties. They may also have event handlers, which are JavaScript expressions that JavaScript executes when a specific kind of event occurs.

THE ANCHORS ARRAY

The anchors array is an array of anchor objects. It is a property of the document object. Anchor objects are reflections of A elements that have a NAME attribute:

```
<A NAME="anchorName">anchorText</A>
```

You can add anchors to the anchors array, but you cannot remove, replace, or modify them.

The anchors array has one property:

length   The number of entries in the anchors array. You cannot change this property directly, but you can create new anchors with the string anchor() method; such newly created anchors are added to the anchors array.

THE BUTTON OBJECT

A button object is a reflection of an INPUT element with a TYPE attribute of "button":

```
<INPUT TYPE="button">
```

button objects are members of the containing form object's elements array.
A button object has two properties:

name   The INPUT element's NAME attribute.

value   The INPUT element's VALUE attribute. This is the button's label in the display. In the absence of a VALUE attribute, this property is an empty string. You cannot change this property.

A button object has one method:

click()   Simulates a mouse click on the button. The onClick event handler is not executed when click() is called.

The button object has one event handler:

onClick   Executed when the user clicks on the button.

THE CHECKBOX OBJECT

A checkbox object is a reflection of an INPUT element with a TYPE attribute of "checkbox":

```
<INPUT TYPE="checkbox">
```

checkbox objects are members of the containing form's elements array.
A checkbox object has four properties:

checked   A Boolean value that indicates whether the checkbox object is on or off. The checkbox object is on if checked is true. You can change checked at any time. Changing checked changes the appearance of the display immediately.

default-
Checked

A Boolean value that indicates the default state of the check-box object. The default state of the checkbox object is on if de-faultChecked is true. The initial value of defaultChecked is set from the INPUT tag's CHECKED attribute. You can change defaultChecked at any time. Changing defaultChecked has no effect on the appearance of the display.

name

The value of the INPUT tag's NAME attribute. You can change it at any time.

value

The value of the INPUT tag's VALUE attribute. value is "on" in the absence of a VALUE attribute. The browser returns this property to the server if the user selected the checkbox. value is not part of the displayed object. You can change this property at any time.

A checkbox object has one method:

click()

Sets the checked property. The onClick event handler is not executed.

A checkbox has one event handler:

onClick

Executed when the user clicks on the display object.

THE DATE OBJECT

Date objects provide a mechanism for dealing with dates and time. At this time, JavaScript does not support dates before January 1, 1970 or after December 31, 1999.

There are three ways to create a Date object:

Date();

Uses the current local date and time.

Date(string);

Uses a string of "month day, year hours:min-utes:seconds"; you can omit the time portion.

Date(year, month, day, hours, minutes, seconds);

The parameters are integers; you can omit the time portion.

Date objects have 20 methods:

getDate()

Returns the day of the month from the date object. The value returned is between 1 and 31.

getDay()

Returns the day of the week from the date object. The value returned is between 0 (Sunday) and 6 (Saturday).

getHours()	Returns the hour from the date object. The value returned is between 0 and 23.
getMinutes()	Returns the minutes from the date object. The value returned is between 0 and 59.
getMonth()	Returns the month from the date object. The value returned is between 0 (January) and 11 (December).
getSeconds()	Returns the seconds from a date object. The value returned is between 0 and 59.
getTime()	Returns the number of milliseconds from January 1, 1970, 00:00:00.000 to the time in the date object.
getTimeZone-Offset()	Returns the difference, in minutes, between local time and Greenwich Mean Time (GMT).
getYear()	Returns the year from a date object. The value returned is the year minus 1900.
Date.parse (*dateString*)	Returns the number of milliseconds between *dateString* and January 1, 1970, 00:00:00.000 local time. The string may be of the form *DDD, dd MMM YYYY HH:MM:SS TZ*. *DDD* is the first three letters of the day of the week. *dd* is the day of the month from 1 to 31. *MMM* is the first three letters of the month. *YYYY* is the year. *HH* is the hour. *MM* is the minute. *SS* is the second. *TZ* is the time zone. parse() recognizes GMT, UTC, and the continental United States time zone abbreviations. You can express the time zone as GMT+*HHMM*, indicating an offset of *HH* hours and *MM* minutes from GMT. If you omit the time zone, the browser assumes local time.
setDate (*number*)	Sets the day of the month in a date object to *number*. If *number* is inappropriate to the date, JavaScript automatically adjusts the month and date. For example, if the month in a Date object is April and you call setDate()to set the date to 31, the date will be May 1 instead of April 31.
setHours (*number*)	Sets the hours in a date object to *number*.

setMinutes (*number*)	Sets the minutes in a date object to *number*.
setMonth (*number*)	Sets the month in a date object to *number*. If the resulting combination of month and date is inappropriate, JavaScript automatically adjusts the month and date. For example, if the date is May 31, and you use set-Month() to set the month to April, the date becomes May 1, not April 31st.
setSeconds (*number*)	Sets the seconds in a date object to *number*.
setTime (*number*)	Sets the date and time in a date object to the value indicated by *number*. *number* is the number of milliseconds since 1 January 1970 00:00:00.000
setYear (*number*)	Sets the least significant two digits of year in the date object to *number*. If the result is a date prior to 1970, the date will be January 1 1970 00:00:00.
toGMTString()	Converts a date object to a string representation using the local platform's GMT conventions.
toLocale-String()	Converts a date object to a string representation using the local platform's locale conventions. You should not use the resulting string to pass a date, as the representation is highly platform-dependent.
Date.UTC (*year, month, day, hour, minute, second*)	Converts the specified date into the number of milliseconds between the specified date and January 1, 1970, 00:00:00.000. The hour, minute, and second parameters are optional and default to 0.

THE DOCUMENT OBJECT

The document object contains information about the currently displayed document. Its properties are derived from the document's BODY element:

```
<BODY>document contents</BODY>
```

The document object has 13 properties:

alinkColor	A string representing the color of an active link. It has the value of BODY tag's ALINK attribute. You cannot change this property after the document has been displayed.

anchors	An array, in source order, of named A tags.
bgColor	A string representing the color of the background. It initially has the value of the BODY tag's BGCOLOR attribute. You can change this property at any time.
cookie	The string representation of an element of the cookie.txt file. You can change this property at any time.
fgColor	A string representing the color of the text. It has the value of the BODY tag's TEXT attribute. You cannot change this property after the document has been displayed.
forms	An array of references to the form objects in the document. The form objects are in source order.
lastModified	A string representing the document's last modification date. JavaScript formats the date for local time. Not all servers make this information available to the browser; in such cases, this property will represent a date of 1 January 1970 00:00:00 GMT, converted to local time. You cannot modify this property.
linkColor	A string representing the color of unvisited links. It has the value of the BODY tag's LINK attribute. You cannot change this property after the document has been displayed.
links	An array of references to the link objects in the document. The link objects are in source order.
location	A string that represents the document's URL. It is not the same as the window's location object. You cannot change location.
referrer	A string that represents the URL of the calling document of this document. You cannot change this property.
title	A string that represents the contents of the document's TITLE tag. If a document has no TITLE tag or if the browser does not display its TITLE element contents (that is, the document is in a frame), this property is null. You cannot change this property.

vlinkColor   A string representing the color of a visited link. It has the value of the BODY tag's VLINK attribute. You cannot change this property after the document has been displayed.

The document object has five properties:

clear()   Clears the document in a window.

close()   Closes an output stream opened by open(). close() forces the stream contents to display if the stream was open for layout.

open()
open
(*mimeType*)   Opens a stream to collect the output of the write() and writeln() methods. open() clears the target window. If *mimeType* is a text or image type, the stream is open for layout. *mimeType* is one of the following:
"*text/html*"—a document consisting of HTML-formatted ASCII text.
"*text/plain*"—a document consisting of ASCII text with end-of-line characters to delimit displayed lines.
"*image/gif*"—a document consisting of a GIF header and pixel data.
"*image/jpeg*"—a document consisting of a JPEG header and pixel data.
"*image/x-bitmap*"—a document consisting of a bitmap header and pixel data.
plugIn—the name of a plug-in.
If you do not specify *mimeType*, the default is "text/html".

write
(*expression*)   Displays *expression* to a document window.

writeln
(*expression*)   Displays *expression* and a new line to a document window.

THE ELEMENTS ARRAY

The elements array contains references to input elements in a form. You cannot add elements to this array, replace elements in the array, or remove elements from the array. The elements array is a form object property. The elements array has one property:

length   The number of entries in the elements array. You cannot change this property.

THE FORM OBJECT

A form object collects input from the user and may send the input to a server. It is a reflection of a FORM element:

`<FORM>`*form contents*`</FORM>`

Each form object is a member of the containing document object's forms array. A form object has six properties:

action	The FORM tag's ACTION attribute. You can change this property at any time.
elements	An array of the form object's input elements in source order. Each radio button is a separate form element and a separate entry in the array.
encoding	The FORM tag's ENCTYPE attribute. You can change this property at any time.
length	The number of elements in the form object. You cannot change this property.
method	The FORM tag's METHOD attribute. You can change it at any time.
target	The FORM tag's TARGET attribute. This is the name of the window that displays the response after the user submits formName. You can change it at any time.

The form object has one method:

submit()	Submits the form's data to the server.

The form object has one event handler:

onSubmit	Executed when the user clicks on the form's SUBMIT button. If the event handler returns false, JavaScript does not send the form's data to the server. If the event handler returns true or fails to execute a return statement, JavaScript sends the form's data to the server.

THE FORMS ARRAY

The forms array is a property of the containing document object. It contains references to all of the form objects in the document, in source order. You cannot add a form to the array, replace a form in the array, or remove a form from the array.

The forms array has one property:

length The number of entries in the forms array. You cannot change this property.

THE FRAME OBJECT

A frame object is a reflection of a FRAME element:

`<FRAME>`

A frame object has six properties:

frames An array of nonempty frame objects in this frame object in source order.

length The number of frames in this frame object. A frame that does not load a document containing a FRAMESET tag has a length of 0. You cannot change this property.

name The FRAME tag's NAME attribute. You can change it at any time.

parent A synonym for the window or frame object that contains this frame object. You cannot change this property.

self A synonym for this frame object. You cannot change this property.

window A synonym for this frame object. You cannot change this property.

A frame object has two methods:

clearTimeout (*timeoutID*) Cancels *timeoutID*, which is a timer reference returned by a previous call to setTimeout().

setTimeout (*expression, time*) Evaluates *expression* after *time* milliseconds. Returns a timer reference that can be used in a call to clearTimeout().

THE FRAMES ARRAY

A frames array contains the nonempty frames within a frame or a window. It has one property:

length The number of nonempty frame objects in this frame array. You cannot change this property.

THE HIDDEN OBJECT

A hidden object is a reflection of an INPUT element with a TYPE attribute of "hidden":

```
<INPUT TYPE="hidden">
```

hidden objects are members of the containing form object's elements array. A hidden object has three properties:

defaultValue	The default value for hiddenName. Initially, it is the value of the INPUT tag's VALUE attribute. You can change this property at any time.
name	The INPUT tag's NAME attribute. You can change it at any time.
value	The INPUT tag's VALUE attribute. You can change it at any time.

THE HISTORY OBJECT

The history object contains information on URLs that the user has visited in a window and provides methods to revisit those URLs. The URLs themselves are not visible to you, and you cannot add URLs to a history object or take URLs away from a history object. The history object has one property:

length	The number of entries in the history object. You cannot modify the length property.

The history object has three methods:

back()	Loads the previous URL in the history list. Performs the same action as selecting the Back button in the navigator.
forward()	Loads the next URL in the history list. Performs the same action as selecting the Forward button in the navigator.
go(*arg*)	Loads the specified URL in the history list. If *arg* is an integer, it is an index into the history list, with positive values indexing forward into the list and negative values indexing backward into the list. history.go(−1) is equivalent to history.back() and history.go(1) is equivalent to history.forward(). history.go(0) forces the browser to reload the current URL. If *arg* is a string, the browser loads the nearest URL in the history list that has *arg* as a substring. The comparison is case-insensitive.

THE LINK OBJECT

A link object is a reflection of an A element that has an HREF attribute:

```
<A HREF=url>anchorText</A>
```

All links are members of the document's links array in source order.

URLs specify the location of documents on the Internet, and the protocol that is used to retrieve them. The general format of a URL is

```
protocol hostname port pathname search hash
```

These are defined as follows:

protocol : The beginning of a URL, up to the first colon. Common protocols include javascript: (JavaScript code), about: (navigator information), http: (World Wide Web), file: (local file), ftp: (ftp), mailto: (mail), news: (Usenet news), and gopher: (gopher). The protocol may be separated from the rest of the URL by two slashes (http:, ftp:, news:), three slashes (file:), or no slashes (javascript:, about:, mailto:, gopher:).

hostname : The host and domain name, or IP address, of a network host.

port : The number of the communications port used by the network host for communication. Many protocols define a "well-known" port number (21 for ftp, 70 for gopher, 80 for the World Wide Web, 119 for Usenet news, to name a few) for the protocol, and because most hosts use the well-known port numbers, the *port* component is rarely used.

pathname : The path of the file, including the file name, on the network host.

search : Query information, beginning with a question mark.

hash : An anchor name, beginning with a hash mark (#)

A link object has nine properties:

hash : The *hash* component of the A element's HREF attribute.

host : The *hostname* and *port* components of the A element's HREF attribute. The strings are separated by a colon. If there is no port component, this property is the *hostname* component of the A element's HREF attribute.

hostname	The *hostname* portion of the A element's HREF attribute.
href	The entire HREF attribute of the A element. You can change this property at any time.
pathname	The *pathname* component of the A element's HREF attribute.
port	The *port* component of the A element's HREF attribute.
protocol	The *protocol* component of the A element's HREF attribute.
search	The *search* component of the A element's HREF attribute.
target	The A element's TARGET attribute. This is the name of the window or frame that displays the document when the browser loads the document. You can change it at any time.

The link object has two event handlers:

onClick	Executed when the user clicks on the display object.
onMouseOver	Executed when the mouse pointer moves over the display object from outside the object. The onMouseOver event handler must return true if it wants to set the window's status or defaultStatus properties.

THE LINKS ARRAY

The links array contains references to all of the links in the document, in source order. You cannot remove a link from the array or replace a link in the array. You can create another link with the string object's link() method.

The links array has one property:

length	The number of entries in the links array. You cannot change this property.

THE LOCATION OBJECT

The location object contains information about a window object's Uniform Resource Locator (URL). It has no methods or event handlers, and its properties consist of the URL and its components. You can change a window object's location, effectively forcing the window to be reloaded from a new URL. Although you can reload a window by changing part of its URL, you should change the entire URL by loading a new URL string into the href property instead.

The location object has eight properties:

hash	The *hash* component of the window's URL.
host	The *hostname* component of the window's URL, plus the *port* component. The *hostname* and *port* components are separated by a colon. If there is no *port* component, this is simply the *hostname* component.
hostname	The *hostname* component of the window's URL.
href	The window's entire URL.
pathname	The *pathname* component of the window's URL.
port	The *port* component of the window's URL.
protocol	The *protocol* component of the window's URL.
search	The *search* component of the window's URL.

THE MATH OBJECT

The Math object provides common mathematical functions, and its properties provide useful mathematics constants. You cannot create a Math object. You cannot modify any of the eight properties:

Math.E	Euler's constant (approximately 2.718281828459).
Math.LN2	The natural logarithm of 2 (approximately 0.6931471805599).
Math.LN10	The natural logarithm of 10 (approximately 2.302585092994).
Math.LOG2E	The base 2 logarithm of Euler's constant, e (approximately 1.442695040889).
Math.LOG10E	The base 10 logarithm of Euler's constant, e (approximately 0.4342944819033).
Math.PI	The ratio of a circle's circumference to its diameter (approximately 3.14159265359).
Math.SQRT1_2	The square root of one half (approximately 0.7071067811865).
Math.SQRT2	The square root of 2 (approximately 1.414213562373).

The Math object provides 17 methods:

Math.abs(*number*) — Returns the absolute value of *number*.

Math.acos(*number*) — Returns the arc cosine, in radians, of *number*. Returns 0 if *number* is out of range.

Math.asin(*number*) — Returns the arc sine, in radians, of *number*. Returns 0 if *number* is out of range.

Math.atan(*number*) — Returns the arc tangent, in radians, of *number*.

Math.ceil(*number*) — Returns the least integer that is equal to or greater than *number*.

Math.cos(*number*) — Returns the cosine of *number*.

Math.exp(*number*) — Returns the value of e^{number}. e is Euler's constant—the base of the natural logarithms.

Math.floor(*number*) — Returns the greatest integer that is equal to or less than number.

Math.log(*number*) — Returns the natural logarithm (base e) of *number*. If number is 0 or less than 0, log returns $-1.797693134862316e+308$.

Math.max (*number1, number2*) — Returns the greater of *number1* and *number2*.

Math.min (*number1, number2*) — Returns the lesser of *number1* and *number2*.

Math.pow (*base, exponent*) — Returns $base^{exponent}$.

Math.random() — Returns a pseudo-random number between 0 and 1. Currently available on UNIX platforms only.

Math.round (*number*) — Returns the next higher integer value if the fractional part of *number* is .5 or greater. Returns the next lower integer value if the fractional part of *number* is less than .5.

Math.sin(number) — Returns the sine of *number*.

Math.sqrt(number) — Returns the square root of *number*. sqrt() always returns 0 if *number* is out of range.

Math.tan(*number*) — Returns the tangent of *number*.

THE NAVIGATOR OBJECT

The navigator object refers to the browser itself, and it has properties that you can use to tailor your JavaScript to the browser. There are limitations and bugs associated with the Netscape Navigator that are specific to the platform it is running on or to specific versions of the browser. The navigator object lets you steer around these problems.

The navigator object has no methods and no event handlers. You cannot modify any of its four properties:

appCodeName	The code name of the browser.
appName	The name of the browser.
appVersion	A string that represents version information about the browser. The information format is *version* (*platform*; *country*) where *version* is the browser version, *platform* indicates the platform (Windows, UNIX, and so on), and *country* is I (international version) or U (domestic United States release).
userAgent	The value of the user-agent header sent in the HTTP protocol from client to server.

THE OPTIONS ARRAY

The options array is a property of select objects. It allows you to manipulate the options of the select object. Individual options objects are reflections of OPTION elements:

`<OPTION>, text to be displayed`

The options array has eight properties:

defaultSelected	The default selection state of an option object. It initially has the value of the OPTION tag's SELECTED attribute. You can change defaultSelected at any time. Doing so has no effect on the appearance of the OPTION element.
index	The index of an option object in the options array. You cannot change this property.
length	The number of entries in the options array. You cannot change this property.

name	The SELECT element's NAME attribute. All OPTION elements are supposed to be contained in a SELECT element. You can change this property at any time.
selected	A Boolean value that indicates an option object's current selection state. It is true if the option object is selected, and false if it is not selected. You can change this property at any time. Changing this property affects the appearance of the SELECT element immediately.
selectedIndex	The index of the first selected option in the options array; −1 if no option is selected. You can change this property at any time; doing so clears all other options in the options array.
text	The text that follows an option object's OPTION tag. You can change this property, but the display does not reflect the change.
value	The OPTION tag's VALUE attribute. You can change this property, but the display does not reflect the change. JavaScript returns this property to the server if the user selects the option.

THE PASSWORD OBJECT

A password object is a reflection of an INPUT element with a TYPE attribute of "password":

```
<INPUT TYPE="password">
```

The data entered by the user is not visible to the display—each character appears as an asterisk—and it is not visible programatically.

password objects are members of the containing form object's elements array. A password object has three properties:

defaultValue	The default value for the password object. It is null initially. You may change it at any time. Changing this property has no effect on the display.
name	The INPUT tag's NAME attribute. You can change it at any time.

value   The INPUT tag's VALUE attribute. You can change it
               at any time. Changing this property immediately up-
               dates the display, but the display shows it as a string of
               asterisks. If you set this property, you can read it back,
               but if the user enters text into the input field, you can-
               not read it.

A password object has three methods:

blur()   Removes focus from the password object.

focus()   Moves focus to the password object. When the password
               object has focus, you can enter a value from JavaScript
               or the user can enter a value.

select()   Highlights the input area of the input field and positions
               the cursor for user response.

THE RADIO OBJECT

The radio object represents a set of INPUT elements of TYPE "radio" with the
same NAME attribute:

```
<INPUT TYPE="radio" NAME=radioName>
```

Each button in a radio object is a member of the containing form object's elements array.

A radio object has five properties:

checked   A Boolean value that indicates whether a specific but-
               ton in the set of radio buttons is checked. You can
               change this property at any time. Changing it changes
               the appearance of the buttons immediately.

defaultChecked A Boolean value that indicates the default state of a
               specific button in the set of radio buttons. The default
               state of the button is checked if this property is true.
               The initial value of this property is the CHECKED
               attribute of the INPUT tag. You can change this
               property at any time. Changing it has no effect on
               the appearance of the buttons.

length   The number of radio buttons in the radio object.
               You cannot change this property.

name   The text following a specific button's INPUT tag.
               You can change it at any time.

value	A specific radio button's INPUT tag's VALUE attribute. In the absence of such an attribute, this property is set to "on". JavaScript returns this property to the server if the user selected this specific radio button. The browser does not display this property. You can change this property at any time.

A radio object has one method:

click()	Selects the specified radio button. The onClick event handler is not executed.

A radio object has one event handler:

onClick	Executed when the user clicks on the display object.

THE RESET OBJECT

A reset object is a reflection of an INPUT tag with a TYPE attribute of "reset":

```
<INPUT TYPE="reset">
```

reset objects are members of the containing form object's elements array.

A reset object has two properties:

name	The INPUT tag's NAME attribute. You can change it at any time.
value	The INPUT tag's VALUE attribute. In the absence of a VALUE attribute, this property is "Reset". You cannot change this property.

A reset object has one method:

click()	Simulates a mouse click on the reset button. The onClick event handler is not executed.

A reset object has one event handler:

onClick	Executed when the user clicks on the display object.

THE SELECT OBJECT

A select object is a reflection of a SELECT element:

```
<SELECT><OPTION>...</SELECT>
```

select objects are members of the containing form object's elements array.

A select object has four properties:

length	The number of OPTION elements within the SELECT element. You cannot change this property.
name	The SELECT tag's NAME attribute. You can change it at any time.
options	An array of the option objects corresponding to the OPTION elements within the SELECT element. You cannot change the elements of this array.
selected-Index	The index of the first selected option object in the objects array. You can change this property at any time; doing so clears all other options in the display.

A select object has two methods:

blur()	Removes focus from the SELECT element. The onBlur event handler is not executed.
focus()	Moves focus to the SELECT element. The onFocus event handler is not executed.

A select object has three event handlers:

onBlur	Executed when the user attempts to leave the select field.
onChange	Executed when the field loses focus and the user has changed the field value.
onFocus	Executed when the display object receives focus if the user tabs to it or clicks on it with the mouse.

THE STRING OBJECT

A string object is a series of characters. You can extract characters in a string, and you can extract pieces of a string, which are called substrings. The string object behaves like a sequence of characters ordered from left to right.

A string object has one property:

length	The number of characters in the string object. You cannot change this property.

A string object has 19 methods:

anchor(*name*)   Creates an anchor string that can be used with docu-ment.write() or document.writeln(). The string object contains the text the user will see. *name* is the anchor element's NAME attribute. An anchor object created with this method becomes a member of the anchors array.

big()   Formats the string object as if it were within a BIG element.

blink()   Formats the string object as if it were within a BLINK element.

bold()   Formats the string object as if it were within a B element.

charAt(*index*)   Returns the character at *index* into the string object. If *index* is out of range, charAt() returns an empty string.

fixed()   Formats a string object as if it were within a TT element.

fontcolor(*color*)   Formats a string object as if it were within a FONT el-ement with the COLOR attribute set to *color*.

fontsize(*size*)   Formats a string object as if it were within a FONT el-ement with the SIZE attribute set to *size*.

indexOf (*searchText*) indexOf (*searchText*, *index*)   Searches a string object for an occurrence of *search-Text*, starting at *index*. If you omit *index*, the browser assumes a starting index of 0. Returns the index where it finds *searchText*. If it does not find *searchText*, it re-turns −1.

italics()   Formats a string object as if it were within an I element.

lastIndexOf (*searchText*) lastIndexOf (*searchText*, *index*)   Searches the string object backwards for an occurrence of *searchText*, starting at *index*. If you omit *index*, the browser assumes a starting index of the string object's length minus 1. It returns the index where it finds *searchText*. If it does not find *searchText*, it returns −1.

link(*href*)   Creates an anchor element. The string object is the contents of the element, and *href* is the value of the an-chor element's HREF attribute. A link created with this method becomes an element of the links array.

small()	Formats a string object as if it were within a SMALL element.
strike()	Formats a string object as if it were within a STRIKE element.
sub()	Formats a string object as if it were within a SUB element.
substring (*index1, index2*)	Returns a part of text defined by *index1* and *index2*. If *index1* is less than *index2*, substring() returns the characters in the string object *index1* to *index2 - 1*. If *index2* is less than *index1*, substring() returns the characters in text from *index2* to *index1 - 1*. If *index1* and *index2* are equal, substring() returns an empty string.
sup()	Formats a string object as if it were within a SUP element.
toLowerCase()	Returns the text of the string object in lowercase.
toUpperCase()	Returns the text of the string object in uppercase.

THE SUBMIT OBJECT

A submit object is a reflection of an INPUT element with a TYPE attribute of "submit":

```
<INPUT TYPE="submit">
```

submit objects are members of the containing form object's elements array.

A submit object has two properties:

| name | The INPUT tag's NAME attribute. You can change it at any time. |
| value | The INPUT tag's VALUE attribute. In the absence of a VALUE attribute, this property is "Submit Query". You cannot change this property. |

A submit object has one method:

| click() | Simulates a mouse click on the SUBMIT element. The onClick event handler is not executed. |

A submit object has one event handler:

| onClick | Executed when the user clicks on the display object. |

THE TEXT OBJECT

A text object is a reflection of an INPUT element with a TYPE attribute of "text":

```
<INPUT TYPE="text">
```

text objects are members of the containing form object's elements array.

A text object has three properties:

defaultValue	The default value for the text object. It is initially the INPUT tag's VALUE attribute. You may change this property at any time. Changing it has no effect on the appearance of text.
name	The INPUT tag's NAME attribute. You can change it at any time.
value	Initially, the INPUT tag's VALUE attribute. You can change it at any time. The browser immediately updates the display.

A text object has four methods:

blur()	Removes focus from the text object. The onBlur event handler is not executed.
focus()	Moves focus to the text object. When the text object has focus, the user can enter a value. The onFocus event handler is not executed.
select()	Highlights the text object's input area and positions the cursor for user response. The onSelect event handler is not executed.

A text object has four event handlers:

onBlur	Executed when the user attempts to leave the field.
onChange	Executed when the field loses focus and the user has changed the field value.
onFocus	Executed when the display object receives focus if the user tabs to it or clicks on it with the mouse.
onSelect	Executed when the user selects any of the text in the field.

THE TEXTAREA OBJECT

A textarea object is a reflection of a TEXTAREA element:

```
<TEXTAREA>... text to be displayed ... </TEXTAREA>
```

textarea objects are members of the containing form object's elements array.

A textarea object has three properties:

defaultValue	The default value for the textarea object. Initially, it is the TEXTAREA tag's VALUE attribute. You can change it at any time. Changing it has no effect on the appearance of the textarea object.
name	The TEXTAREA tag's NAME attribute. You can change it at any time.
value	Initially, the TEXTAREA tag's VALUE attribute. You can change it at any time. The browser immediately updates the display.

A textarea object has three methods:

blur()	Removes focus from the textarea object. The onBlur event handler is not executed.
focus()	Moves focus to the textarea object. When the textarea object has focus, the user can enter a value.
select()	Highlights the input area of the textarea object and positions the cursor for user response.

A textarea object has four event handlers:

onBlur	Executed when the user attempts to leave the field.
onChange	Executed when the field loses focus and the user has changed the field value.
onFocus	Executed when the display object receives focus if the user tabs to it or clicks on it with the mouse.
onSelect	Executed when the user selects some of the text in the field.

THE WINDOW OBJECT

The window object is a top-level object that contains a document object, a history object, and a location object. It may also contain a frames array, which is an array of frame objects. The term "window" is somewhat ambiguous. It refers to the entire browser display on the user's screen. The browser can spawn additional displays; those displays are also windows. Each FRAMESET and FRAME element also defines a window.

The browser display window has several components to which the window object's properties and methods refer. One component, the status bar, has two values that you can manipulate: a default message that normally appears, and a transitory message that overrides the default message.

The window object has eight properties:

defaultStatus	The message that appears in the window status bar when nothing else is in the status bar. If you change this property within an onMouseOver event handler, the event handler must return true for defaultStatus to be changed.
length	The number of frames. You cannot change this property.
name	The window's name.
parent	A synonym for the window or frame object that contains this window object. You cannot change this property.
self	A synonym for this window object. You cannot change this property.
status	The transitory message that appears in the window status bar—for example, when a mouseOver event occurs. If you change this property within an onMouseOver event handler, the event handler must return true for status to be changed.
top	A synonym for the topmost window that contains frames or nested framesets. You cannot change this property.
window	A synonym for the this window object. You cannot change this property.

The window object has seven methods:

alert(*message*)	Displays *message* in a dialog box that requires no user decision.
clearTimeout (*timeoutID*)	Cancels the timeout specified by timeoutID.
close()	Closes the window. In event handlers, you must specify a window reference (windowRef.close()). If you do not specify a window reference, the browser assumes you meant document.close().

confirm (*message*)	Displays *message* in a dialog box that requires the user to select either OK or Cancel. Returns true if the user selects OK and false if the user selects Cancel.
open(*URL, windowName, features*)	Creates a new browser display window. *URL* is the URL to open in the new window. *windowName* is a name that a FORM or A element can use in its TARGET attribute. *features* is a column-delimited list of window options. Do not use spaces. The options are *directories*—Creates the standard Navigator directory buttons, if true. *height=pixels*—Specifies the window height in pixels. pixels must be a positive number. *location*—Creates a location entry field, if true. *menubar*—Creates the menu at the top of the window, if true. *resizable*—Allows the user to resize the window, if true. *scrollbars*—Creates horizontal and vertical scrollbars when the document is larger than the window, if true. *status*—Creates the status bar at the bottom of the window, if true. *toolbar*—Creates the standard Navigator toolbar, if true. *width=pixels*—Specifies the window width in pixels. pixels must be a positive number. The Boolean options (all options except height and width) are true if included as *option, option*=1, or *option*=yes. Boolean options are false if omitted or if included as *option*=0 or *option*=no. Exception: if you list no window options and you omit *windowName*, all options are true. open() returns a window object reference.
prompt (*message*) prompt (*message, inputDefault*)	Displays a dialog box that displays *message* and receives user input. *inputDefault* is the default value. If you do not specify *inputDefault*, the browser displays the value <undefined>. prompt returns the text entered by the user.
setTimeout (*expression, time*)	Evaluates *expression* after *time* milliseconds. setTimeout returns a timer ID that can be used in a call to clearTimeout().

The window object can have two event handlers:

onLoad	Executed when a window or all frames in a frameset have finished loading.
OnUnload	Executed when the user exits the window.

BUILT-IN FUNCTIONS

JavaScript provides six built-in functions. These functions are unrelated to the built-in objects.

escape (*string*)	*string* is a string in the ISO Latin-1 character set.	Returns a string. escape() converts non-alphanumeric characters in *string* to the form %xx, where xx is the hexadecimal representation of the character's value. escape() passes alphanumeric characters in *string* to the return string intact.
eval (string)	*string* is a string containing a Java-Script statement or expression or sequence of statements.	Evaluates *string* and returns a value.
isNan (*value*)	*value* is a value returned from parseFloat() or parseInt().	Returns true if *value* is NaN. NaN is a special value returned by parseFloat() and parseInt() to indicate that the evaluated value is not a number. parseFloat() and parseInt() do not return NaN in Windows platforms.

parseFloat (*string*)	*string* is a string representing a numeric value.	Returns the floating-point number that *string* represents. It stops parsing *string* when it encounters a character that is not part of a valid numeric expression. parseFloat() returns NaN (not a number), under all platforms except Windows, if it cannot create a valid floating-point number. parseFloat() returns 0 under Windows when it cannot create a valid floating-point number.
parseInt (*string*) or parseInt (*string*, *radix*)	*string* is a string representing a numeric value. *radix* is a nonnegative integer.	Returns the integer that *string*, in the specified *radix*, represents. The browser guesses a radix if you omit *radix* or specify a value of 0. The browser assumes a value of 16 if *string* begins with 0x, 8 if *string* begins with 0, and 10 if *string* begins with any other digit. JavaScript assumes that letters are digits, such as A–F for a radix of 16, when *radix* is greater than 10. parseInt() returns NaN (not a number), under all platforms except Windows, if it cannot create a valid floating-point number. parseInt() returns 0 under Windows when it cannot create a valid floating-point number.

| unescape (*string*) | *string* is a string that contains sequences of "%number", where number is a value from 0 to 255, or "0xnumber", where number is a hexadecimal value from 00 to FF. | Returns a string with the escaped values in *string* converted to ISO Latin-1 characters. |

APPENDIX F:
ONLINE RESOURCES

This appendix lists some URLs that provide further information about JavaScript.

- The ATLAS JavaScript FAQ (http://www.freqgrafx.com/411/atlas/jsfaq. html) is Andy Augustine's excellent attempt at tracking Frequently Asked Questions about Netscape ATLAS, which will eventually become Netscape 3.0.

- The Dead Eye Saloon (http://www.lhouse.com/~jbloomberg/stud/), a Web page game by Jason Bloomberg, is a good example of a game written in JavaScript.

- Do You Have JavaScript in Your Browser? (http://www.cris.com/~raydaly/ javatell.html) is a cute little demo by Ray Daly. Try it out!

- Doctor HTML (http://imagiware.com/RxHTML.cgi) is a very handy site. It will perform a number of validation checks on your Web page, including spell checking and verifying that your element tags are properly nested and contained. Particularly noteworthy is its ability to check your IMG tags and tell you how to set the WIDTH and HEIGHT attributes. Probably 90 percent of JavaScript pages that don't work fail because of the infamous "missing HEIGHT and WIDTH" bug.

▶ Gamelan (http://www.gamelan.com/) is Earthweb's Java Directory. There are an impressive number of JavaScript links collected here, and it was one of the key sites I used to track down JavaScript details.

▶ The hIdaho Frameset (http://www.hidaho.com/frameset/) is a set of functions written by Bill Dortch. The functions provide global function registration and a calling mechanism for multiframe applications. This is a very impressive body of work that is design to make life in multiframeset applications less of a headache.

▶ How to Do Forms (http://www2.ncsu.edu/bae/people/faculty/walker/hotlist/forms.html), written by Joseph C. Walker of North Carolina State University, contains a great deal of information about creating forms. Much of this material is beyond the scope of this book, so you should definitely check this site if you need help with forms. In particular, there is a wealth of information about creating the CGI scripts in Perl, which is one of the more popular scripting languages for writing CGI applications.

▶ Jamie's Calculator (http://www1.mhv.net/~jamihall/calc2.html) is a calculator written in JavaScript. I almost included a chapter explaining how to construct a calculator, but after I saw this page, I gave it up. This is such an elegant solution, I just couldn't surpass it.

▶ JavaScript 411 (http://www.freqgrafx.com/411/) is Andy Augustine's JavaScript Information home page. You could spend a day or two just following and reading the useful links from here.

▶ The JavaScript FAQ (http://www.freqgrafx.com/411/jsfaq.html) is Andy Augustine's compilation of Frequently Asked Questions about JavaScript. This is a very useful page when you're struggling with code that you know should work but doesn't. It can be comforting to know that you've just tripped over a bug in the browser, that the problem is not your code, and that there's a workaround for the bug on this page.

▶ The JavaScript Index (http://www.c2.org/~andreww/javascript/) is Andrew Wooldridge's index of JavaScript links. I learned a lot from browsing here.

▶ Netscape's Frames Documentation (http://www.mcom.com/assist/net_sites/frames.html) is a good introductory document on using FRAME and FRAMESET elements.

▶ Netscape's JavaScript Authoring Guide (http://home.netscape.com/eng/mozilla/2.0/handbook/javascript/index. html) is Netscape's online documentation of JavaScript for Netscape 2.0. This is the authoritative documentation for what's in this book. Just be careful: Not everything described in this site was actually implemented as described!

▸ Netscape's JavaScript Authoring Guide (http://home.netscape.com/eng/mozilla/3.0/handbook/javascript/) is Netscape's online documentation of JavaScript for Netscape 3.0. By the time you get this book in your hands, Netscape 3.0 should be right around the corner, if not already available. The new version of Netscape includes some neat things that I wished I could have used in this book.

▸ The Snippet Library (http://www.freqgrafx.com/411/library.html) is Andy Augustine's ongoing effort to collect useful pieces of code that you can incorporate into your pages. I highly recommend checking out this site from time to time to see what's new.

▸ The Tiger Mapping Service Instructions (http://tiger.census.gov/instruct.html) contains the specifications for using the Census Bureau's Tiger Map Service. In Chapter 8, I created a simple interface that only uses the rudimentary capabilities of the Tiger Map Service; investigate this site to find out what else you can do.

▸ The WWW HTML Archive (http://fox.nstn.ca/~tmonk/weaver/html.html) is an impressive list of HTML links. Although it's not as useful as some of the other sites listed here for dealing with JavaScript itself, it includes some good tips on writing HTML.

▸ Odyssey Systems Corporation (http://www.iliad.com) is a high-end Web service provider that does custom JavaScript development.

In addition to the URLs mentioned here, you can often find useful information on the JavaScript newsgroup, comp.lang.javascript (all the major JavaScript authors seem to post there), and you can write me at marcj@nando.net or the technical reviewer for this book at l@luke.org; we don't mind answering questions. Just be patient; if I'm in the middle of another book, I might not be able to get back to you instantly.

Index

A

A (anchor) HTML element, 199
addition operator (+), 225
ADDRESS element (HTML), 199–200
adult material, 29–31
alert windows, 19, 20
ALIGN attribute (HTML), 195–196
alignment of HTML elements, 195–196
ALT attribute (HTML), 33
anchor objects, 237–238
anchors array, 237–238
AND operators
&, 226
&&, 230
announce() function, 18
APPLET element (HTML), 200
applets, 8
architectures, and running JavaScript, 8
AREA element (HTML), 200–201
arrays of objects, creating, 61–62

assignment operators
=, 225–226
op=, 234
attributeSelector() ONCHANGE event handler, 97
attribute tables (colors), 95, 96

B

bandwidth considerations, 83
BASE element (HTML), 201
BASEFONT element (HTML), 202
B (boldface) HTML element, 201
Bed of Procustes, 34
BIG element (HTML), 202
bitmap structure, 59
bitwise AND operator (&), 226
bitwise exclusive–OR (XOR) operator (^), 226
bitwise negate operator (~), 227
bitwise OR operator (I), 227
BLINK element (HTML), 202
BLOCKQUOTE element (HTML), 202
blur event, 18

BODY element (HTML), 35, 203
   assigning a color to, 95–98
   load event, 45
BORDER attribute (HTML), 5
branch nodes, drawing, 65–66
branch objects, tree–structured outline, 57
BR (line break) HTML element, 203
browser display window components, 260
browsers, downloading, 32
browser support for JavaScript, 31
built–in functions (JavaScript), 263–264
built–in objects (JavaScript), 237–262
BUTTON fields
   event handlers, 89, 90
   INPUT elements, 133
   plus and minus event handlers, 90, 91
   set and reset, 98–99
button object, 238

C

CAPTION element (HTML), 203–204
catalogs, online, 21
ceil() method, Math object, 36
CENTER element (HTML), 204
CGI (Common Gateway Interface), 6–7
CGI programs, 43–44, 52–54, 81–82, 104–106,
      130–131, 155–156
change event, 18
change event handler (TEXT field), 90
changeLongitude() function, 140
character set (ISO Latin–1), 185–191
checkbox object, 238–239
CITE element (HTML), 204
CLEAR attribute (HTML), 196–198
click event, 18
client, 3
client pull, 7

clock display, creating, 23–24
clocks, 23–24
close() method, 60
code
   consistency of style in, 38
   documenting, 37–38
   hiding, 31–32
CODE element (HTML), 204
codeOf() function, 166
color attribute tables, 95, 96
color chooser example, 79–101
   assigning a color, 95–98
   the form, 83–100
   improving, 100
   with JavaScript, 83–100
   without JavaScript, 81–82
   modifying, 101
   requirements, 80–81
   selecting a color, 84–95
   setting and resetting color, 98–99
colors
   assigning to <BODY> attributes, 95–98
   creating, 89
   HTML tag, 195
   Netscape, 80
   screen, 33
color selection table
   creating, 85–89
   detailed, 85
   high–level, 84
commenting your code, 31–32, 37–38, 193
compass controls (map example), 137
concatenation operator (+), 227
conditional operator (?), 228
consistency in code style, 38
container element (HTML), 194
content, 27–31
cookie feature, 20–21

countdown timers, 24–25, 45

counters, hit, 6

createCookie( ) function, 159

credit card validation, 111–116

customer order form validation, 103–126

D

data.htm file listing, 67–73

data types in Java, 8

date object, 239–241

dateOK( ) function, 114–115

DD (definition description) HTML element, 204

decrement operator (—), using, 32

depth functions, tree–structured outline, 60–62

depth objects

    arrays of, 61–62

    tree–structured outline, 60–62

destination field, 16

DIR (directory) HTML element, 205

dir.htm, 13

displayScoreBoard( ) function, 159–160

dithering, 79

DIV (division) HTML element, 205

division operator (/), 228

DL (definition list) HTML element, 205

documenting your code, 37–38

document instances, 4

document maintenance, 37–38

document object, 241–243

document object's referrer property, 29–30

documents

    creating interactive, 14–16

    frame, 12, 55–76, 83, 138

    live, 21–25

    with memory, 20–21

    multipart with frames, 11–16

    parts of SGML, 3

    protecting from users, 35–37

    self–updating, 25

Document Type Definition (DTD), 3

double quotes ("), 6

drawBreak( ) function, 100

drawLine( ) function, 100

drawPlayingField( ) function, 164–167

DT (definition term) HTML element, 205

E

elements array, 243

EM (emphasis) HTML element, 205–206

empty element (HTML), 194

empty nodes, drawing, 62–63

end tags, HTML, 194

equality operator (==), 228

escape( ) function, 159, 263

eval( ) function, 91, 263

event handlers, 18–20, 45, 89–95

events, user, 16–20

examples of Web pages, 41–181

    color chooser, 79–101

    form content modification, 129–151

    form validation, 103–126

    games, 153–181

    outlined document, 51–77

    URL patch, 43–48

exclusive–OR (XOR) operator (^), 226

F

floor() method, Math object, 46
focus, 16, 18
focus event, 18
focus event handlers, 19
FONT element (HTML), 206
FORM elements (HTML), 206–207
  events, 20
  input fields, 16
  in map example, 133
form handling, 6
form modification example, 129–151
  control functions, 139–144
  improving, 150–151
  with JavaScript, 131–150
  without JavaScript, 130–131
  laying out the controls, 134–138
  laying out the window, 138–139
  modifying, 151
  requirements, 130
form object, 244
forms array, 244–245
form validation, 7, 103
form validation example, 103–126
  improving, 126
  with JavaScript, 107–126
  without JavaScript, 104–107
  modifying, 126
  requirements, 103–104
frame documents, 12, 55–76, 83, 138
FRAME elements (HTML), 12, 207–208
frame object, 245
frames, 11
  examples of, 17
  multipart documents with, 11–16
frames array, 245
FRAMESET elements (HTML), 12–13, 208–209

function comment block, 37
function loading, 35
functions (JavaScript built–in), 263–264

G

gameOver() function, 168–169
games. *See* hangman game example
gatekeeper page, 29–30
getCookie() function, 158–159
getLongitude() function, 141
getMagnification() function, 141
GIF file example (form modification), 129–151
grammar, 29
greater than or equal operator (>=), 229
greater than operator (>), 32, 228–229
guess() function, 167

H

hangman game example, 153–181
  improving and modifying, 181
  with JavaScript, 156–180
  without JavaScript, 155–156
  JavaScript listing, 169–180
  in progress, 180
  requirements, 153–155
HEAD element (HTML), 35, 209
hexadecimal numbers, 80
hidden object, 246
hiding your code, 31–32
history object, 246
hit counters, 6
H1..H6 (heading) HTML element, 209
HR (horizontal rule) HTML element, 210
HTML content, 193

HTML elements, 194
   alignment, 195–196
   Netscape–supported, 199–224
HTML (an HTML element), 210
HTML (Hypertext Markup Language), 3
HTML 1.0 and 2.0, 4
HTML review, 193–224
HTML tag attributes, 193–194
HTML tag colors, 195
HTML tags, 193–194
HTML 3.0, 4

I

I (italic) HTML element, 210
image is everything, 27–35
IMG (image) HTML element, 210–211
inequality operator (!=), 229
initializeScoreBoard() function, 159–160
INPUT element (HTML), 212–214
input fields, form, 16
input.htm, 16
input validation, 35–36
interactive documents, creating, 14–16
ISINDEX (is indexed) HTML element, 214
ISO Latin–1 character set, 185–191

J

Java data types, 8
Java vs. JavaScript, 8
Java programming language, 8

JavaScript
   browser support for, 31
   built–in functions, 263–264
   built–in objects, 237–262
   evolution of, 6
   history of, 3–6
   vs. Java, 8
   operator order of precedence, 235–236
   operators, 225–236
   platforms, 8–9
   reserved words, 192
   a scripting language, 6, 8
   what it is not, 6–8

K

KBD (keyboard) HTML element, 214

L

Latin–1 character set, 185–191
layout documents. *See* frame documents
leaf nodes, drawing, 63–65
leaf objects, tree–structured outline, 57
less than or equal operator (<=), 230
less than operator (<), 229–230
LI (list item) HTML element, 214–215
LINK element (HTML), 215
link object, 247–248
links array, 248
live documents, 21
LiveScript, 6
load event (BODY element), 20, 45
location controls (map example), 136
location object, 248–249
location property, window object, 45

logical AND operator (&&), 230

logical NOT operator (!), 230

logical OR operator (II), 230–231

M

main.htm, 12

main2.htm, 15

MakeArray() function, 61, 161

map controls (map example), 138

mapctrl.htm file listing, 145–150

map GIF file example, 129–151

MAP element (HTML), 215

markup tags, 3–4

math object, 249–250

   ceil() method, 36

   floor() method, 46

   random() method, 162

memory, documents with, 20–21

MENU element (HTML), 215

messages, scrolling, 21–23

META element (HTML), 215–216

minus ONCLICK event handler, 92

misspellings, 27–29

model–view–controller (MVC), 94

modulo operator (%), 5, 46, 231

mouseover event, 20

multipart documents with frames, 11–16

multiplication operator (*), 231

N

NaN (Not a Number), 36

navigator object, 251

negation operator (–), 231–232

Netscape colors, 80

Netscape extension for HTML 2.0, 4–6

Netscape Navigator platforms, 8–9, 36–37

Netscape–supported HTML elements, 199–224

neverPlayed() function, 159

newWord() function, 162

NHTML, 4–6

NOBR (no break) HTML element, 216

node objects

   arrays of, 61–62

   tree–structured outline, 57–67

nodes, drawing, 62–66

NOFRAME element (HTML), 33, 216

NOT operator (!), 230

O

objects (JavaScript built–in), 237–262

OL (ordered list) HTML element, 216

ONCHANGE event handlers, 89, 91, 95, 97

ONCLICK event handlers, 89, 91, 92

online catalogs, 21

online resources, reference to, 265–267

ONLOAD event handler, 46, 169

open() method, 36, 60

operating systems, and running JavaScript, 8

operator order of precedence, 235–236

operators (JavaScript), 225–236

OPTION element (HTML), 217

options array, 251–252

order form validation example, 103–126

order of precedence of operators, 235–236

OR operator (II), 230–231

outline document example, 51–77
  drawing the tree, 74–75
  improving, 76
  with JavaScript, 55–76
  without JavaScript, 52–54
  loading, 67
  modifying, 77
  navigation aids, 55–76
  requirements, 51
  tree structure, 55–76
output.htm, 16

P

page examples. *See* Web page examples
page redirection example, 43–48
  with JavaScript, 44–48
  without JavaScript, 43–44
pages, keeping simple, 34
page structure, 193–196
page validation, 5
PARAM element (HTML), 217
parseFloat() function, 35, 36, 141, 263
parseInt() function, 35, 36, 142, 264
password object, 252–253
pixels, 33
platforms for Netscape Navigator, considerations, 8–9, 33–37
plus and minus event handlers (BUTTON field), 90, 91
plus() ONCLICK event handler, 91
popup windows, 19–20
post–decrement operator (—), 232
post–increment operator (++), 232
P (paragraph) HTML element, 217
pre–decrement operator (—), 232–233

PRE element (HTML), 218
pre–increment operator (++), 233
presbyopia, 33
presentation, 31–35
programming language, Java as, 8
protect.htm, 30
protecting documents from users, 35–37

Q

quotes ("), 6

R

radio object, 253–254
random() method (Math object), 36, 162
readDecimal() function, 90
readHex() ONCHANGE event handler, 91
reading the screen, 33–34
readSelector() ONCHANGE event handler, 94–95
redirecting visitors to your page, 43–48
redirection page, 44
referrer.htm, 30
referrer property (document object), 29–30
reloading part of a window, 14
reserved words (JavaScript), 192
RESET button, 98
reset object, 254
ResetViewScreen() function, 99, 100
resources, online, 265–267
RestoreAttribute() function, 98
RGB color values, 79–80, 89
rogue users, protecting documents from, 35–37

S

SAMP element (HTML), 218
screen, reading, 33–34
screen colors, 33
screen resolution, 33
SCRIPT element (HTML), 35, 66–67, 218
scripting language, JavaScript as, 6, 8
scrolling messages, 21–23
SELECT element (HTML), 218–219
select event, 18
SELECT field event handlers, 94
select object, 254–255
self–updating documents, 25
server, 3
server push CGI, 7
setAttribute() function, 97
setColor() function, 92, 95
setDec() function, 92
setDefaults() function, 99
setHex() function, 93
setLongitude() function, 142
SGML documents, 3
SGML (Standard Generalized Markup Language), 3
shift left operator (<<), 233
shift right operator
   sign–propagating (>>), 234
   zero–fill (>>>), 235
shorthand assignment operator (op=), 234
sign–propagating shift right operator (>>), 234
SMALL element (HTML), 219
source field, 16
spelling, 27–29
splitting windows. *See* frame documents
STRIKE element (HTML), 219
string object, 255–257

STRONG element (HTML), 219
style, 27–38
SUBMIT button, 98
submit event, 20
submit event handler, 20
submit object, 257
SUB (subscript) HTML element, 219
subtraction operator (–), 234
SUP (superscript) HTML element, 220

T

TABLE elements (HTML), 220–221
   creating, 85–89
   in map example, 134–138
tag attributes, HTML, 193–194
tags, HTML, 193–194
TD (table data) HTML element, 221–222
TEXTAREA element (HTML), 222
textarea object, 259
TEXT field change event handler, 90
TEXT field event handlers, 89, 90
TEXT INPUT elements (map example), 133, 136
text object, 258
TH (table header) HTML element, 221–222
timers
   countdown, 24–25, 45
   for scrolling messages, 21–23
TITLE element (HTML), 223
toHex() function, 94
toHex2() function, 93
tree–structured outline
   creating, 55–76
   drawing the tree, 74–75
   improving, 76
   loading, 67
   modifying, 77
   node objects, 57–67

treeview.htm, 74–75
TR (table row) HTML element, 223
TT (teletype) HTML element, 223

U

UL (unordered list) HTML element, 223
unescape() function, 264
Uniform Resource Locators (URLs), 194–195
unload event, 20
updating, document self–updating, 25
URL patch for redirecting visitors, 43–48
user events, controlling, 16–20
user interaction, controlling, 16–20
users, protecting documents from, 35–37

V

validateCreditCardNumber() function, 113–114
validating forms example, 103–126
validating input, 35–36, 103–126
validating Web pages, 5
validation, form, 7, 35–36, 103–126
VAR (variable) HTML element, 224

W

WBR (word break) HTML element, 224
Web page examples, 41–181
    color chooser, 79–101
    form modification, 129–151
    form validation, 103–126
    games, 153–181
    outlined document, 51–77
    URL patch, 43–48

Web page redirection example, 43–48
Web pages, keeping simple, 34
Web page structure, 193–196
Web page validation, 5
welcome.htm, 13
window objects, 259–262
    location property, 45
    properties, 261–262
window reloading, 14
windows, popup, 19, 20

X

XOR operator (^), 226
Xwindow platforms, browser windows on, 36

Z

zero–fill shift right operator (>>), 235
zip code validation, 110
zoom buttons, 143–144
zoom controls, 135